BLOODY PROVOST

BLOODY PROVOST

An account of the Provost Service of the British Army, and the early years of the Corps of Royal Military Police

R.A.J. Tyler

Phillimore

1980

Published by
PHILLIMORE & CO. LTD.
London and Chichester

Head Office: Shopwyke Hall,
Chichester, Sussex, England

ISBN 0 85033 359 8

Printed in Great Britain by
UNWIN BROTHERS LIMITED
at The Gresham Press, Old Woking, Surrey
and bound by
THE NEWDIGATE PRESS, LTD.
at Book House, Dorking, Surrey

CONTENTS

LIST OF ILLUSTRATIONS

(between pages 118 and 119)

FOREWORD

By Brigadier Michael Matthews, C.B.E., R.M.P.
Corps of Royal Military Police, Provost Marshal

I am delighted and honoured to be asked to provide this foreword to *Bloody Provost* for my old comrade and fellow Corps member, Major Roy Tyler. He has spent many years carefully delving into the past to research the origins of my Corps and my ancient Office, and has produced an excellent and unique book.

The publication of an authorative work about the Provost service and my ancient Office from Saxon times until the end of the Boer War in 1902 will prove a welcome addition to many libraries and private book shelves, and will fill a gap in the knowledge of the history of our Provost service.

Bloody Provost describes so well and so fully those early days when Provost Marshals were to be feared and avoided, for it was only in comparatively recent times that the Provost Marhal's power of summary execution was removed.

There are 56 names of Provost Marshals on the board outside my office, stretching in an almost unbroken line from Henry Guyldford, who was sent in 1511 by Henry VIII to Spain as Provost Marshal, to Lord D'arcy and his army. For his services during this short campaign, Henry Guyldford was knighted in 1512 by both Ferdinand and Henry VIII and was eventually promoted to Master of the Horse and Comptroller of the Royal Household—regretfully no such opportunities seem to exist today for Provost Marshals.

London, August 1979

M. MATTHEWS
Brigadier
Provost Marshal

PREFACE AND ACKNOWLEDGEMENTS

There is no doubt that after 39 years in the Army one can become a bore to civilian friends, and if 35 of those years are spent in one Corps there is a risk of becoming a specialised bore. Perhaps this is true in my case. I do not write this as an apology, quite the opposite in fact. My years in the Military Police changed me from a boy into a man and went a long way towards giving me the education denied by the circumstances of the late 1920s and early 1930s.

Early in my Military Police service I became interested in the origins of Provost, my appetite having been sharpened by Major A. V. Lovell Knight's *History of the Office of Provost Marshal and the Corps of Military Police,* published in 1943, which, although dealing cursorily with the early days, induced me to start reading. When the war was over and I had attained a position where doors not previously available became accessible, I was able to make a positive start. Let me therefore pay tribute straight away to the Army Library Service of the Royal Army Education Corps, who obtained books from many libraries, even Harvard, and let me down on only one occasion when it was found that the book I sought had been stolen from the library to which it had been traced!

In addition to sources referred to in the text I acknowledge with gratitude hundreds of authors and many publishers who through the years have recorded the clues that have made *Bloody Provost* possible. In particular I am grateful to Gale and Polden for permission to use the work referred to above as a source, and also to use material from *Neills Blue Caps,* by H. C. Wylie, and the *History of the 8th Gurkha Rifles,* by H. J. Huxford.

H.M.S.O. very kindly authorised use of *Record of the* *Expedition to Abyssinia, 1867-68,* by T. J. Holland, *Military History of the Campaign in 1882 in Egypt,* by J. F. Maurice, and *History of the Sudan Campaign,* by H. E. Colville.

Longmans generously permitted extracts from *The Military Memoirs of Edward Costello,* by A. ·Brett-James, and from *The Napoleonic Wars of Thomas Morris,* by John Selby.

To Manchester University Press go my thanks for authority to reproduce certain letters from *The Sergeants of the Peace in Medieval England and Wales,* by R. Stewart-Brown. In particular I am indebted to Major A. S. Robertson, M.A., R.M.P., for translating the letters from their original Latin into English.

Extracts from *The Despatches of the Duke of Wellington,* by Lt.-Col. Gurwood, are reproduced by permission of John Murray, the publishers. The Oxford University Press kindly agreed to the use of material from Cartes's *Life of the Duke of Ormonde,* Volume VI.

Major T. M. W. Burnham, Intelligence Corps, stepped into the breach and translated various documents published in medieval French, and Major Keith Kidd (Retd.) was good enough to guide me through the maze of the Lord Chamberlain's Office, and to that Office I am grateful for information on the Royal Marshalmen.

To Brigadier M. Matthews, C.B.E., the current Provost Marshal, and the staff of his Headquarters, go my thanks for use of the R.M.P. archives and R.M.P. journals, and, in particular, I am grateful to Major R. J. R. Whistler, M.B.E. (Retd.) and Col. A. G. Akerman (Retd.) for their ready assistance.

R.H.Q., the King's Regiment, kindly provided details of the service of Capt. H. N. Robinson, and Lt.-Col. W. W. Leary, B.E.M. (Retd.), Curator of the Intelligence Corps Museum, directed me to Lord Burghley's Port Regulations of 1593.

To the ladies of the Army Libraries in Singapore, Bielefeld, and Dusseldorf—thank you all for your trouble, and to Mr. Yang of Kowloon Army Library. I will always be grateful for his very kind assistance.

Frau Tosca Baum of Dusseldorf, Mrs. Peggy Cooley of Singapore, Mrs. Annie Cheng Law of Sham Shui Po, Mrs. Pat Reeves of Chichester, Mrs. Mary Powell of Mill Hill, and my daughter Deirdre, all typed or re-typed drafts, no doubt murmuring 'Bloody Provost'; nevertheless, thank you, ladies, you have made this possible.

Lt.-Col. Howard A. Cole, O.B.E., T.D., D.L., F.R.S.A., F.R. Hist. S. permitted references from his *Story of Aldershot,* and gave me some very welcome advice.

W.O.2 T. Suckling, and W.O.2 D. Harmon, D.C.M., of R.M.P./S.I.B. volunteered photographic assistance in their spare time, and for this I am very grateful. Both I, and my Corps, are exceedingly grateful to Major G. C. C. Coleridge (Retd.), for providing details of his father's service as an A.P.M. and for the photograph which is reproduced elsewhere.

Finally I would point out that this book is merely an account of general interest and makes no claim to be an academic record, and for this reason it has not been referenced. I look forward to the day when this important part of our constitutional history receives the professional research and record that has for so long been neglected.

CHAPTER I

IN DAYS OF OLD

Justises did he maken newe,
Al engelond to foren throw,
Fro douere into rokesborw,
Shireues he sette, bedels and greves,
Grith-Sergeans, wit long gleves,
To yemen wilde wodes and pathes,
Fro wicke men that wolde dou scathes.

The Lay of Havelock the Dane

THIS 8th CENTURY POEM tells how, 600 years before, Ethelfrith, King of Northumbria, created Grith Sergeants as State policemen. This is probably the earliest reference to the embryonic Constables and his importance in our story will become apparent later, but he provides an ideal starting place for the narrative. The old English word *Prafost* comes from the Latin *Praeponere*—placed before, to superintend—which is a most effective description of a Peace Officer. Historically a Marshal was second in importance of the King's Officers, coming after the Constable, or High Constable, as he was sometimes called. Many other Marshals later appeared, Earl Marshal, Knight Marshal, Marshal of the Hawks, and so on. Eventually only the former—the senior Peer in the Realm—remained. He is now responsible for ceremonial, but still has to approve the appointment of the Provost Marshal who compared to all others, is a recent innovation and now purely a military office. 'Marshal' came to mean the commander of a military force, even of comparatively small bodies of troops. In civilian usage it denoted a Peace Officer, as it still does

1

today in the United States. The surviving example in Britain
is London's City Marshal, who was created originally as a
Provost Marshal, but more of him anon!

A Knight Marshal first appeared in the mid-seventh
century and in part was the forerunner of the Provost
Marshal General, as the head of the Military Police was called
until 1829. The office of Provost Marshal pre-dates the
appearance of the title in 1511, but we do not know when
it came to be adopted. Originally the Knight Marshal was
responsible to the Earl Marshal for Law Enforcement within
the Court, in due course creating a Provost Marshal to assist
him. Additional Provost Marshals were created for more
general use as and when a need arose. In those far-off days
military organisation was rudimentary and developed along
the following lines. In Saxon times a king was protected
by a number of thegns, who were mounted minor nobles,
and during the 11th century a bodyguard, known as huscarls,
was formed and kept near the king's person. All men owed
an obligation of service to the Crown and were embodied
when required under what was termed the 'Fyrd'. Men were
raised in the shires under ealdormen and reeves and addition-
ally could also be called out for police duties. From this
evolved the system of Writs of Watch and Ward, so common
during the 12th and 13th centuries. Desertion was a problem,
then as now, and the Statutes V Ethelred 28 and VI Ethelred
35 created various punishments, including death for quitting
the king's command. Under III Edmund 3 penalties were
established for absence from police duty call-out. The Shire
Sheriffs assisted by Parish Constables, though not then so
named, became responsible for mobilisation. Command
fell to the High Constable and Marshal, and so it was when
Harold fell.

In those days the parish was the smallest division for
tax and administration purposes. Churches only became
associated with parishes when someone came along with
an inclination to build one. Today, of course, the term
describes a solely ecclesiastical unit of responsibility. Of
far greater antiquity are territorial divisions called Hundreds,
which often cover several parishes. The parish headman was

known variously as Tythingman, Headborough, Borsholder, Bororeeve, Chief Pledge, Provost, or Constable. Provost was in general use from about 1100, but had been replaced by Constable by the end of the 15th century, although it lingered on in the West Country for many years. Provost in its law enforcement context was alluded to by the printer William Caxton (1422-1491) when he referred to St. Michael as the Provost of Heaven!

Each Hundred had a Head Constable who, whilst no superior of the village constable, could refer problems to him. Overall responsibility lay with the Shire Sheriff. After the Restoration in 1661 village constables were superseded in importance by Churchwardens to whom they were answerable locally. Parish officials were elected annually at the Court Leet, which had the power to punish certain minor offences, usually with financial penalties. Indeed records show that on 13 April 1416 Constable John Brewer was fined 6s. 8d. (33½p) for neglect of duty. The main difference between ancient and contemporary constables is that the former was elected annually by his neighbours, whilst the latter joins for a career, has authority within the county, and is a State Officer.

Henry I (1100-1135) created the system known as 'Provost and Four' in 1100. Each parish had four men and a Constable assisting the Hundred Jury of Twelve in tax assessment, collection, and affairs where local knowledge was necessary. Edward I (1272-1307) modified the system in 1297 and 1306, and Edward II (1307-1327) made each parish responsible for producing, when ordered, one soldier equipped for 60 days' service. Edward III (1327-77) shifted the onus for this to the Provost and Four. His enactment referred to the Constable/Provost as the 'Provost in Oyer', signifying that he was required to represent his Provostwick in Sheriff's and Coroner's Courts, in addition to the Court Leet. Edward also made the Provost and Four responsible for investigating reported crime and for raising the Hue and Cry when necessary. This ancient authority for hot pursuit, which is still extant, is defined in *The Compleat Constable*, published in 1708 thus:

'Hue and Cry' signifieth the pursuit of one having committed
felony by the highway; and if the party robb'd, or any in the
company of one murthered or robb'd, come to the Constable
of the next town, and will him to raise Hue and Cry, or to make
pursuit after the offender, describing the party, and shewing, as
near as he can, which way he is gone, the Constable ought forthwith to call upon the Parish for aid in seeking the felon. And if
he is not found there, to give the next Constable warning, and he
the next, until the offender be apprehended, or at least until
he is pursued to the seaside. The Constables of every town to
which Hue and Cry shall come, ought to search in all suspected
houses and places within their limits; and as well the officers,
as all other persons, which shall pursue the Hue and Cry, may
attach and stay all such persons as in their search and pursuit
they shall find to be suspicious, and thereupon shall carry them
before some Justice of the Peace of the county where they are
taken, to be examined where they were at the time of the felony
committed; and if any default be in the officers, they may be
fined by the Justices for their neglect.

The Provost was made responsible for billeting when Royal
or other progresses were undertaken. Later these powers
were revised, and permitted the Provost to arrest anyone
found cheating as the result of being provided with billets
or forage. Simultaneously with the above system, where
we have seen the earliest use of 'Provost' in a law-keeping
context in eight counties, the Welsh Marches and, after
conquest, Wales, another form of Peace Officer existed.
These were 'Sergeants of the Peace' and were in two forms,
Royal, where they had Shireal authority, and Baronial, with
jurisdiction within their lord's land. There was overlapping,
tyranny and corruption, whilst at the same time many
Sergeants were conscientious and efficient. Master Sergeants
equated to Hundred Head Constables and Sergeants to Parish
Constables (Provosts). This comparison is only general. Much
research needs to be done in this area of complexities and
divisions. All we can say in this brief account is that these
two systems, existing simultaneously, but often under
dissimilar circumstances, worked to a common end, keeping
the Peace.

The demise of the Sergeants of the Peace system and loss
of much of the Sheriff's powers came as a gradual result of

the Statute of Westminster of 1285. This brought into existence, as a continuing process, Justices of the Peace. However, in Cheshire and Wales Sergeants of the Peace were not abolished until 1536, as the result of 27 Henry VIII Cap 5. Whilst Sergeants of the Peace have no claim to kinship with the Military Police of today, a further contemporary Peace Keeping Officer has—Military Sergeants of the Peace, whose role was similar to those just described, but they were soldiers, not civilians like all the others. In Shropshire and the West Derby Hundred of Lancashire we have 13th-century references to Grith Sergeants as Sergeants of the Peace. That this old Scandinavian name was used contemporaneously with Provost raises an exciting thought, did the same apply during the period described in the Lay—the late sixth century? That would make the law enforcement usage of 'Provost' over 1300 years old!

Here is part of a letter of 1293, which shows how a particular family by custom appointed Grith Sergeants, and called on local residents to help pay for them:

> And he said his ancestors had followed the custom as is laid down in that manor for the preservation of the Peace in these parts, namely the appointment of a Servicium called Grithser-gauns of greater or lesser number as their predecessors saw fit, and that this Servicium was maintained by the bondmen and members of the manor, etc.

Military Sergeants of the Peace originally had fortress affiliations, but in due course became responsible for the local area and were in effect a Military Police. They were the only Peace Officers paid by the Crown. When Richard I (1189–1199) was on the Crusades, Prince John greatly increased the numbers of these men, until the eventual strength was: Yorkshire, 8; Northamptonshire, Buckingham-shire, Gloucestershire, Lincolnshire and Sussex, 6 each; Essex, Norfolk, Suffolk, Hertfordshire, Oxfordshire, Berkshire, Warwickshire, Leicestershire, Worcestershire, Herefordshire, Nottinghamshire and Derbyshire, 4 each. An overall total of 92 men.

When John (1199–1216) eventually became king he again increased the establishment. Certain Orders and establishments were expected to assist the Crown to maintain the Peace Officers. King Henry III (1216–1272) ordered the Sheriff of Yorkshire not to collect from the Knights Templars. His letter reads:

> At Windles on 15 July 1238
>
> Concerning the exemption of the men of the Knights Templar. The Sheriff of Yorkshire is commanded that he is not to require the men of the Knights Templars in his jurisdiction to contribute towards the maintenance of those assigned to keep the Peace in those areas, although their men are as ready as others to defend the King's Peace, in so far as it concerns them.

One wonders how such a conditional support of the Common Law requirement to keep the Peace would be received today? The following letter from Henry III shows how men were ordered and maintained:

> 28th May 1241
>
> The King to the Sheriff of Yorkshire, greetings.
>
> On receipt of this letter, and in the presence of your legal and Military Knights, and on their advice, you are commanded to select eight Serjeants and to retain them, horsed and armed, for the maintenance of the Peace, and to travel to those places where it is necessary.
>
> Should they hear or know anything of malefactors or disturbers of our Peace, all neighbouring townships are to rally under arms to the Hue and Cry, and are to join the aforesaid Serjeants in the pursuit and capture of such malefactors and peacebreakers. Those who are captured in this manner and likewise those who are suspected are to be received by you notwithstanding any event or difficulty, and held safe in prison until you receive our further order.
>
> And so that honest men should not be troubled by the aforesaid Serjeants in any way, each of them is to have 6d per day for the maintenance of themselves their horses, and their men. This is to begin on the date of this order; the Sunday preceding the feast of St. Barnabas the Apostle; and to continue up to the feast of the Exaltation of the Holy Ghost.
>
> You are also to arrange in each of your townships night-watches up to the feast of St. Peter ad Vincula following the receipt of this order. These night-watches are to be diligent in arresting wrong doers, and holding in arrest all suspects and strangers until dawn.
>
> Concerning the above you are to act speedily, notifying us of the names of the above Serjeants.

Similar letters were sent to 18 other Sheriffs, raising a total of 85 Military Sergeants of the Peace during 1241. One of those representing Essex was asked for by name; therefore, until the contrary is proved, one William of Casingham can be held to be the first named Military Policeman.

As was earlier recorded, the Statute of Westminster was the death knell for existing peace keeping methods, though no date for their end can be set. However, if we have learned that 'Provost' for hundreds of years denoted a Peace Officer, that for ages there was a Military Peace Officer, and that the term 'Marshal' could indicate various Crown appointments, then we are equipped to proceed further into this historical maze, but as so much remains unknown we are never likely to establish the exit beyond doubt.

When, in 1152 Henry Plantagenet married Eleanor of Aquitaine, lands stretching to the River Loire in south-western France came to him as dowry. By the time the groom arrived in his new possessions in 1156 he was Henry II (1154–1189). Our French territory was governed by a Seneschal, with a variety of lesser officials under him. These included Constables of Castles, who were in fact guardians of their fortresses and Law Enforcement Officers. There were local Provosts as in England, and another appointed directly by the king, known as the Royal Provost of Ombriere Castle in Bordeaux, whose duties were similar to the Provost Marshals we shall meet later in our story. He had his own executioner and had authority over the castle, its immediate precincts, and visitors to the town. Bordeaux town had its own Provost, who did not always see eye-to-eye with his Royal appointed neighbour. The Royal Provost of Bordeaux is the first Provost we have met with power of life and death. After the accession of Richard I a Royal Provost was created for Bayonne, who also had a Court independent to that of the bishop and town, and his own executioner. The right to collect the king's taxes in the town was given to the Royal Provost.

One of our earliest military codes was that issued by Richard in Chinon during March 1190 before departing for the Crusades. It is of interest that one of the military punishments provided was that of tarring and feathering, which today survives as a favoured punishment of subversives in Ireland.

Our French administration was not very effective outside the large towns. Local officials exercised authority far beyond their proper place in the order of society and much tyranny resulted. An example of this occurred during 1277 in Barsac where the Provost arrested a Crusader and hanged a priest, both matters within the jurisdiction of the Bishop of Bordeaux. It will be noted that the Provost had already reached the stage where no compunction was felt about hanging a person not under their jurisdiction. In England, however, this was not so, and 200 years would pass before the Provost assumed powers of life or death.

During the reign of Edward I one Bertram de Podernac became Mayor, Royal Provost and Constable of Bayonne Castle simultaneously, and Hugh de Broc did the same in 1287. The Seneschal, Armaury de Craon, had to intervene in a boundary dispute between the Municipality of Bordeaux and the Royal Provost in 1314. In 1373 the Black Prince headed the King's Council which drew up a table of fees that the Royal Provost of Ombriere could charge. In those days all official offices were self enriching, and the Royal Provost must have been very pleased to be put in charge of the Castle stores, over the head of its Constable! Relations between the Royal Provost and Bordeaux remained a source of friction right until the end of the English presence. By 1204 the foolishness of King John had resulted in much of our territory being lost to the French.

Richard I appears to have founded the first actual Military Police, a body 30 strong, known as the Household Sergeants at Arms, who were responsible for the king's person and for law and order within 12 miles of his presence. They were on the staff of the Knight Marshal and each carried a crown-topped mace as a badge of office. The Knight Marshal ran his own Court, the Court of Verges, for offenders apprehended within the 12-mile limit. It was this Court that, with the passing of time, gave rise to the Provost Marshal's Court.

In various parts of the country memorials exist depicting Sergeants at Arms, but it must be remembered that only after the 16th century attempts to produce likenesses were made. A brass effigy of Thomas Stable, erected in 1371, can be seen at Shopland, Essex, and in Wandsworth, Surrey, one Nicholas was commemorated in 1420; the mace in particular is very well preserved in this instance. In Broxbourne, Herts., is a particularly fine stone memorial to John Borrell, who clasps his mace in both hands.

In the Middle Temple is an illustration of the coronation procession of Charles II (1649–1684) on 23 April 1661. No less than 20 Sergeants at Arms can be seen. All are mounted and ride with maces resting on right shoulders. The maces are about three feet long and the heads are formed entirely as crowns. In due course Sergeants at Arms gave way to another body with similar responsibilities, except that these were restricted to Royal residences. This little force, Royal Marshalmen, existed until quite recently. They also carried a mace, no bigger than a policeman's truncheon, and this had the Royal Arms on one end and those of Westminster on the other. Previously under the control of the Knight Marshal they passed, when his office was abolished in 1846, under the authority of the Comptroller of the Royal Household. At the coronation of Queen Victoria (1837–1901) the Marshalmen marched in ranks of four behind the Earl Marshal.

The Earl Marshal often influenced the course of history. One such instance occurred in 1164, when John, Marshal of England, coveted Pagham Manor, now under four miles from the home of the Royal Military Police, and within 10 miles of the seat of the Earl Marshal. Thomas, Archbishop of Canterbury, owned the land. John invoked legislation permitting those in dispute with the Church to take their case to the king, and substituted a prayer book for the Bible when taking the oath the law required. The archbishop refused to appear when summoned by the king, having heard of John's ruse. The king was infuriated by Thomas's defiance, and this led to the break which terminated with the archbishop's murder and eventual canonisation as St. Thomas à

Becket. There is a link with those far-off days still. John had a son, William, known commonly as William the Marshal's son! This eventually became William Marshalson, thus establishing this as an English surname.

In due course officials were created known as Commissioners of Array, whose responsibility it was to raise troops when men were required. An early appearance of such a Commission is evidenced by a Writ of Henry III of 13 June 1230 authorising Constables/Provosts in villages outside city or borough limits to muster able-bodied men. The onus of overseeing Arrays was originally on Head Constables, but later special Shrieval Commissioners were established for the purpose. For centuries Writs were the means by which citizens were called out for peace-keeping purposes. On 4 August 1233 one such Writ was issued raising men for a Hue and Cry to apprehend the rebel Richard Marshall and his adherents. Under another such writ issued on 24 August 1238 one Nicholas de Bolevil took 10 Sergeants at Arms from the Court, and assisted by Chippenham men searched local woods for bandits. These two examples illustrate the wide use of Writs, one being issued for State security and the other for thief taking. Edward I issued several Peace Keeping Writs, one of 16 June 1306 specified just how this should be done. Between 21 June 1308 and 13 June 1385 20 Writs were issued for police purposes. Edward II once called out High Provosts and Provosts in Norfolk, plus two men from each port in the county, for the purpose of planning operations against Queen Isabella and Mortimer, her lover. Perhaps one day the absorbing subject of Writs for Hue and Cry will be thoroughly researched; until then we can do no more than mention them in passing.

CHAPTER II

WHEN KNIGHTS WERE BOLD

COURTS OF CHIVALRY are often encountered when reading contemporary accounts of medieval history, and as their organisation concerned the forbears of today's Provost Marshals it is right that we glance briefly at them. William I (1066-1087) allegedly introduced Trial by Combat, which was the usual outcome of these Courts. Originally they catered for felonies committed by nobles and military classes, but they gradually assumed competency for State and chivalric transgressions, losing sight of their primary function. By the accession of Richard II (1377-1399) the Treason Duel had become recognised as an extension of the system. Courts were conducted with precise ceremonial by the Constable and Marshal, though eventually it was the Knight Marshal to whom the responsibility fell. The king's uncle, Thomas of Woodstock, had drawn up the Woodstock Ordinance, which regulated the conduct of Trials by Combat. These contained a table of fees for the Constable and Marshal, and stipulated conditions under which the arms and mounts of defeated contestants were forfeited to them. Richard reinforced the rules by his 8 Richard II Ch. 5, and 13 Richard II Ch. 2. That he rigidly enforced these is evidenced by the execution, on 30 November 1384, of Martigo de Vilense, who was hung, drawn and quartered for having falsely accused another man of treason, merely for the opportunity to settle a private quarrel by combat. The king consented to the execution 'Lest such appeals become many in the land'. In this instance the king used the appropriate Criminal Court, but his tendency to ignore them was one of the arguments used by Henry IV

(1399-1413) in support of his seizure of the throne. Article 26 of these accusations accused Richard of contravening Magna Charta by using Trial by Combat to remove political opponents. This was particularly obnoxious when one considers that the king's champions were lusty young knights whereas their opponents were normally past their prime.

Henry also misused these Courts. During 1401 he brought William Clark of Canterbury before the Court for slandering him. Clark was convicted, tortured and beheaded. Henry's I Henry IV Ch. 14, published in the first year of his reign, restricted Chivalric Courts to particular offences committed overseas, and directed that the appropriate Civil Courts should have jurisdiction in all other cases.

The last official Trial by Combat was in 1492 before Henry VII (1485-1509) when Sir Hugh Vaughan killed his opponent. Henry VIII (1509-1547) was thwarted in an attempt to revive the system. An encounter by private agreement occurred in Ireland on 12 September 1583, when the victor sent his opponent's head to the authorities in Dublin. Private duelling continued for a long time, but the passing of the Courts of Chivalry brought an end to many of the tyrannical powers inherited by the Knight Marshal.

Edward III had done much to improve our mobilisation methods, nominating 'Keepers of Maritime Land' to watch the coast and raise men for local defence when necessary. It was he who suggested church bells as an early-warning system, permitting the use of one for services. This concession was not permitted in 1588 and 1940 when history repeated itself. Edward introduced a system of voluntary enlistment in the Army and permitted convicts to enlist. These men were used in the most dangerous situations and pardoned if they eventually returned home. He introduced the contractual system, of which we shall read more later. It was a step forward, but open to abuse. He also forbade litigation against men on active service, and appointed lawyers to manage estates of landowners serving abroad. Henry of Lancaster was sent on an expedition to France in 1345 and many of the ships in his fleet had a constable, then a mixture of bosun and master-at-arms, among the crew. The custom of living off the land, combined with the antecedents of many of the soldiers, did not endear them to the French, but what today would be outrageous was then considered commonplace during operations. Discipline was enforced by the commander, and Edward had no scruples. When, at Beauvois in 1346, a monastery was looted against his orders, he personally traced and hanged 20 of the men concerned. Native criminals emulated the invaders, and contemporary records reveal many instances of rape and atrocity by French monks. In England profiteering, particularly on routes used by troops, was rife. During 1355 every wine store and inn in London was visited by the Royal Butler, who catalogued and priced all stocks. When purveyors arrived to victual expected troops, woe betide those who attempted to raise their prices! Returning soldiers robbed and raped as they dispersed to their homes, often combining in bands, causing village Provosts to call out men to resist them.

For many months the coronation feast of Henry V (1413–1422) on 9 April 1413, held in Westminster Great Hall, was the talk of London. The Marshal and his tipstaffs were forced to ride horses to make paths for the staff and guests to get to the tables. It is one of the unsolvable questions of history that we do not know what kind of Marshal he was. Obviously both the Marshal and Knight Marshal would have been guests, the Marshal of the hall was but a head butler, and contemporary writers would be unlikely to equate sergeants-at-arms with tipstaffs, possibly therefore it was the, as yet unnamed, Provost Marshal, who did have tipstaffs in his establishment. As this occurred 98 years before a Provost Marshal is first referred to as such we can only guess.

On 14 August 1415 Henry landed at Harfleur with the largest army since the days of Edward III, his great-grandfather. He was intent on regaining our lost French possessions. Henry and his staff occupied seven vessels, each of which carried a constable, and he sailed from Southampton on 7 August in the *Trinity Royal,* captained by Stephen

Thomas. Sir H. Nicholas published in 1832 his *History of the Battle of Agincourt*. This contained Henry's disciplinary code, which was obviously modelled on that of Chinon. Henry appreciated that for a law to have any effect it must be known, his Ordinance therefore concluded:

> Also that these pointe afore writtene, which be nedefall, are to be cryed in the Coste, and also it is nedefull that the cupie be given to every governour of men in the coste, so that they may have playne knowledge to enforce their men of the aforesaid ordenance.

Today officers commanding are still required to periodically acquaint their troops with certain sections of the Army Act 1955.

One section of the code required all Royal staff, including those of the Marshalsea (Marshal's prison), to wear scarlet. Five-and-a-half centuries later Military Police still wear scarlet cap covers on duty. The Marshalsea had its own clerk, Robert Castell. Thus we have a Marshal's prison with a uniformed staff so soon after the appearance of a disciplinary Marshal at the coronation feast. Who then can doubt that, by 1415, a Provost Marshal was in being, even if not then so named?

Harfleur surrendered on 22 September, having undertaken to do so if not relieved. Henry immediately organised a marine patrol on the Seine to prevent surprise. One vessel concerned was the *Lytyll John,* hired from one William Soper for three months at a cost of £140. Among the crew was a constable.

Records show that Henry used the Hue and Cry to apprehend a soldier, who had despoiled a church. The man was hanged immediately. Thus we learn that this system of hot pursuit was not confined solely to civilian use in England.

Many of the punishments under Henry's code resulted in financial gain for the Constable and Marshal, viz. Section 13:

> Also that no man escrie which is called Mounte, nor no other unreasonable escrie in costes upon payne that he may be founde begynner of such an escrie by under arrest of conestable and mareschalle, and also be put from his horse and harnies, unto

the tyme that he hath made a fyne with them, and moreover his body to the Kynges will of his liffe. And who that certifieth who is the begymner shall have one hundred shillings for his travaille of the conestable and mareschalle.

Therefore not only did the Constable and Marshal gain a horse and harness if the fine was not paid, but anyone who informed received five pounds.

The subsequent march of Henry across France deserves more credit than has been given. Realising the importance of traffic control he personally supervised the Seine crossing by his fighting men, whilst two of his best officers oversaw the crossing of stores and followers at another point.

On 25 October 1415, 6,000 English, mainly archers, defeated 25,000 French killing over 7,000 of them. The battle of Agincourt dealt French nobility a blow that took several generations to recover from. There can be no doubt that our soldiers were generally well disciplined during this period. Let the French historian, 'the monk of St. Denis', tell what our enemies thought of us before the action:

> They considered it a crime to have bad women in their camp. They paid more regard than the French themselves to the welfare of the inhabitants who declared themselves in our favour. They closely observed the rules of military discipline and scrupulously obeyed the orders of their King. His words were received with enthusiasm, and not only by the leading men, for the common soldiers also promised to fight to the death.

The dictates of self survival caused the massacre of many of the prisoners after the battle. It is therefore unlikely that Article 16 of the Ordinance would have been invoked. This said:

> Also if any man take prisoner, and another man come upon hym, asheying parte, menacing that ellees he will slay hym, he shal have no parte, though it were so that parte had to be grant unto hym, and if he shal slay the prisoner he shal be arrested by the Conestable and Mareschalle without deliverance, tylle that he have made gve with the partie, and a fyne after the awarde of the conestable.

Henry returned in triumph to London on 23 November 1415. The crowds in London welcoming him were so dense that it was not possible to pass from Poultry to Cheapside despite the efforts of tipstaffs and sergeants. To whom did these officials belong? London did not have its own Sergeant-at-Arms before 1419. From 1338 one had been loaned to the mayor from the Royal Household, and was used mainly as crier. The City still has only one Sergeant-at-Arms, who today carries the mace before the Lord Mayor. Possibly the unsuccessful street clearers had returned with the king and were his sergeants-at-arms, while tipstaffs were those on the establishment of the Knight Marshal and led by an official yet to be named as a Provost Marshal.

The following January the Earl of Dorset made a raid on the French coast, using two ships, the *Holy Ghost* and the *Trinity*, each carrying a constable, both of whom were paid 6d. (2½p) per day. The earl later joined up with the Harfleur garrison and was badly wounded in a sally from the town.

Henry returned to France on 30 July 1417, landing where Trouville now stands. The Duke of Clarence was Constable, and a special Commission authorised him to punish all who broke the army regulations. Together with the Earl Marshal, that term now being in use, he ran a military court. The applicable records state, 'obedience to their commissioned subordinates was vigorously enforced, violent resistance to arrest being punishable if a Royal Officer was hurt'. Surely this suggests that 'duly commissioned subordinates' were members of the staff of the Earl Marshal and Constable, and the reference to a Royal officer, not just any officer, also infers this; one feels that the Provost Marshal had indeed arrived; who else was likely to be present when military offenders resisted? The Duke of Clarence died on 22 March 1421, and with him lapsed the ancient office of Steward of England. Thereafter it was revived only occasionally for a particular state function, or as a reward for a Court favourite.

The offence of resisting a State officer in his disciplinary capacity is echoed today, for Section 15 of the Army Act

1955 creates the specific offence of resisting a Provost Marshal or his subordinates, which it seems is exactly what the 1417 code of conduct intended. That code was somewhat hard on prostitutes—any caught in camp could be robbed and have an arm broken before being turned out!

Rouen surrendered on 20 January 1419, and the English immediately fed the starving inhabitants. Apart from five defiant castles the whole of Normandy was subjugated by the end of February. Garrison life caused, as always, a lessening of discipline. This led to the king drawing up a Code of Conduct for Garrisons in Nantes during 1419.

To a great degree the control exercised over troops is reflected in their behaviour. This is true whether we are dealing with an army or a platoon. In this period tenants and serfs owed allegiance to their lord, and he made the political decisions that affected their lives. It is not surprising therefore that control by the commander was often tenuous. Throughout history events have been influenced by notables changing sides during a passage of arms, decisions which underlings never thought to query, if they thought at all on the issues of the day!

The indenture system, introduced in the late Middle Ages, did much to weaken parochial affiliations. This introductory period of contracts led to today's enlistment procedure. An officer contracted to provide fully equipped men for a specified period, and whilst this was fine for short engagements, it did not meet the needs of prolonged occupation, as in France. Modifications led to the system of Muster and Review, whereby those contracted were periodically counted and inspected. Personalities could change between musters provided the set number was maintained. Payment was made to the Captain according to the number produced and the conditions of the arms, equipment and horses. Thus pay was reasonably regular and, being in arrears, deterred desertion. Musters were normally quarterly, but on active service monthly. Regular pay made it less likely that the troops would live off the land. Once the inspection was over the troops were said to have 'passed Muster', an expression still used today. Musters were also used occasionally in

England to check the availability of men should they be required for service. A Seneschal, not to be confused with the Seneschal mentioned earlier, held the muster in France. A Commission still survives dated 27 August 1419, directing Sir Huge Lutteral, Seneschal to the Treasurer of Normandy, to muster the Normandy garrison half yearly or quarterly at his discretion. Musters were prone to sharp practices; sometimes the same men and equipment appeared in different stations, having been passed from one Garrison Captain to another. Those holding musters began preparing the Rolls in duplicate and drawing lines under the last entries to prevent additions. Here, translated from quaint Norman French, is a muster certificate:

> Be it known to those whom it concerns that I, Guillame Harman, Equerry and Controller, ordained and established by most noble, exalted and powerful Prince, His Royal Highness, the Regent of the United Kingdom of France, Duke of Bedford, and Lord of Nante, to see and know about the soldiers ordered and charged with the guard of the town of Nante, in the company of the late Edward Makwilliam, laterly departed, during his days as Bailiff and Captain of the aforementioned Nante, witness and certify that the persons whose names and surnames are listed in a parchment schedule attached to this present Certificate, written in my hand, and signed with my signature, have carried out their duties and continue to serve the King, my Sovereign Lord, and my Lord the Duke of this town of Nante, as soldiers in the Company and under the Command of the said late Edward, since the first day of January, and until the nineteenth day of the following February, excepting certain absences, which as declared in the Muster Roll of the said period of time.
>
> Witness the seal of my Arms this Monday the twelfth day of the month of April in the year one thousand four hundred and twenty eight.

Presumably the new Captain took over the recently mustered Company as seen!

On 22 November 1425 the office of local Seneschal was abolished, Sir William Oldhall being the last known holder of such a situation. The Earls of Warwick, Salisbury and Suffolk were each directed to issue 'Commissions of Array' for their respective military districts. These Commissions were authorities for holding musters, and later were used for mobilisation at home when danger threatened. A Controller of Musters was appointed as a permanent official. Originally an assistant to the Commissioners, he often officiated at musters, and had to supervise garrison guard duties in his normal station.

The word 'Captain' then described the commander of a body of troops of any size. Many years were to pass before today's ranking system came into being.

A Commission of Array in St. Lo, dated 23 May 1429, reports that the Controller ordered to assist himself failed to pass muster! Following redistribution of offices after the Earl Marshal, the Duke of Arundel, was killed at Gerberoy on 7 May 1435, the Seneschal was reintroduced with Lord Scales as the first incumbent. Unfortunately the records do not show whether he was responsible for mustering, and it is likely that he was not. In those days the fiscal year started at Michaelmas and that became a convenient time to hear disciplinary charges, as musters were held then. Even today few troops miss pay parade, so witnesses were likely to be available. Muster records show that on 3 June 1436 eighteen archers were disciplined at Fresney for leaving their place of duty on various occasions to visit the village of Villaine-la-Juhel. History does not record their punishment, but it does nominate their officer as 'the Lieutenant and Marshal of the said place'. Clearly here we have an official who is both a military officer and a Peace Officer charged with the maintenance of discipline. Is he, perhaps, our first definitely identifiable Provost Marshal? Certainly the process of evolution is speeding up, for we are only 75 years away from the first Provost Marshal whose office is beyond doubt!

Our journey through the years leaves so many questions unanswered; for instance, who organised the execution, after sentence of death was passed on 30 May 1439, of Joan of Arc. Such events fell under the jurisdiction of the Earl Marshal, through the Knight Marshal, whose officer subordinates were Provost Marshals, and they supervised executions. However, it is a point that must, for the time being at least, remain obscure.

One failure of the Contract, or Indenture, scheme was
the ease with which troops could desert in France and return
to England, merely forfeiting any pay due. If apprehended
and returned to their Captain he could only stop the pay
that they had already decided to do without. In severe cases
a Commission to imprison offenders could be obtained, but
this meant financial loss to the Captain. Desertion was particularly annoying when troops, who were all volunteers,
were assembling for a crusade. Cardinal Beaufort when
recruiting for what became known as the 'Hussite' crusade
in Normandy, produced a military code, and this told those
who joined for religious reasons and were unpaid that they:

> Stande under the lawes, Statutes and Ordinances to be maed
> by the Contable and Marshal as is above said, as well as thei
> that go for wages. Considered that with or be the King's people
> it is as necessary to kepe under goode reule and preserve from
> all mescheife and inconvenience on as other.

Thus the military code became applicable to all members
of the Army for the first time. Through the subsequent years
the position fluctuated, but ceased to become arguable on
1 January 1957, when wives, Red Cross, N.A.A.F.I., and
other officials became subjects to Military Law under certain
circumstances through the provisions of Section 209 of the
Army Act 1955.

The offence of desertion became a statutory offence in
1439 under 18 Henry VI Cap 19, which enacted that once a
soldier had received part of his pay (the King's Shilling) and:

> So have mustered and been entered on Record as the King's
> Soldiers before his Commissioners, for such terms as their Masters
> (Captains) have indented, have presently after their Muster and
> Record and receipt of part or whole of their wages, departed
> and gone where they could—and long within their terms
> departed from their Captains and the King's Service, without
> apparent licence granted to them by the said Captains. It is
> therefore enacted that every man Mustering and receiving the
> King's wages who leaves his Captain in this way, except that
> notorious sickness or impediment by the visitation of God,
> which may be reasonably known, suffer him not to go and
> which he shall certify to his Captain and shall repay his money,
> so that he shall provide for him another soldier in his place,
> shall be punished as a felon.

A further provision covered the arrest of deserters who returned to the United Kingdom under their own steam. They could be arrested by the Chief in the County having 'Royal Power' and brought before the magistrates. It also made their unlawful return a felony in its own right.

Thus overnight desertion changed from being a very minor offence to a felony, and therefore punishable by death. Today the essence of Section 186 (4) of the Army Act 1955 is that deserters arrested by the Civil Power must be brought before a magistrate—no change in well over 500 years!

CHAPTER III

TO THE END OF THE TUDORS

ON ST. GEORGE'S DAY 1509 Henry VIII (1509-1547) came to the throne. His disabilities were many, but his influence on military development does, in my view, far outweigh contemporary disenchantment and disgust. An early military involvement occurred in 1511 when Lord D'arcy was sent with an army to Spain, and Henry Guyldford of Leeds Castle in Kent was commissioned as his Provost Marshal. Thus in May of that year, we at last encounter the office nominated in today's terms. The English army landed in Cadiz on 1 June, and:

> Some ran to the stewes, some brooke hegges and spoyled orchardes and wyneyardes and orynges before they were ripe, and did many other outrageous dedes, whereof the chief of the towne of Cadiz came to complain to Lord D'arcy on hys shippe, which sent forth his Provost Marshal with scarclie with payne refrayned the yoman archers, they were so hot and wilfull, yet by commandment and policy they were all brought on bord their shippes.

During the last war the author was one of the Military Police who, by 'commandment and policy', coerced many a drunken soldier back to his ship—times may change, soldiers never!

For his services Henry Guyldford was knighted, both by Ferdinand of Spain and Henry. He also became a founder member of the new Royal bodyguard, the 'Spears'. The army that went to Fuentarrobia, Southern Spain, the following year under the Earl of Essex had a Provost Marshal on its strength. The force was sickly, mutinous, and consistently beaten, and it returned to England by Christmas, the troops having insisted that: 'after Michalmas we will abide for no man', a reference to the end of their indentured period. As was usual in those days the returning soldiers left a record of disease and upheaval from the ports of disembarkation to their homes.

Henry produced 'Articles of War' for his invasion of France in May 1513. Two provisions affecting the Provost Marshal were that, on orders from the High Marshal, he would mark out camping places, and arrange a market place on a site allocated by the Lieutenant-General. Control of Sutlers and market organisation was a Provost responsibility for hundreds of years. The Articles also made the Provost Marshal responsible for camp defence, for visiting sentries 'Twise or thrise in the night', for enforcing silence after 'lights out', the signal for which was 'the Watchepiece shotten off'. His tipstaffs were to maintain order in camp, and he was responsible for administering punishments, for which purpose he maintained his own prison (marshalsea). Discipline, security, messing, even sanitation, all were the responsibility of this ancient office. It is ironic that the Articles referred to his 'Provost Company', a term not officially adopted in the Army until 1936!

Like earlier Codes the Articles encouraged informers:

> . . . men found playing at dise, cardes, tables, closhe, handout or any other game whereby they shal waste theyr monie, would lose all such monie as he or they playe for, the one halfe to the Provost of the Marshall, the other halfe to hym that so fyndeth them playing.

This is the first instance where we have a reference to the fact that Provost (meaning the Service as opposed to an individual) was part of the organisation of the Marshal, so there can now be no doubt as to its origins.

An entry in State accounts for 1514 proves that a marshalsea was not necessarily a permanent structure. It records that Richard Gybburn purchased a hale (marquee) for the Provost Marshal's marshalsea. The tent measured 34ft. by 12ft., and presumably its inmates were made responsible for raising and striking it? That a marshalsea was part of the

Court administration is proved by the Domesday Book,
which show that in 1086, during the reign of William I
(1066–1087), one Godfrey held the manor of East Worldham
for running the Court marshalsea. He was described as the
Royal Marshal and this provides another link in the inter-
rupted chain of our Provost Marshal's ancestry, for the
Royal Marshal was within the gift of the Crown through
the Marshal, just as today in theory is the office of Provost
Marshal, each nominee being approved by the Earl Marshal.

When Henry met Francis I of France, a few miles south
of Calais on 7 June 1520 in an attempt at reconciliation,
history was made. The meeting has been remembered as
'The Field of the Cloth of Gold', and our Provost Marshal,
Sir Henry Guyldford, led the English procession, his counter-
part leading the French. Both were responsible for security
in their respective camps and this early co-operation in law
enforcement is probably quite unique. We now know,
incidentally, that Sir Henry was issued with his spectacular
dress from the Royal Wardrobe on 11 August 1518, as was
Carew, Master of the Horse, a post later held by Sir Henry,
who went on to become Comptroller of the Royal Household. Identification of Royal officers becomes much easier
after the execution of the Duke of Buckingham in 1521,
for his office of Constable died with him.

Sir Henry befriended the Protestant reformer, William
Tyndale, after his acquittal in 1521, and introduced him
to Tunstall, Bishop of London, through whom Tyndale
made contacts that enabled him eventually to publish his
English translation of the Bible. Sir Henry died in 1532,
and on 6 December 1536 Tyndale was strangled and burnt
as a heretic in Belgium. It was on 1 May that year that Anne
Boleyn was sent to the Tower prior to her execution for
adultery.

Resentment at changes in land laws, dissolution of the
local religious establishments and other matters led to revolt
in Lincolnshire and Yorkshire. Known to history as 'The
Pilgrimage of Grace', the trouble started at Louth on
1 October 1536 and spread rapidly. Energetic action by
the Duke of Suffolk restored order locally by 13 October,

but the revolt simmered until the following March. Robert
Aske from the East Riding led the Yorkshire outbreak on
9 October. Suffolk's Provost Marshal, Sir Ralph Ellerker, was
ruthless in his punishments, a fact which later rebels foolishly
lost sight of.

During 1544 our Provost Marshal in Guisnes, France, was
Thomas Audley, brother of Chancellor Thomas Audley.
This old custom of giving brothers identical names may
have served a purpose years ago, but it has little to commend
it to those of us interested in historical research today.
On 25 August 1544 in France, Sir Ralph Ellerker again
appeared, where he hanged one of his men, a member of
the Scout Watch, for failing to give warning that the French
were coming. In today's parlance this duty would be known
as an outlaying picket. Sometimes the Provost Marshal was
responsible for these, but with time the responsibility passed
permanently to the Scout Master. Our Irish contingent in
this campaign had pipers, surgeons and a Provost Marshal
on their establishment, and each soldier had a boy servant.

Edward VI (1547-1553) came to the throne on 28 January
1547, and Provost Marshal Thomas Audley later dedicated
a book 'Treatise on the Art of War' to him. This can be seen
in the British Museum Library (Add. MSS. No. 23971).
Here are the responsibilities of a Provost Marshal according
to Audley:

> And when the High Marshall is appointed and for every
> Battail (main body of Troops) one Provost Marshall with his
> Under Marshall, with his necessaries VZ a Hale (Marquee), with
> Jornes (Irons), with the Safe Keeping of the prisoners and
> carriage of the same at his Majesties charge. A sufficient number
> of Tipstaffs or Sergents for the apprehension of offenders and
> Safe Keeping of theme. A Clarke of the Watche, a Clarke of the
> Market, and an executioner, these being the necessary Officers
> that be under a Provost Marshall.
> And there be appointed for every Battail or Warde one High
> Harbinger to appoint the place where the men shall lodge after
> the High Marshall hath appointed the ground. Also the said
> Harbingers ought to appoint ways and streets for the men to
> passe through within the campe. And in specific overlook that
> you have faire and easie passage for the men of the Artillery,
> where men do assemble together in Battail at the time of the

Larme, all saving the Watche or the Warde. Also there must be
Scotmasters appointed for every Battail or Warde.

And the High Marshall and Provost Marshall must see all
these Officers do their duty, for thei be all of the Office of
Marshall lykwyse, if it be so that you think it good to appoint
Forage masters thei shall also be under the Marshall.

Obviously this instruction was influenced by Henry VIII's
Articles of War. However, as the first recorded catalogue of
a Provost Marshal's duties they are of great value historically.
It is also interesting that every 'Battail', or large body of
troops, had its own Provost Marshal, as indeed an army has
today. In those far-off days a Provost Marshal had many
duties that have since become military appointments in
their own rights. However, from this point on there will
be no confusion over offices in this narrative, for wherever
a Provost Marshal is referred to he is called so in the records
of the day.

Shortly after the death of Henry VIII our army advanced
into Scotland. The Duke of Somerset was in command, with
James Wylford as the Provost Marshal. Judges of the accompanying Military Court were Sir William Patten and Sir
William Cecil, who later as Lord Burghley became Queen
Elizabeth's famous Chancellor. Discipline appears to have
been rigid, for on the march north Wylford hanged a soldier
in Newcastle market place for the simple offence of quarrel-
ling! Wylford was later knighted for his services at the battle
of Pinkie Cleugh in September 1547, when the Scots were
defeated with heavy loss. Records do not tell us what
happened to the garrisons of Douglas and Thornton, who
after surrender were handed over to the Provost Marshal.

An incident, smacking of the old Trial by Combat,
occurred in Haddington early in 1548. A prisoner named
Newton was to be executed for making rude remarks about
young King Edward VI (1547–1553). Newton protested that
a man named Harrison was responsible, whereupon Harrison
challenged him to combat. Lists 40ft. by 40ft. were erected
in the market place and after both men swore they were
innocent the fight commenced. There are different versions
of what occurred, but Harrison died and Newton was

released. The Commander, Lord Grey, gave him the coat off his back and a gold chain as compensation. Sir James Wylford, after governing Haddington Castle, was wounded and taken prisoner by the Scots several months later.

Rebellion broke out in Sampford Courtney, Devon, on Whit Sunday 1549 when liturgical changes came into effect. Led by their tailor, Edward Underhill, the villagers forced the vicar to say the old Mass. Within days thousands had flocked to Bodmin, where the mayor joined them. The rebels then marched to Exeter and set up two camps outside the city. These camps were commanded by the mayors of Bodmin and Torrington respectively, but the acknowledged leaders of the Cornish Rising, as is known to history, were John Winslade of Tregarrick and Squire Humphrey Arundell of Helland. The rebels submitted a list of 14 religious demands and one secular demand to the authorities, the latter requesting that gentility should be permitted but one personal servant each. An attack on Exeter by 20,000 men led by a local priest was repulsed. Soon after this loyalist forces under the command of Lord Russell chased the rebels back to Crediton, where they were crushingly defeated. The last resistance was where it had all started, in Sampford Courtney. Then the Provost Marshal, Sir Anthony Kingston, came into his own. His conduct has been likened to Judge Jeffreys of later years. In one instance he hanged a miller's servant for pretending to be his employer, saying the wretch was 'a double false knave, false in two tales'. The priest who had led the assault on Exeter was hanged from his own church, St. Thomas's, dressed in full vestments, with holy water stoup, sprinkler and sacring bell fastened to him. The mayor of Bodmin was in due course visited by Sir Anthony and asked to have a gallows built whilst they dined together. After the meal the Provost Marshal asked the mayor whether he thought the structure was strong enough, and on being assured that it was Sir Anthony said, 'Well then, get you up, it's for you', and shortly afterwards Bodmin was without a mayor. Winslade and Arundell were apprehended and taken to London for execution.

On the night of 20 June 1549 Robert Kett raised a rebellion in Attleborough, near Norwich, over new Land Laws, and within six weeks 10,000 men rallied to his banner. Royal forces commanded by the Marquess of Northampton re-took Norwich on 30 July. The same night Kett attacked and routed the Royalists, but fresh troops under the Earl of Warwick recaptured the town three weeks later. The Provost Marshal was again Sir Anthony Kingston, and in no time 59 rebels were hanging in the market place. Two days after this Kett was defeated in Dussins Dale, and his peasants slaughtered. He was captured and in due course executed in Norwich Castle, his brother being hanged from the tower of Wymondham church, the true Kingston touch. Thus ended the Norfolk rising.

Sir James Wylford arrived in York on 21 November, having been released from his captivity. The following year, on 24 March, one James Dewar was tried in Edinburgh by the Scots for accompanying Sir James when he burned Dalkeith and Newbottil in December 1548. Other Scots were also punished for assisting Sir James, who finally died from his wounds in London on 24 November 1550. His portrait can be seen today in the Council Room of St. George's Hospital, London.

Mary (1553–1558) came to the throne on 6 July 1553 and died, generally unmourned, five years later. Early in her reign, on a February morning in 1554, a charge down Charing Cross by a hotch-potch of cavalry, among whom was the Provost Marshal, Sir Anthony Kingston, helped seal the fate of the rebellion raised by William Wyatt the younger. Dozens of rebels were later executed, including Wyatt, whose speech from the scaffold helped remove suspicion from the young Princess Elizabeth. Another potential threat to the throne, Lady Jane Grey, was executed on 12 February. Harsh Sir Anthony Kingston may have been, but he was among those brave enough to bid farewell to Bishop Hooper before his martyrdom on 8 February the following year. Soon after this he was appointed to the office of Knight Marshal. Eventually he turned against the queen and was arrested for treason, dying at Cirencester, allegedly, by his own hand, on 14 April 1556, whilst being brought back to London for trial.

Our Provost Marshal in St. Quentin during 1557 was paid 20s. a day. If he had to pay for his staff he was not overpaid, for it consisted of two judges, a chaplain, two gaolers, a hangman, and four tipstaffs. Calais, our last possession in France, fell on 5 January 1558, and Bloody Mary passed away soon afterwards. It is during her reign that we first encounter civilians being punished by Provost Marshals when not in rebellion in England. Later we will come across similar circumstances in Ireland. A classic case at home occurred during 1558, when the Marquess of Winchester was permitted by Royal Proclamation to appoint Provost Marshals to try by martial law any person considered a traitor, but action was not taken to suspend the civil authority. Appointments were accordingly made for 27 counties. Sir Giles Poole was commissioned for the London post and was ordered by the Privy Council to go with his tipstaffs to St. James Fair on 9 August to put down a disturbance. This was simple police work and had no connection at all with military discipline. Provost Marshal George Penruddock was sent to attend the Wiltshire musters, but as that was one of the counties that did not have a Provost Marshal appointed, it is possible he was commissioned purely for musters under the new Militia system then being brought into use. Disorders at musters was one of the reasons for creating this crop of Provost Marshals—indeed the Cambridgeshire Provost Marshal was particularly directed to punish trouble-makers on those occasions. Mary had earlier repealed the Statute of Westminster and created Lords Lieutenant to govern counties, although the idea had been Henry VIII's. Sheriffs lost many of their ancient powers, and the onus of raising troops was henceforth vested in the new Lords Lieutenant. Commissions in the new Militia were granted by these new Royal representatives, who also were required to purchase and store arms for use in times of need. Mary died heavily in debt, and was succeeded by Elizabeth I (1558-1603), and thus the golden age of England was born. Musters became yearly mid-summer events when all males between 16 and 60 years of age were required to report. This was not very popular, and when Launceston endeavoured to obtain exemption by pleading an ancient Charter, the reply from the Privy Council was ominous:

> Moreover, you shall be well advised, touching upon the curious standing upon your Charter, lest you cause the same to be called in question, and in contending for some part you lose all!

Men were mustered in their Hundred divisions, with local gentry as their officers. These were referred to as Captains of the Hundreds, which soon became known as Companies. Two paid officers were commissioned solely for controlling musters at the various assembly points in each county. These were the Muster Master and Provost Marshal. Both checked and signed muster certificates once they were satisfied with the state of the men's arms and training. In due time the Companies became known as Train Bands, not 'Trained Bands', as is so often stated in contemporary and subsequent accounts. Henceforth these Train Bands were to play an increasingly important part in the history of England, militarily and constitutionally.

Other than the Royal bodyguard there was no standing army at this stage; troops were raised under indenture of levy from the Militia when required. The General was a Royal nominee, all other officers being appointed by the Privy Council. Normally these were the Lieutenant-General of Infantry, a Master of Ordnance, and a Sergeant-Major General. The General, or Marshal, was responsible for supply and discipline. His personal responsibility for investigating serious crime was usually restricted to those attracting the death penalty. However, his principal assistant, the Provost Marshal in practice relieved him of these duties. The matters for which the Provost Marshal was accountable fell into the following categories:

Disciplinary	Administrative
Maintenance of Discipline	Liaison with Merchants
Arrest	Price Control

continued next page

continued—

Disciplinary	Administrative
Prison arrangements	Camp Control
Provost Marshal's Court	Hygiene
Punishments	Supervision of Settlers and Fol-
Executions	lowers

He was truly a man of many parts, undertaking duties currently covered by the R.A.O.C., R.A.M.C., M.P.S.C., and Camp Commandants.

Also on the staff of the Marshal and subordinate to the Provost Marshal was a Trench Master, with responsibility for fortifications; a Scout Master, who organised intelligence matters; and a Master of the Horse, who controlled the cavalry, which generally consisted of independent units answerable to particular members of nobility.

A foretaste of what was to come, and which indirectly contributed to the use of civilian Provost Marshals, came in August 1563 when, after the fall of Le Havre, our last bridgehead in France, troops returning to southern England brought the Black Death with them.

When Lord Bothwell was awaiting trial for murder, Mary, Queen of Scots, was in touch with Queen Elizabeth. At 6 a.m. on 12 July 1567, the day of the trial, our Berwick Provost Marshal arrived at Holyrood Castle with a letter from Elizabeth to Mary. The letter was accepted by the Scots Courtier, Leatherington, but he refused to waken Mary. The Provost Marshal was unable to obtain an answer and had to return empty-handed to Berwick, which in those days was a paramount border station, where the Provost Marshal was a most important Crown officer whose signature was required before any local Peace Keeping Ordinance became law. After Queen Mary's later escape to England she was moved from Carlisle, which was too near the border, to Bolton Castle, escorted by Sir George Bowes, of whom we shall read more later, and several other notables. The queen subsequently expressed her gratitude to Sir George, who brought furniture and textiles from his own home to make her more comfortable.

During 1568 forces under Lord Warwick seized Le Havre and were quickly besieged themselves. Articles of War produced for the garrison introduced a new twist in military punishments: adulterers were to receive six days' imprisonment, and then be sent out of the town into the hands of the enemy!

What is known as 'The Rebellion of the Northern Earls' occurred in late 1569 when the Lords Westmorland and Northumberland rose in support of Mary. However, Elizabeth was forewarned and had her rival moved to Tutbury Castle. Expected support did not materialise and an army under the Duke of Somerset moved towards them. Sir George Bowes raised a force for the queen, and in retaliation his home at Streatham was destroyed. Retreating to Barnard Castle he held out until hunger and widespread desertions forced his capitulation. With 400 loyal survivors he was permitted to march away and eventually joined the Duke of Somerset and was appointed Provost Marshal. Another Royalist force commanded by Viscount Hereford had a Mr. Highfield as its Provost Marshal. Resistance soon crumbled and the rebellion petered out. Early in 1570 Sir George executed over 600, mainly peasants. As far as possible all were killed near their homes as an example to others. It was the queen's express wish that no mercy should be shown; in Durham alone 341 men were hanged. Sir George suffered great personal financial loss through the rebellion and was never fully compensated. The two months long struggle had cost the Crown £200,000, but the estates of 58 influential rebels were seized to offset this. When Sir George later wrote to Sir William Cecil (who on 25 February 1570 became Lord Burghley), referring to his employment as Provost Marshal, he complained, 'I was first a Lieutenant. I was after little better than a Marshal, I then had nothing left to me but to direct hanging matters'. Here he refers to himself as a 'Marshal'; no wonder ambiguity exists now when attempting to establish personal identifications after the space of several hundred years.

We have touched on the 'County Provost Marshal', created mainly for annual muster duties. These men were usually without military backgrounds. Their duties increased as the Lords Lieutenant developed, and as a matter of expediency many Poor Law commitments were passed to them. During 1570 London was authorised to appoint several Provost Marshals to clear the streets of 'rogues, vagabonds and maimed soldiers'. These officials were also civilians and are the forerunner of today's City Marshal. They received 6s. 8d. (33p) per day, and each of their six tipstaffs was paid 1s. (5p). By then Provost Marshals were a recognised part of the Scottish scene. In Edinburgh Castle a Provost Marshal's house still exists, and the steel breast-plate of one is preserved in the museum there. English prisoners from Sir William Drury's army were kept in the castle in 1571 and the following year the Scottish Regent ordered anyone apprehended trying to supply Queen Mary's supporters in Edinburgh, to be publicly branded in Leith market place. If again apprehended they were to be executed by hanging or drowning—the choice was the Provost Marshals! He was also told to punish rogues posing as discharged soldiers, a form of begging which appears to have been common on both sides of the Border.

Signs of regimental organisation in the English Militia appeared during 1572. Colonels are noted as commanding 'Regiments', and the following year Queen Elizabeth confirmed the Militia age limits, and ordered legislation to be passed permitting their use overseas. Successful musters were held in 37 counties that year, and 12,000 men picked for special training, thus creating the first selective Train Bands.

Sir William Drury besieged Edinburgh Castle in 1578 and his eight Articles of War issued for that campaign still survive. Our military headquarters were in Berwick, where there was constant friction between the Provost Marshal and mayor over who had the right to try soldiers for civil offences. The Provost Marshal argued that his Court was established by Privy Council Writ in the days of Edward I (1272-1307). This surely confirms that a Provost Marshal then existed, if not so named, 204 years before Henry Guyldford enjoyed the title.

Extremely comprehensive Articles of War were issued by

the Earl of Leicester for his 1585 campaign in the Lowlands.
The main sections dealing with his Provost Service were:

> Article 5.—This authorised the Provost Marshal to whip and
> banish anyone bringing prostitutes into encampments.
> Article 9.—The Provost Marshal could execute anyone com-
> municating with the enemy.
> Article 11.—Those leaving the ranks without permission could
> be executed by the Provost Marshal.
> Article 16.—He could inflict a like punishment on those
> quarrelling in garrison, town or camp.
> Article 25.—Anyone trying to buy supplies before the Provost
> Marshal had had the chance to do so could be executed.
> Article 30.—Soldiers must not resist the Provost Marshal or his
> men, and must aid them if requested. Anyone responsible
> for the escape of a prisoner became liable to suffer the
> punishment the prisoner would have received.
> Article 47.—Prisoners must be handed over to the Provost
> Marshal, who must render a return to them every eight days
> to the General.
> Article 51.—Officers detecting soldiers of offences against the
> Articles must hand them over for punishment to the Provost
> Marshal.

For this campaign the Provost Marshal had a staff of 30 men,
all equipped with firearms. In the same year our expenditure
on Secret Service matters was £20,000, a considerable sum in
those days, which suggests that the queen was not par-
simonious where her security was concerned.

Fears of Catholic traitors, intrigue by the continental
Catholic League, bad harvests, disgruntled former soldiers,
all combined to create unrest and alarm in southern England,
and from 1585 onwards increasing use was made of Provost
Marshals permitted under the Militia regulations. A Mr.
Humphrey Moore was appointed Provost Marshal of Devon.
In Shropshire Deputy Lieutenants were permitted to create
Provost Marshals without reference to the Lord Lieutenant,
so great was the need, and this delegation of authority was
copied in other counties. Thus the last 10 years of the queen's
reign produced a host of County Provost Marshals, who were
in effect Chief Constables. Thereafter their importance
quickly waned, and there are few references after the early
years of King George II (1727–1760).

CHAPTER IV

ELIZABETHAN CIVILIAN PROVOST MARSHALS

Pray for the soul of Sir Hugh Johns and Dame Mawde his wife. Sir Hugh was made Knight at the Holy Sepulcure of our Lord Jesus Christ in the city of Jerusalem the XIIIj of August the year of our Lord XIj and the said Sir John had continued in the wars for a further five years, that is to say, against the Turks and Saracens in the parts of Troy, Greece, and Turkey, under John, that time Emperor of Constantinopole, and after that was Knight Marshall of France under John, Duke of Somerset, by the space of five years, and in likewise after was Knight Marshall of England under the good John, Duke of Norfolk, which John gave unto him the manor of Ladymore, to him and to his heirs for evermore, upon whose soul Jesus have mercy.

Inscription on a tomb in Swansea—*circa* 1500

IT WAS in Elizabeth's time that the powers to create Provost Marshals under the Statutes 4 and 5 Philip and Mary Cap 3 were fully utilised. They were authorised to police the counties at other than muster time, and summarily to execute wrongdoers. Moreover only six Privy Councillors were necessary to issue a Proclamation of establishment. The use of Provost Marshals in time of peace was extraordinary, though from 1585 until the end of the century conditions were unusual to say the least. On the credit side they brought a semblance of security to the countryside, and it now appears evident that the beacons that flared across England when the Armada was sighted were supervised by Provost Marshals. Purely military Provost Marshals were still being created when required; one executed three soldiers during 1586 in Utrecht for trying to rescue a prisoner. The following year a contemporary writer, Barnaby Rich, defined

a Provost Marshal in a manner to which we are becoming
accustomed:

> The Provost Marshal is to have charge of the Marshalsea and
> he must be provided with fetters, gyves, handlockes and al
> manner of irons for Safe Keeping of such prisoners as shall be
> committed to his keepinge. He is to see due execution of all
> malefactors having received sentence of death, and to apprehend
> the authors of any disorders. He must rate the price of any
> victuals as shall come into the campe. He is to see the campe
> cleanly kept. The Watch being set he is not to suffer any noise
> or great stirre.

Thirty soldiers returning from service in the Lowlands in
1587 demonstrated outside the gates of Greenwich Castle,
refusing to leave until they received outstanding pay. Once
the Earl of Leicester confirmed that the pay had been
advanced to the soldiers' captains the queen directed that
they be paid. She then requested that the Lords Lieutenant
look for other instances of abuse and send any who had been
cheated to London for payment.

About this time the queen explained to her representatives
why Provost Marshals were necessary for civilian duties. The
letter concerned can be seen in Report 15 of the Hist. MSS.
Commission dealing with the Saville-Foljambe MSS. Here is
the explanation:

> And because in such doubtful times it falleth out commonly
> that divers false rumours and reports are given forth and spread
> abroad, which so distracts the mind of the people and breeds
> confusion, it is thought very requisit a care should be had thereof
> and that the authors of such rumours and tales should be diligently
> found out from time to time, and severally and speedily punished.
> For the better execution whereof, because there are many idle and
> vagrant persons that go about the country fit to be evil instru-
> ments of all bad actions, it is thought very requisite at this
> present for the chastising of such lewd persons and preventing
> these inconveniences that by them may rise, that you shall
> appoint a Provost Marshal, according to the authority your
> Lordship hath, by your Commission of Lieutenancy to peruse the
> country, and to be assisted in all cases by Justices and Constables,
> for the apprehension and stocking and imprisoning of them if
> they will not give themselves to labour, wherein, praying your
> Worship that speedy direction be given in this behalf, we wish
> your Lordship heartily farewell.

Thus we have Provost Marshals acting as Chief Constables—'to be assisted in all cases by Justices and Constables'—which is very different from the relationship between Chief Constables and Justices that exists today.

In 1588 the threat of a Spanish invasion resulted in the Train Bands being called out to a camp in Tilbury. A Captain Peter Crisp was appointed Provost Marshal of the force with a salary of 13s. 4d. (66p) a day, with a gaoler at 1s. 8d. (8½p), and eight tipstaffs each at 8d. (3½p) daily. Six halberdiers from the Train Bands were detailed to assist him. The Train Bands were very slow in answering the call up, causing the General, the Earl of Leicester, to complain 'if it takes five days for local men to report, how long will it require for men coming from miles away?' Local merchants hesitated in supplying the camp, and a promised bridge of boats across the Thames was not available when required. The apathy went right to the top, for even the queen forgot to sign her General's commission, thus making all his orders illegal. About this time a Mr. Twiddye was appointed as Provost Marshal for Essex, and on 4 October a Mr. G. Acres was nominated to replace Captain Crisp who had been selected as Provost Marshal of a force to proceed to the Lowlands under the command of Sir John Norrie.

It appears that the gentry were not contributing towards the upkeep of Provost Marshals with the regularity that the queen would have liked, as the following directions from the Privy Council to a queen's messenger on 21 December 1588 evidence:

> . . . repair unto certaine gentlemen and others inhabiting the County of Middlesex which refuse to contribute unto an assessment made towardes the charges of a Provost Marshal there, and command them to make payment of the same according to a schedule subscribed by one of the clerkes to the Councell, which was delivered him there with al or els that they fail not to attend upon the Lords of the Councell to showe the cause of their refusal.

The queen, not trusting large assemblies of men, ordered that in 1589 no more than 300 men were to be mustered at any one time unless the Lord Lieutenant was present. It was during this year that Mr. Humphrey Coningsby and Mr. Henry Goodyer became Provost Marshals of East and West Hertfordshire respectively.

They were appointed by Sir John Brockelt and Sir Henry Cocks, Deputies to Lord Burghley, Lord Lieutenant of the county. All Justices and Constables were ordered to assist the Provost Marshals, and Justices were to keep meticulous accounts in order that eventually costs could be distributed evenly among those subject to levy. Lord Burghley later took Sir John to task for failing to co-operate with the Provost Marshals, and ordered him to hold special Sessions in order to empty the over-crowded prisons in the county. These Provost Marshals were each paid 10s. (50p) per day and allowed six armed assistants. Burghley dismissed the suggestion that previous Peace Keeping arrangements were inefficient, and when the crime rate in Hertfordshire fell off he ordered that the Provost Marshals need ride out on their rounds on only three consecutive days every fortnight. He reduced their armed retainers from six to four and cut their pay by half.

Sir Henry Cocks later wrote a long report on Peace Keeping which contained a very interesting account of a conversation between two criminals, overheard by a farmer who had hidden behind a tree. One of the men said:

> ther was greate speches aboute London that there sholde be Provoste Marshalles in every sheare, to hang them uppe. But saithe he, I warrante thee they dare not doe it, for theie are as much afrayed of us, as we are of them, they knowe ther very many of us, and ther are many ennymes abroade and at home also, therefore I will warrante you they dare not hunt us.

The Mr. Twiddye mentioned earlier was employed as the Essex muster Provost Marshal for 1589, at which the officials of the Train Bands in that county were:

Colonel	Sir John Smythe
Muster Master	Robert Recock Esq.
Provost Marshal ..	Will Twytte Esq.

Although the spelling differs there is little doubt that Twiddye and Twytte are one and the same person. The pay for the Provost Marshal on this occasion was also 10s., and each of his 10 assistants received 2s. 0d. (10p) per day. What appears to be an excessive number of assistants could suggest that musters were inclined to be lively affairs—no wonder the queen would not have more than 300 men together at any one time! In Norfolk at this time the Provost Marshal was paid a pound a day, but from this had to pay a gunner and four foot soldiers 2s. 0d. a day each, so, in effect, his pay equated to that of his Essex and Hertfordshire counterparts, but not, in the latter instance, after Lord Burghley made his financial cuts.

During our campaign in the Iberian peninsula in 1589 the Provost Marshal held a weekly court at which he dealt with offenders from each of the 14 regiments in the army. When the dispirited troops later returned to England they brought disease with them, and their condition was such that the queen ordered that they were to be paid at the ports of disembarkation and ordered to return immediately to the towns and villages from which they were levied. Few did so, and they caused such disruption in the Home Counties that all Provost Marshals were ordered to be retained in office. In London 2,000 men of the Train Bands were called out to deal with 500 former soldiers who were terrorising the Palace of Westminster. It was necessary for the Provost Marshal to hang four of the men before the remainder would disperse. Another former soldier was hanged at Kingston-on-Thames on 27 August, and later two more met their deaths at Tyburn, two on Tower Hill, and a further two outside Westminster Palace.

That autumn 4,000 men were levied from London, Sussex, Kent and Hampshire and sent to France under the command of Lord Willoughby. Thomas Wilford, of whom we shall read more later, commanded the Kent men. The Articles of War drawn up by Lord Willoughby on this occasion followed closely those issued by the Earl of Leicester at the time of the Tilbury camp, and numbered a total of 29 clauses. At Alencon Lord Willoughby and Thomas Wilford jointly invented a machine for forcing drawbridges, thus adding another engine to the train available for siege purposes. Disorders following the return of this army to England caused the queen to issue a Proclamation 13 November ordering the Knight Marshal, and County Provost Marshals, to execute former soldiers who, within two days of disembarkation, failed to obtain a passport authorising their return home. Rogues apprehended in the guise of ex-soldiers were also to be executed. This was the final solution, and cheap. No doubt it pleased the mayor of Rye, for he had been complaining of the cost to his town of keeping destitute former members of the army. It was also provided that employers of men who had been levied were to take them on again when they returned home— failure to do so rendered them liable to punishment by the Provost Marshal. Parish councils were reminded of their obligations towards distressed ex-service men. Genuine well-conducted former soldiers were to be given passports 'to the ende that they might not fall into the danger of the Provost Marshall'.

The Lord Mayor of London was particularly ordered to ensure that discharged soldiers were made aware of the Proclamation. They were to be told that if they got into trouble after the expiration of their passposts the Provost Marshal would treat them just like any other rogue. Although the Privy Council were not happy at having to keep the peace this way it ordered that each county was to recruit as many Provost Marshals as the requirements of the day warranted.

On 15 November the queen wrote to each Lord Lieutenant in the Home Counties on the subject of Provost Marshals. She stated why their continued employment was necessary, the rates at which they were to be paid, the amount of assistance they were to be afforded, and how money for their support was to be raised. Each Provost Marshal had to be commissioned for a three-month period, but this could be extended if there was a continuing need for his services. It was stressed that Provost Marshals and their men must 'have knowledge of the countries wayes and passages', a reference to the local knowledge that is still so very necessary for law enforcement to be effective. This very important letter is far too long to be reproduced here and may be found in Acts of the Privy Council, New Series, Volume XVIII, 1589–1590, page 224.

By this time Humphrey Coningsby had become the Provost Marshal for the whole of Hertfordshire, answerable direct to Lord Burghley, the most powerful individual in the Realm. Most fair-minded men agreed that Provost Marshals had made a vast difference to the country; indeed Essex endeavoured unsuccessfully to retain one permanently. It was acknowledged that travel had become far safer, but it is likely that county enthusiasm was influenced by fear of what the queen would do to any who did not assist. In London, ever jealous of its independence, there were grave doubts about the legal position of Provost Marshals. A Mr. Coates even sued Provost Marshal John Read for trespass and was awarded minimal damages, but history does not say whether the City or its Provost Marshal paid, that is assuming that someone did!

Lord Cobham, the Lord Lieutenant of Kent, appointed Thomas Nevinson of Eastry as Provost Marshal for East Kent and Canterbury on 5 December 1589. He instructed the Deputy Lieutenants to give their orders to the Provost Marshal in writing, ensuring that both he and the Justices concerned got copies. The manner in which the local notables were to be assessed towards the upkeep of the Provost Marshal and his men was stipulated for the three-month period, with a lower contribution for the final month, as shown in the following table:

Assets	1st month	2nd month	3rd month
(a) Value of lands held	2d.	2d.	2d.
(b) Value of goods owned	1½d.	1½d.	1d.
Total assessment for each pound of (a) and (b)	3½d.	3½d.	3d.

Thomas Nevinson died in 1590, and in Eastry church a very fine memorial brass was erected. It is still extant and a photograph is reproduced in this book. The text is in English and shows quite clearly that he was both Provost Marshal and Scoutmaster of his area. There are no other known brasses referring to a Provost Marshal. His steel helmet is also preserved in the church.

It was during the January of 1590 that Lord Burghley remonstrated with our Governor in Bergen-op-Zoom for not reporting an attack on Lord Norriss's Provost Marshal. The Governor, Sir Thomas Morgan, replied to the effect that as a Provost Marshal was only a hangman he did not think it worth reporting!

London by this time was employing several Provost Marshals regularly. Two of the most prominent during 1590 were Mr. Gurney and Mr. Warne. Their pay was 30s. (£1.50) per day, and this is so high that it suggests that they were responsible for paying their own staff. Mr. Gurney was a man of some importance who later became an alderman, after which he held the office of Provost Marshal for a second period. Provost Marshals finally vanished from the London scene during the early part of the 18th century.

In 1591 the Earl of Essex took an army to France and published Articles of War that followed what had by then become an established pattern. One wonders if assaults on Provost Marshals were commonplace, for a provision that had been used in earlier years, but not recently, reappeared, soldiers being warned that:

> No man shall resist the Provost Marshal or other of his officers in apprehending any malefactors, but if need be shall aid and assist him.

This is currently a requirement under military law, and today's soldier failing to assist the Military Police if called upon to do so commits an offence under the Army Act 1955.

Despite all the precautions taken by the Privy Council returning former soldiers still gave much trouble, robberies and murders marking their dispersal routes across the countryside. A Proclamation raising Provost Marshals was published on 28 February 1591 and again on the 5 November the same year. Provost Marshals were instructed to take great care in order that genuine impoverished former soldiers were not confused with villains, but at the same time they were enjoined to spare rogues posing as former soldiers no mercy, but to hang them forthwith.

The passing of the Pensions Acts of 1592/3 was a serious attempt to solve the problems of former soldiers, and they are evidence that thinking men realised that resort to the rope was not the answer. The following year Lord Burghley passed legislation to control access to ports and royal residences. Clause 10 of the Document is reproduced here, the original can be seen at the Public Record Office under S.P. Dom. Eliz. (S.O. 12), Vol. 247, No. 66:

> 10. Item to avoyde the over greate resort of persons to lodge near the Court, the Knight Harbinger and Marshall with some company of tipstaves and, if nede be, with the ayd of some of the yeoman of the gard shall twise or thrise everye weeke, make a view and serche what are lodged, being no householder, nor their ordinary servants in any town within two miles of the court; And if they shall fynd either lodged or that shall hawnt the court, that are not allowed in the porters books, not by the masters of Requests, nor by speciall warrant from any lord or other having lodging in the court, the same person shalbe first examined in the cause of his cominge nere the court, and finding no juste cause, he shalbe committed to prison, and not be delivered untill uppon his examination be he lycenced.

A most unusual appointment was made on 18 January 1595 when Sir Thomas Wilford—the inventor whom we last encountered in Alencon—was commissioned as a Provost Marshal.

> To be Provost Marshall, and to exercise Martiall Lawe upon the significance of rebellious offenders in London, Essex, Kent, and Surrey, and to apprehend vagrant persons.

The troubles in this instance were not being caused by former soldiers but by rioting apprentices and servants. Sir Thomas was further ordered to:

> Apprehend all such as will not be readily reformed and corrected by the ordinary officers of justice, and without delay to execute them upon the gallows by order of Martiall Lawe.

Here we have a situation where a Provost Marshal is appointed for the sole purpose of punishing a particular class of citizen in violation of the established judicial system of the country. Of this Hallam has recorded that 'no other measure of Elizabeth's reign can be compared in point of violence and illegality'. The Provost Marshal we have encountered here is quite unlike any that we have so far met. He was answerable only to the Privy Council for powers that extended across several counties and was in effect a Royal Provost Marshal. A further Proclamation on 4 July 1595 authorised him to arrest and execute any person trying to free a prisoner from his custody. That he had no hesitation in using his awful authority is evidence by the fact that on 22 July he and his tipstaffs arrested five young ruffians in London and, having convicted them of high treason, hung, drew and quartered them on Tower Hill two days later. Another of his unconstitutional rights was that of being able to execute any arrested persons previously pardoned on another account. His duties extended to the obligation to keep beggars away from London's theatres. Later, when his powers had lapsed and the beggars flocked back to theatreland, the Lord Mayor commented that 'this would not have happened had Sir Thomas Wilford still been in office!'. During 1596 a committee sat in London to advise on the employment of Provost Marshals, and it was agreed that the responsibility for impressing men for overseas could rightly be given to them.

It was during 1596 that the City of London became exasperated because rogues from Middlesex were flocking into the City. This was a result of Middlesex discontinuing the use of Provost Marshals. London therefore posted their Provost Marshals at the gates from 6 a.m. until 8 p.m. to keep migrant criminals out. The City also complained that offenders arrested there and handed over to local constables were being released unpunished. This led to a tightening up all round, and a parish constable being imprisoned for neglect. One of London's Provost Marshals appears to have been very officious and on one occasion arrested Lord Cromwell for arguing with him! This man, a Mr. Simpson, was later sued by one of the queen's grooms for wrongful arrest, but it does not appear that the plaintiff obtained satisfaction. By this time each City Provost Marshal had his own establishment, some even provided their men with liveries, and there is little doubt that this was a period when law enforcement in the capital was well in advance of that experienced in other cities in the Realm.

There appears to have been another Royal Provost Marshal appointed in 1597, again with the power of life and death over civilians, though the occasions on which he could exercise these were reduced.

We are therefore encountering a period when three classes of Provost Marshal existed contemporaneously. These were:

(a) Royal. With a roving Commission within counties specified by the Privy Council.
(b) County. Operating within Shire boundaries, authorised by Royal Proclamation, but appointed by Lords Lieutenant (those appointed for London being nominees of the Lord Mayor).
(c) Military. Appointed to a particular garrison or army.

Within the second classification come those appointed solely at times of county musters. We have seen examples of all three, and a further instance of the third category is the appointment of William Bredyman as Provost Marshal of the Berwick garrison in 1597. That year saw the passing of 39 Elizabeth I, Cap. 17, which consolidated the law on the issue of passports to returning soldiers. They were required to report to a magistrate at their disembarkation port; he would compute the time that it should take them to return home, add 14 days, and then issue the document. Anyone who did not report as directed or who forged a passport, and who was apprehended within one year, could be summarily executed by a Provost Marshal. A further Poor Law Act passed that year tidied up various Proclamations and authorised Provost Marshals to arrest and return home anyone found outside their own parish without excuse. The onus for supporting returning soldiers was put squarely on their home authorities. Improvements in the Poor Law during the final years of Elizabeth's reign and in the early years of James I (1603-1625) greatly increased the work load of Provost Marshals, but as their services were gradually dispensed with enforcement of the Poor Law provisions declined with a resultant deterioration in the condition of the destitute.

At this time county Provost Marshals appear to have been paid at a standard rate of 10s. (50p) a day, yet those operating on the continent with our forces received only 6s. 8d. (33½p). In London it was decided to levy all merchants and householders in order that funds could be raised for peace keeping. It appears that in the City Provost Marshals were paid less than the going rate, for one office holder, John Reade, was paid only 6s. 8d. out of which he was required to provide his own horse. In the spring of 1598 it was decided to dispense with his services on 24 June, and in the meantime to reduce his staff to eight men, who would each receive 1s. (5p) a day.

In September 1598 when the queen's erstwhile favourite, the Earl of Essex, languished in the Tower of London, the Privy Council sought his opinion, as the Earl Marshal, on the subject of the appointment of Provost Marshals, as the right to do so was historically his. Their letter, dated the 6th, is here reproduced in entirety as it discloses the motivation behind the appointments of recent years:

> Uppon notice lately given unto Her Majestie of divers notorious and outragious misdemeanours of certain rogues, vagabondes and other dissolute persons that in some place not farre distant from London have committed such violences, even to the assayling and slaying of some of Her Majesties Officers, as the ordinary course of justice sufficeth not to suppresse them, it hath pleased Her Majestie to give orders for the appointing of a Provost Marshall for London and for some of the counties neere adjoyning.
>
> Hereuppon we have proceeded thus farre by Her Majesties commaundment as to cause a commission to be drawn for a Provost Marshall, to be signed by Her Majestie, and certaine letters to be written by us unto the said counties to give them knowledge of the commission and to require theire service in redressing of the said disorders.
>
> But because we do consider that this maie in some sorte appertaine to your Lordships office of the Earle Marshall of England, and would by no means take any course herein that maie be prejudiciall to the right and authoritie of your place, we have thought meete to acquaint your Lordship herewith before we go any further with the business, and doe praie your Lordship to certifie us both of your opinion concerning your own particular right and interest, in the ordering and executing

of this service, by virtue of your office, and also in the generalitie to give your good advise for our better proceeding herein.

Essex replied, apparently on 8 September, and approved the appointment of Provost Marshals by an authority other than his own. He suggested that perhaps the Knight Marshal could be employed instead of Provost Marshals, as the Knight Marshal was in effect the Knight Provost Marshal! This is of course what had been happening for years; the Knight Marshal, a Deputy of the Earl Marshal, himself had a Deputy, the Knight Harbinger, and several assistants who were originally known as Vergers and later as Provost Marshals. The Knight Marshal was responsible for law and order within 12 miles of the king's person. He ran his own Court—the Court of the Verges—in addition to the ancient Marshal's Court. The Court of the Verges could commit offenders to prison. In 1630 when Sir Edmund Verney was Knight Marshal, both Courts merged and became known as the King's Court of the Palace of Westminster, using the old marshalsea, situated in Southwark High Street, as its place of correction. We know that in the days of King Richard III the Knight Marshal and his tipstaffs committed prisoners to the marshalsea, so it is very likely that the establishment served the Knight Marshal in both his roles. The letter from the Earl of Essex mentioned above is too lengthy to be reproduced here, but anyone wishing to read it is referred to page 125, Volume VI of the *Journal of the Society for Army Historical Research*.

This chapter commenced with an inscription from a Swansea tomb which records that the deceased served as Knight Marshal at home and abroad. This suggests that athough the appointment was that of assistant to the Earl Marshal, it did not necessarily have to be carried out in the presence of the king. It appears therefore that it was duplicated as a purely military office, which if we agree with the clue contained in the Earl of Essex's letter, was probably mainly a disciplinary appointment.

The Earl Marshal referred to in the inscription was killed, together with King Richard III, on 22 August 1485 at the battle of Bosworth. The title then fell into disuse until

1 February 1514 when it was bestowed on Thomas, Earl of Surrey, who was created Duke of Norfolk and Earl Marshal. It became hereditary to the Dukes of Norfolk over 160 years later.

John Reade, of whom we have read earlier, appears to have had his term of office extended, for he was still a Provost Marhal in the City of London in 1599. It seems that he served at least 11 years in the appointment and can therefore be considered a professional Provost Marshal.

During 1600 the City took over responsibility for providing liveries for Provost Marshal Reade's men, and this may well be the first uniformed police paid from public funds that the country had seen.

Four Provost Marshals were commissioned on 13 August 1599, one for each of the administrative divisions of Cornwall; they were:

> For Penrith and Kerrier—Thomas Penrose.
> For Trigg, Lostwithiel and Stratton—John Hender.
> For the Hundred of East and West Redruth—William Coade.
> For Pyder—Gilbert Holcom.

Provost Marshals commissioned in February 1600 for the Home Counties were:

> Kent—Sir Thomas Waller.
> Essex—Mr. William Smithe.
> Surrey—Sir Thomas Morgan.
> Middlesex—Sir Francis Daralla.
> Hertfordshire—Mr. Ralph Connisby.

One wonders if Sir Thomas Morgan was the same man who once thought it not worth reporting an assault on a Provost Marshal as he was only a hangman? These Provost Marshals were ordered to apprehend beggars obviously heading for the metropolis, but if they were harmless to return them to their home parish. Seditious beggars were to be prosecuted, but any who were begging in the guise of a distressed former soldier were to be summarily executed. It is small wonder that Provost Marshals were feared when one considers that their power of life and death was not subject to appeal and, irrespective of the opinion of the

Privy Council, were quite outside the stated law of the Kingdom.

Sir Thomas Wilford, our first Royal Provost Marshal, died in 1601 after having held many important offices under the Crown. His book *A military discourse whether it is better for England to give an invader present battle, or to temporise and defend the same,* was published in his name 133 years after his death. His views on anti-invasion measures were very similar to those actually prepared in 1940. He also conceded that firearms had come to stay.

The Earl of Essex paid for his treason on 25 February 1601 when he was executed, and was survived by his queen for only two years, for Elizabeth, last of the house of Tudor and creator of much of England's greatness, died on 24 March 1603.

Note: Much of the information in this chapter is derived from the researches of the late Brigadier H. Bullock, F.R.Hist.S., late Indian Army, and from his contributions in a series of articles in various issues of the Journal *of the Society for Army Historical Research. To Brigadier Bullock and the S.A.H.R. must go the credit for revealing so much of this fascinating period in the history of the office of Provost Marshal, and I am very grateful to the S.A.H.R. for their permission to use their publications as source material for this work.*

CHAPTER V

IRELAND—WITHIN AND WITHOUT THE PALE

Oh—she'd make a mott for the Provost Marshal
Or a wife for the Major on his couch so high
Or a Queen of Andalusia
Kicking her heels in the Cardinal's eye
I'm as blue as cockles, brown as herrings
over a grid of glimmering coal
And all because of the Spanish Lady
so mortal neat bout the sole.

Joseph Campbell

THE HISTORY of this beautiful but malignant island is a monotonous record of rebellion and sectarian strife. In over 450 years there have been many Provost Marshals in Ireland and they have been woven into its history since the days of Henry VIII.

Originally English influence was strongest in the Pale, as the 20 by 30 mile coastal strip around Dublin is known. Those living outside were 'beyond the Pale', an expression currently denoting social outcasts. The administration was headed by Viceroy, later titles being Lord Deputy and Lord Lieutenant, the latter lasting from Commonwealth times until Partition. Installation was conducted by the Archbishop of Dublin, power being assumed on receipt of the Sword of State. Councils of Regency governed during the absence of the Lord Lieutenant, who often ruled through Deputies. The Duke of Richmond, appointed in 1526, was but six years old at the time.

The only regal power denied the Head of State was the right to mint currency. Considering the corruption of former times this is easily understandable. A Council assisted in

50

government, the most powerful members of which were the Lord Chancellor, Lord Chief Justice, the Marshal of the Army, and the Treasurer at Wars. Army organisation at the top was quite good, but logistical support often was non-existent, a not unusual state of affairs in those days.

The Marshal was assisted by a General of Horse and Lieutenant-General of Foot, and himself was responsible for discipline, organisation and camps, etc. From the early 16th century there was a Provost Marshal to assist him, overseeing discipline, billeting and provisioning, including control of Sutlers. A Sergeant-Major General made and actioned tactical decisions, with a Scoutmaster-General for intelligence gathering. Troops were raised by a Muster Master General, whilst the Master of Ordnance provided guns and ammunition and controlled fortifications, assisted operationally by the Master Gunner. Ordnance did not then mean clothing, vehicles, rations, accommodation and clerks, as it does today.

When Sir Henry Poynings was Lord Deputy he enacted what became known as 'Poynings Law'. This made English laws applicable to Ireland, but Irish laws had no force nor could the Irish parliament sit until approved by the king in England. These restrictions existed for over 300 years and, together with religious bigotry on both sides, caused much of the hatred and bloodshed that has plagued Ireland ever since.

The first mention of a Provost Marshal in Ireland is found during Lord Deputy Sir Richard Skeffington's time. In March 1535 he trapped leaders of a Catholic uprising in Maynooth Castle, of which he gained possession through treachery on the part of Christopher Paris, brother of Lord Kildare. Sir Richard promised Paris and the rebels their lives, but handed all notables over to his Provost Marshal, who executed 95 of them, including the Archbishop of Dublin, a successor of whom was also executed by a Provost Marshal 50 years later. For years in Ireland 'The pardon of Maynooth' was used to express bad faith. Viscount Crane had been Marshal of Skeffington's army and it was particularly well disciplined, but whether this was due to the presence of a Provost Marshal history does not record. Osborne Itchingham was a Provost Marshal in Ireland during 1540 and he complained that he had to bear the cost of his 12 assistants. In due course 12 men were allotted to him from another officer's command, and he was reimbursed for his outlay.

Two years later martial law was proclaimed in Munster and at a meeting between officials, one of whom was the Provost Marshal, and local notables, the latter promising to keep the peace among themselves instead of resorting to arms, but in the event there was little improvement.

The accession of Mary Tudor convinced Catholics in Ireland that the Church would again come into its own. Although her reign was too short to give effect to this, unrest became widespread, and the Provost Marshal was ordered to 'search the country and punish suspects, vagabonds and all idle and masterless folk, by the law Martial according to their deserts'. At that time there was no war or revolt in being; thus the punishment of civilians by Provost Marshals would appear to be completely illegal. The accession of Elizabeth on 17 November 1558 was followed by trouble in Ireland, and the following year one Shane O'Neil went into open rebellion. He successfully ambushed our Marshal, Sir George Stanley, whose rearguard was routed and its commander, Sir Jacques Wingfield, Master of Ordnance, was unjustly accused of cowardice. The Earls of Desmond and Ormonde then commenced operations against each other over disputed territory, and as they were the two most influential men in the area Sir George Stanley marched against them. By 1562 many inhabitants were incensed at the disorder and punitive action caused by the O'Neil outbreak. One complaint was that a soldier charged with murder had been rescued by the Provost Marshal and punished by being put in the stocks hooded so that he could not be recognised. Although the complaints were mainly against the military for over-riding civil law, the queen replied that the governor must support the Provost Marshal who had power over soldiers in all matters. The Provost Marshal did not always get his own way, for despite his support, in 1565 Sir Henry Radclyffe, brother of the Lord Deputy, was imprisoned by a Royal Commission for muster frauds.

By the end of 1566 the O'Neill rebellion was finally crushed, by which time the Treasury was £300,000 in debt. About this time Connaught and Munster were made Presidencies with Sir Edward Fitton and Sir John Perrott the respective Presidents. Sir Edward immediately alienated the Catholic clergy by forbidding them to continue the ancient custom of keeping unofficial wives. He ordered a general census, instructing his Provost Marshal to hang malefactors and any others who could not be vouched for. Ralph Rokely, a notable of the period, reported to Sir William Cecil in 1570 that the Provost Marshal had executed many, having been ordered to 'trusse upp such as he thought of those horseboyes, woodkernes and proclaimed rebells that wyll not come into any government'.

Sir John Perrott took action against those who came out in the Fitzmaurice uprising in 1569. During his campaign he lost only 18 men, but his Provost Marshal executed over eight hundred, including seven Cashal merchants who had supplied the rebels.When the Earl of Essex became President of Munster in 1575 he found that lack of funds and Irish distrust of English settlers made his task very difficult. He received much assistance from Henry Davells, Constable of Dungarron Castle, who laboured to repair the ravages of the Fitzmaurice Rebellion in his area. When the Lord Deputy, Sir Philip Sidney, toured the troubled areas in 1576 he left a Provost Marshal with 24 mounted men and 24 foot soldiers to put down lawlessness in Galway, and another Provost Marshal with 12 mounted men and 24 infantry for similar duties in Clare, saying 'that country swarmed with idle men, and by this means they thought to suppress them'. Later, after Sir William Drury became President of Munster, he reported on the state of his Province, saying that his Provost Marshal had been riding about from place to place and not been idle, but had hanged 80 men who had been so!

By July 1579 there were only 1,211 ill-clad, half-starved English soldiers in Ireland, and it was then that James

Fitzmaurice landed at Smerwick from his self-imposed
exile to raise a second rebellion. In no time it was underway
with all the rape, arson and looting so familiar in Ireland on
those occasions. English settlers rushed to the Pale for safety,
and Queen Elizabeth levied 800 men for Ireland. Henry
Davells, then one of the Commissioners for Munster,
persuaded a reformed pirate, Captain Thomas Courtney, to
attack Spanish vessels accompanying Fitzmaurice. The
Spanish quickly sailed away, leaving the rebels in the lurch.
The Munster Provost Marshal was ordered to execute by
martial law 'all Harpists, Bards, Idle and masterless persons,
and leaders of blind people', as these were considered
possible rebel propagandists and spies. The Provost Marshal,
Arthur Carter, was then sent with Henry Davells and an
escort to test the loyalty of the Earl of Desmond, who
entertained them civilly, but had not declared himself by
the time they left. On the return journey the party lodged
at an inn in Tralee kept by a Mr. Rice. During the night,
having bribed the door-keeper, Sir John and Sir James
Desmond, brothers of the Earl, crept into the inn accompanied by their men. A page gave the alarm; 'What son,
what is the matter?' said Davells. 'No more son, no more
father, but make yourself ready, for die you must', cried
Sir John, and in no time the government party were
slaughtered, the page died defending his master. According
to records Davells and Carter were sharing the same bed—
not uncommon in inns in those days. Desmond accepted
loot from the murdered mens' possessions, but Fitzmaurice
was very angry at the murders. Sir Warham St. Leger then
became President of Munster and also assumed the office of
Provost Marshal, leading a force into Desmond country
where he put the town of Youghal to the sword, but sparing a
Friar who had given Davells and Carter a Christian burial. By
this time the whole province was in flames and loyalists were
murdered whenever found. Then occurred one of those little
things that change the course of history: Fitzmaurice was killed
while trying to steal the horse of a ploughman. The insurgents
lost the services of a man who had developed into an outstanding guerrilla leader and as such was irreplaceable.

Although there was much hard fighting ahead the Desmond Rebellion, as it had become known, started to collapse. When Carrigafoyle Castle fell in early 1580 the Provost Marshal executed all prisoners. Stronghold after stronghold was taken, and the pursuit became a hunt. Sir James Desmond was taken at Muskerry and hung, drawn and quartered without loss of time. Sir Warham St. Leger retained the Provost Marshalship until the end of the rebellion and was remembered for his dedication to exterminating all who had supported it. Dr. Sanders, a priest who had landed at Smerwick with Fitzmaurice, was passed from family to family, no one giving him away, until he died of dysentery in April 1581, still in hiding. Sir John Desmond was betrayed and killed on 3 January 1582; his body then hung in chains in Cork.

During 1582 Barnaby Googe became Provost Marshal of Connaught, with £40 a year salary and the right to eat with the President. Income from the Marshal's gaol in Galway brought him a further £40 annually, but he did not receive an expected £100 a year for ransoms, and only after many complaints was given 12 tipstaffs to assist him.

The Earl of Ormond became Governor of Munster on 21 February 1583 and promised amnesty to all remaining rebels, other than the Earl of Desmond, who had offered to submit. St. Leger suggested they accept the offer, then tempt him to commit treason, and execute him. Discussion on this ungentlemanly proposal soon became academic, for a government supporter, Owen Moriarty, captured Desmond and killed him when rescue seemed likely. In Dublin the Provost Marshal executed Desmond Huxley, the Archbishop, on 19 June 1583. He was the last surviving notable supporter of the Desmond rebels, and that ended the uprising. Two years later Barnaby Googe sold his appointment to Captain Francis Barkley for one hundred pounds.

In 1588 many surviving vessels of the Spanish Armada tried to return home round Ireland, and came to grief on its rugged coast. Two galleons came ashore together in Connemara and 300 survivors were taken to Galway for execution by the

Provost Marshal. He was then sent to the O'Flaherty country to salvage stores and execute survivors. Both tasks had already been carried out by the O'Flahertys very efficiently, except that they 'lost' the stores. Other officers were sent on similar fruitless errands to Mayo. One of three vessels wrecked in Sligo Bay had Don Martin de Arandon, Provost Marshal of the Armada, on board, but he did not survive. Many who did were terribly treated by the natives before being granted the privilege of death. A very few were kept as slaves, and those, with the Spanish survivors of the second Fitzmaurice uprising, were absorbed into the race, and traces can still be detected in certain West Coast families.

Towards the end of the century a rising by the Earl of Tyrone very nearly succeeded. At the Battle of Yellow Ford on 14 August 1598 the English were defeated and the commander, Sir Henry Bagenal, killed. Colonel Currey, the Sergeant-Major General, took over, but his troops broke up and ran. A new commander was appointed, but died before he could assume his duties. Queen Elizabeth was very concerned at the state of Ireland, where her subjects had much cause for complaint. Much of the blame lay on the queen's parsimony, for the troops were months in arrears, without footwear, nearly naked, and forced to live off the land in order to survive. Corrupt officials battened on the inhabitants and Provost Marshals were tyrannical. Their pay of 4s. per day was insufficient for them to exist in a manner befitting the office and this led to extortion on a large scale. The queen promised funds and sent the Earl of Essex with a staff of proved officers to retrieve her fortunes. Both Essex and his Marshal, Christopher Blount, were later executed. Essex created an army out of nothing; his arrival in Ireland can be equated to that of General Bernard Montgomery in Egypt in 1942. On 9 May 1599 he commenced operations and within 48 hours Ashley Castle capitulated. Lords Cahir and Mountgarrett, supporters of Tyrone, came in to surrender, and their lives were spared, in return for which they assisted Essex to gain control of their family castles, during which time they were in custody of the Provost Marshal. Within two years peace was restored, but mayhem, rapes and robberies—ever the Irish way of life, continued under the label of Liberty.

Essex's plans, though successful, were not those laid down by the queen. Later he` returned to England where his involvement in matters best left alone led him to the block.

During 1600 George Newgent (Newcomen) was Provost Marshal in Ballyshannon. His was a prominent name in Longford where George was often used as a Christian name. We do not know if our Provost Marshal came from that family, which became extinct in 1823 with the death of Sir Thomas Newcomen Bart. Lord Mountjoy became commander in Ireland during 1600 and did what he could to restore normality. His comprehensive Articles of War directed that after 24 hours prisoners in civil custody must be handed over to a Provost Marshal for speedy trial. For a first offence drunken soldiers should be imprisoned, and fined for a second transgression; subsequently they should be handed to the Provost Marshal 'for the Marshals Court to decide'. In 1601 George Newgent (Newcomen) asked the Privy Council for a Provost Marshal's appointment in Ulster. This was granted because of his long service and familiarity with the Presidency.

Within a few days of the death of Elizabeth on 24 March 1603 the fugitive Earl of Tyrone surrendered. Mountjoy became Lord Deputy, and Ormonde was sent to pacify the country, for the Irish, believing that a Catholic resurgence was at hand, came out again. Protestant clergy were deposed and robbed as parish after parish declared for the Pope. Ormonde arrived before the locked gates of Waterford and announced that he would hang every notable if not admitted. This had the desired effect; he handed the town keys to his Provost Marshal for safe keeping. His troops, in their ill-clad, half-starved condition, were very well behaved, despite immediate raising of prices. When Ormonde marched on he left 150 men to guard the town, which remained peaceful. Mountjoy in the meantime had entered Cork with a second column, and there he arrested three leading disaffected notables and handed them to his Provost Marshal for execution. Tales of the sternness and fairness of both columns preceded them and the countryside became quiet as they advanced, remaining so as they passed on.

George Paulet, son of the Marquis of Winchester, bought the Vice Provost Marshal's office among others from Sir Henry Docwra when he left Ireland. Paulet was an obnoxious individual and when Sir Cahir O'Dogherty complained that he had been slandered by him, the reply was that 'O'Dogherty is a violent man who should best be dealt with by a Provost Marshal with a halter'. On 19 April 1608, when O'Dogherty was in rebellion, he captured Derry together with its Vice Provost Marshal, whom he immediately executed, together with the city's Protestants. The historian Bagwell says they totalled only 10, including Paulet.

An expedition was organised against O'Dogherty and all prisoners taken were immediately executed by the Provost Marshal. O'Dogherty was cornered in Donegal and in due course his head appeared over New Gate, Dublin. The rising gradually petered out and eventually Paulet's killer, Owen O'Dogherty, was one of 20 surviving rebels captured and hanged at Lifford.

King James I during 1611, ostensibly to raise money to support his army in Ireland, offered to sell titles to those whose annual income exceeded £1,000—the normal charge for a knighthood was between £1,000 and £2,000. In 1614 he sent a Commission to Ireland to examine the situation there, stating that he wished to encourage the people to make petitions to the throne whenever they sought redress for a grievance instead of 'after the old fashion of that country to run upon every occasion to bog and wood and seek their remedy that way'.

During 1628 certain Catholic and Protestant notables offered the king, then Charles I (1625–1649) £120,000, payable in quarterly instalments of £10,000, for assurance that certain complaints would be remedied. These assurances, known as 'Graces', would have made life more bearable for the inhabitants. One promise sought, number 33 in the Schedule, reads:

> But one Provost Marshal to be in a Province, because he hath a sufficient number of horse in our pay for the execution

of that place, and the said Provost Marshal is to take no money for booking, nor cess his horse or foot without paying for it in such sort as is ordered for our soldiers; and such as may be brought to trial of law are not to be executed by the Marshal, except in time of war or rebellion.

The king agreed, but payments ceased on 1 April 1629 when it became obvious that he was not keeping his word. Apart from anything else, Provost Marshals had continued executing people even though the country was at peace.

A Royal Commission freed Phelim MacPheagh from prison in 1628 on finding charges of treason by Sir Richard Graham, Sit William Parsons and others were false, and merely an attempt to extort certain Wicklow lands. The case highlighted the corrupton of named Provost Marshals, one of whom was the son of Sir Richard Graham, and can best be summarised by the evidence of the seventh witness:

Hugh MacGerald, being duly sworn and examined deposeth that he was apprehended by William Graham, the Provost Marshal, who kept him seven days in his custody, tied with a hand lock, and two several times the said Graham threatened to hang the examinant if he would not do service against Phelim MacPheagh, one time sending for a ladder and another time showing a tree whereupon he would hang him, and the ropes and withes, but the examinant, making protestations of having no matter to lay to the said Phelim's charge did choose rather to suffer than to impeach without a cause. He said that there was present at one time Mr. Calcott Chamber the elder and younger, and Mr. Sandford, when the said Graham threatened to hang this examinant, and at that time the examinant verily believed he had been hanged if Mr. Chamber, observing this examinent to be on his knees to prepare himself by prayer for death, had not dissuaded the said Graham from it for that time, the examinant being told by some present who interpreted to him Mr. Chamber's speeches, that Mr. Chamber would not have the examinant hanged on his land without better ground [of his guilt]. He further saith that he was committed to prison where he remained for twenty-two weeks. He was at divers times solicited by Sir Henry Hellings and Mr. William Graham, promising that he should have from the Lord Deputy such favour, means of livelihood, and his liberty, if he would do service against Phelim's MacPheagh and his sons, which having nothing whereof to accuse them. He saith that he was several times brought to the Right Hon. the Lord Deputy to be examined, many fair promises being made to him by the said Sir Henry and Mr. Graham, so as he would do service against the said Phelim and his sons, which he, the examinant, was not able to do.

One of the most deplorable aspects of this incident was that the king's representative in Ireland, Lord Falkland, was an active member of the conspiracy, using his vast powers to subvert and coerce witnesses, and it is to their lasting credit that they refused to be intimidated into breaking the ninth Commandment. Another witness, Dermot O'Toole, told how, after a Provost Marshal, Sir Henry Hellings, had unsuccessfully tried to get him to give false evidence, he was taken before Lord Falkland who, after having also unsuccessfully endeavoured to persuade him to lie, asked which of his three Provost Marshals he would like to be hanged by, Sir Henry Hellings, William Graham, or a Mr. Bowen? The witness replied that he was innocent of any crime and therefore hoped not to be hanged by any man!

Lord Wentworth, a renegade Irishman, arrived as Lord Deputy on 23 July 1635. He was universally hated. The governor of Tralee Castle recorded in his diary at this time:

> 23 July 1635—The Lord Viscounte Wentworth came to Ireland to govern ye Kingdom. Manie men feare.

Wentworth embarked on a career of deception to keep Ireland quiet whilst obtaining the maximum revenue to support the Protestant army. An example of his tyranny occurred on 11 December 1635 when he objected to a remark made by a dinner guest, Lord Mountnorris, an Irish peer, who, although a civilian, commanded a company of soldiers. Wentworth had the table cleared, convened a court martial and sentenced Mountnorris to death, saying, 'nothing now remains but to order the Provost Marshal to execute him'. Mountnorris appealed against this travesty of justice to the king, who upheld him. The incident was one that later supported treason charges which sent Thomas Wentworth, Earl of Strafford, to the block on 11 May 1641.

Rebellion broke out in Ireland on 21 October 1641, except in Dublin, where an informer enabled the authorities to forestall the plotters. The most documented leader of the uprising was Ulster's Phelim O'Neil, who took on the lapsed title of The O'Neil, Earl of Tyrone. There are differing accounts of the number of Protestants slain, but it certainly exceeded 37,000, many of whom died in obscene cruelty. These figures are well established and much below those accepted at the time, but contemporary records are available for all who care to consult them. Today it is fashionable to reduce the figure to a fraction of the original; such is the disregard for truth exhibited by modern propagandists. One of the most terrible facets of the story was that priests and women led murder gangs containing children to surround their Protestant friends and beat them to death with sticks and stones.

There were only 943 cavalry and 2,297 infantry in Ireland when the uprising came. The Earl of Ormonde assumed overall command on 17 November 1641 and at the end of that month previously quiet Munster was invaded by rebels from Leinster. Sir William St. Leger defeated a rebel force at Mothill, sending 70 prisoners for execution to the Provost Marshal in Waterford. By 18 February 1642 Sir Frederick Hamilton had executed 56 rebels, one a woman, at Manor Hamilton.

Sir Charles Coote, whose many appointments included that of Provost Marshal, pacified the area around Dublin executing many and filling the city's three gaols to over-flowing. The Lords Justices ordered all prisoners other than members of the nobility or large landowners to be executed. Sir Charles was already known for his fearlessness and cruelty, but his actions now put him in the pages of Irish legend, for thereafter a live prisoner became a rarity. One of those executed was Father O'Higgins, a Franciscan priest, who had been sent to Dublin for his own safety for repeatedly risking death saving Protestants from his co-religionists, who therefore considered him a traitor. The Justices ordered his arrest on 24 March, and Coote executed him immediately. Ormonde was aghast at this, for he had sent O'Higgins into Dublin. His efforts to bring Coote to account were thwarted by the Justices. However, on 7 May Coote was surrounded by a large body of rebels and killed, he and his small escort fighting till the end. His eldest son, also Charles, became Provost Marshal of Connaught in his place.

Rebels took Ardmore Castle in September and hanged 117 of its Protestant defenders. On 24 October the rebels held an Assembly and declared their prime allegiance to the Pope, and secondly to the king. They then elected Commanders for each Presidency, these being:

> General for Ulster—Owen Roe.
> General for Leinster—Thomas Preston.
> General for Munster—Colonel Gerald Barry.
> Lieutenant-General for Connaught—Colonel John Bourke.

As the rebellion progressed its organisation improved and success was very nearly achieved. Catholic army Provost Marshals were appointed, and it soon became evident that they had no compunction about emulating their English counterparts. Possibly the most infamous rebel Provost Marshal was Patrick McLoughlin Mahon who was responsible for the deaths of many Protestants in Carrickfergus. He was rivalled by Turlough Groom O'Quinn for cruelty. O'Quinn was Provost Marshal for the Ardha area in Tyrone. In Ballybarney, Wicklow, Provost Marshal George Hacket had a well-merited reputation for brutality, whilst Richard Cantwell, Provost Marshal of Ballygarrett, undertook the slaughter of Protestants with enthusiasm, once hanging a 16-year-old boy against the orders of his commander, Richard Butler, son of Lord Mountgarrett. When Butler was captured he revealed that in December 1641 Cantwell hanged seven Englishmen and one Irishman together, the latter for being found in the company of the former. This occurred in Kilkenny, the frame of a partly-built house being used as a gibbet. When Lord Mountgarret heard of the killings he was furious and galloped into the town, the looting of which he stopped, and then, riding up to Cantwell, shot him dead.

A Friar Malone, who had been involved in many murders in Skerry, told various of his victims that he had been planning the rebellion for 14 years.

Although nothing can excuse the savagery generated by the rebellion one must remember that the ordinary people had been misled into believing that King Charles had agreed to the creation of an Irish Catholic State, with England to follow later. Fear and distrust begat fury, and the animalism to which certain Catholics reverted was duplicated by many Protestants, as the retaliatory murders of Catholics on Magee Island testify. So Catholic fought for their religion against those they wrongly believed to be in opposition to the king, and the Protestants attacked those they believed to be exterminating Protestants on the orders of Rome, and contrary to the orders of their king. This unhappy episode of Irish history was overtaken by the Civil War in England. Generally in Ireland Catholic sympathies were for Charles, with Protestant support for parliament. On 13 November 1643 Lord Ormonde became Lord Lieutenant, beset by a crisis of conscience. His decision was made easy for him, however, when Archbishop Queely, one of the Catholic commanders, was killed at the Battle of Sligo on 17 October 1645, for on his body was found a copy of a document, now known as the Glamorgan Treaty. Apparently the king had commissioned Lord Glamorgan to negotiate with the remaining Irish rebel nobles that would leave himself free to deal with the parliamentary rebels in England. Unbeknown to Charles, Glamorgan had exceeded his authority and committed him to return the Government and Church in Ireland to its pre-Henry VIII status. This placed Ormonde in the impossible position of leading the loyalist forces, of both denominations, against the Catholic rebels, who were now known to be supported by the king, Ormonde's master! The effect on public opinion of the Treaty of Glamorgan enabled Ormonde to act with honour. For the sake of good government of the country he surrendered the Sword of State to a parliamentary commission, and Dublin to General Michael Jones, parliamentary commander, leaving for exile in France on 28 July 1647.

CHAPTER VI

IRELAND–COMMONWEALTH TO 1900

THE MILITARY SITUATION then existing in Ireland was that parliamentary forces held the Pale, and had little intention of proceeding further until the English Civil War was over. There was a small royalist force in Ulster, and the remainder of the country was dominated by various Catholic rebel factions.

In 1644 Dublin's Provost Marshal, Lawrence Lambert, was convicted by the Irish House of Commons for assaulting a member, the sentence was 'to be conveyed from the Marshalsea by the Sheriffs on the next Market Day, without hat or cloak, unto the Gibbet in the Corn Market, and there to make an acknowledgement of his offence'. This infers that at the time the civil power was predominant, and that enforced self confession is not a recent innovation from behind the iron and bamboo curtains.

Lord Ormonde wrote from the Continent on 20 February 1649 to Lord Clanricard, royalist commander in Ulster, recommending an old officer, Captain Thomas Leicester, for an appointment as Provost Marshal, saying that although the old man was fit, it was unlikely that he would keep the position too long! Shortly after his father's execution Charles II (1649-1684) recognised Ormonde's loyalty and reappointed him Lord Lieutenant of Ireland, albeit in exile.

The victorious Commonwealth, as they became known, forces in England were now able to turn their attention to Ireland. An army under their best general, Oliver Cromwell, arrived in Dublin on 15 August 1649. Preparations for the campaign immediately commenced, the estates of the king's

supporters being sold off to provide funds. Cromwell became
the rival Lord Lieutenant of Ireland, and on 3 September
besieged Drogheda. His Provost Marshal of Horse was Colonel
Richard Lawrence, and there were 24 men on his staff. The
town refused to submit and was attacked, falling on 11 September, but street fighting carried on a further two days,
as the defenders fought from house to house. They knew
that, under the laws of war, their fate was sealed once their
commander, Sir Arthur Ashton, refused to submit. In all
3,552 defenders were killed, including priests and women
under arms. Commonwealth dead and wounded are said to
have totalled only sixty-four!

Wexford, after refusing to parley, was betrayed by Captain
James Stafford, one of its defenders, and it fell after a
four-day resistance on 11 October. Again the fighting surged
from street to street, leaving over 2,000 defenders dead
for a loss of 20 government soldiers. The news of these
two successes spread rapidly and New Ross surrendered when
summoned on 19 October.

The events of Drogheda and Wexford are still remembered
in Ireland, but although horrific were within the rules of
warfare then universally recognised, and once each town had
refused to submit the outcome followed a permitted course
of events. Briefly the rules were on the following lines:
a threatened town could be taken by Treaty, an arrangement
to surrender on mutually agreed terms. This gave rise to the
current expressions of 'Treating' and 'Parleying'. An emissary
of the attacking force would confer with the defenders and
between them draw up a Treaty of Capitulation. How often
have we not read of a garrison marching out with the
honours of war? Sir George Bowes did during the Rebellion
of the Northern earls. So did our men in Yorktown during
the American War of Independence; the fact that Congress
repudiated the Treaty later does not reflect on the honour
of their commander in the field. The Treaty of Cintra in
1808 permitted the French to leave the Peninsula, in our
ships, carrying spoil looted from our allies! What uncon-
ditional surrender means will be described by any former
prisoner of the Japanese in most explicit terms!

To return to our theme—once a town had refused terms
the attackers had the right to destroy all within. Only
churchmen and their property were exempt, unless they
too bore arms, as was the case in Drogheda and Wexford.
Sacking of a town ceased when the commander gave the
word. However, it took Wellington four days to bring his
enraged troops under control after the fall of Badahos. In
Ireland the contestants were mainly Catholics against
Protestants, but in Badahos the British troops were mostly
Irish Catholics, fighting a Spanish Catholic town defended
by Protestants, atheists and Catholics, although the Spanish
townspeople were Catholic to a man. In Rouen Henry V
made a treaty that, if not relieved by a certain date, the
town would capitulate and pay an enormous fine, which
is what happened, and not one life was lost!

Before one condemns Cromwell the whole story should
be read in the light of contemporary standards. One will
then learn of the defence of Clonmel by Sir William Butler,
who had refused to treat and was later forced to surrender
through treachery on the part of his own townspeople. The
town was not sacked and Cromwell personally congratulated
Butler on his spirited defence. Cromwell had suffered more
casualties before the town than had been incurred in the
whole campaign to date. Yet he chose to spare the inhabitants. This, and the surrender of New Ross, reveals the other
side of the coin, for those prepared to turn it over!

At a Dublin court martial on 19 March 1651 Evan Jones, a
soldier, was accused of stealing an iron and socket from a
water pump. He was convicted and sentenced—

> That hee shal ride the wooden horse at the Main Guarde, with
> two musketts att each heele, with the iron and sockett at his
> necke, and an inscription on, his breaste, for one hourer.

Truly a case of punishment fitting the crime!

Another army under General Ireton took Limerick in
1651, the town being betrayed by one of its defenders,
Colonel Fennel. The terms granted were generous, but did
not include any who had committed outrages before the
Catholic Assembly on 24 October 1642. As many of the

clergy in Limerick had been out with O'Neill in 1641 they ordered the inhabitants, under pain of excommunication, to fight on, but the people had had enough. These were the same clergy who, in 1650 when Ormond had returned to Ireland for a time, refused to let him and his small force into the town. Under the exemptions to the treaty there were many executions by the Provost Marshal, the traitor Fennel being one to suffer death. About ten priests were executed, including the Bishop of Galway who had hidden in a pest house. The Bishop of Limerick dressed as a soldier and escaped. Later the heads of all the executed clergy appeared on spikes over one of the town's gates.

Clare then surrendered, and Galway on 12 May 1652, after Father Anthony Geoghegan had been in treasonable contact with the Commonwealth commander. Ross Castle surrendered on 20 June, Cromwell then appointing a Commission to enquire into the atrocities of 1641. Dr. Henry Jones, Cromwell's Scoutmaster-General, was appointed to the Commission—in intelligence matters he had been supreme. At this time the Scoutmaster-General with Fairfax's army was Leonard Watson who is remembered more for his antecedents than his efficiency: some years previously he had to leave Lincoln, where he was a goldsmith, precipitately, as he had been adulterating precious metals.

The royalist cause died in Ireland with the Leinster Articles signed on 12 May 1652. The main royalist army of 17 assorted regiments surrendered on 1 June, a second force on the 22 June, and a third, little more than bandits, on 14 August. By then many Catholics were in the royalist forces. Most of the men went to Spain as mercenaries under their commander, Colonel Richard Grace. He died a soldier's death eventually in Athlone during 1691, fighting William III (1688-1792).

The Provost Marshal General of Horse, Colonel Richard Lawrence, Scoutmaster John Jones, and others were commissioned on 1 August 1653 to see how the oppressions could be removed and Irish colonisation forwarded. By the

time Henry Cromwell had become Lord Lieutenant in Ireland
and Richard Cromwell had succeeded his father as Lord
Protector the Commonwealth was disintegrating, and the
about face by General Monck resulted in Charles II being
proclaimed in London on 8 May 1659.

For his great service Ormond became a duke and Lord
Lieutenant of Ireland in December 1661. The restoration
of the monarchy did not, unfortunately, bring peace to
Ireland. A party of officers, upset by the upsurge of
Catholicism, planned an uprising, but it was betrayed 12
hours before it should have commenced. All except
Lieutenant Richard Blood were arrested. Blood later ensured
a place in history by attempting to steal the Crown Jewels.
One of those arrested was Major Richard Thompson, Deputy
Provost Marshal of Leinster. He confessed and was sentenced to death. At his trial an escort's pistol was accidentally
discharged, killing a bystander. On the scaffold he said he
had been fooled by Blood, and after praying for the king
died with dignity.

The Duke of Ormond hurried to Carrickfergus in May
1666 to quell a mutiny, to find that his son, the Earl of
Arran, had already accepted the surrender. One hundred
and ten men were court martialled on 30 May, nine were
immediately executed by the Provost Marshal and the
remainder shipped to the West Indies as slaves.

During 1684 Colonel Richard Lawrence died. He was
buried in St. Werburgh's church, Dublin, but a fire in 1754
destroyed his tomb and all church records.

With the accession of James II (1684-1688) on 6 February
1684 strife returned to Ireland. A favourite, Richard Talbot,
Earl of Tyrconnell, became army commander, and then
Lord Lieutenant. Seizing on the Monmouth rebellion as a
pretext he disbanded the Militia, making their arms available
for Catholic volunteers. Protestant officers in the army were
replaced by Catholics and Ireland was firmly in Catholic
hands when James was ousted by William of Orange. James
arrived in Ireland in 1690 from France, and by 14 June
William had landed at Carrickfergus. He set up his head-

quarters at Lisburn, where the Provost Marshal was the Dutchman, Assarias Van Velthaven. The king laid down a strict military code; those contravening were to be taken to the Provost Marshal and made to run the gauntlet through his regiment on three separate occasions.

Tradition has given the Battle of the Boyne on 1 July 1690 a military importance it does not deserve; nevertheless, politically its effects are felt today. A fair summation of the event is that William led the advance and James the retreat. His army lost 1,500 men, and that of William over 500, and unfortunately included his ablest commander, Marshal Schomberg. James left Ireland on 4 July, but Stuart Pretenders were to appear on the stage of history for many years to come. Many accepted a pardon offered on 7 July. However, William remained in Ireland completing pacification for several months.

Complaints piled up against his Provost Marshal who had mistreated soldiers complaining at the excesses of their officers. An investigation was made into expenses claimed by the Provost Marshal who, it was alleged, charged £7 6s. 0d. (£7.30) for comforts for 26 men awaiting execution, when in fact he spent £1 6s. 0d. (£1.30). He then claimed £24 as fees for the executioner, when only £6 was due. Also, although claiming expenses for funerals, bodies of executed men were thrown in a river. A nice touch was his claim for £9 for a blue-lined tent for use by a prostitute. Van Velthaven contested the allegations, claiming that in Holland such fees were customary. The king agreed and ordered the account to be paid without further delay. There is another similarly inflated account still in existence. Condemned men were referred to as patients, which presumably was an allusion to their forthcoming cure!

The signing of the Treaty of Limerick on 13 October 1691 officially ended the campaign in Ireland. Had the Protestant soldiers at the Boyne known that 32 years later those of them who had defended Derry would still be waiting for their pay, what would the outcome have been? Apparently the sums embezzled were immense and totalled:

				£	s.	d.
Baker's regiment	..	..	..	16,274	9	8
Mitchelburn's regiment	..	..		9,541	16	0
Walker's regiment	..	..	..	10,188	13	0
Munroe's regiment	..	..	..	8,360	2	0
Crofton's regiment	..	..	..	7,750	11	0
Hamill's regiment	..	..	..	8,969	13	6
Lane's regiment	..	..	..	8,360	2	0
Murray's regiment	..	..	..	5,312	9	6

£74,757 16 8
(£74,756.83p)

On Christmas Day 1718 John Martyn became Provost
Marshal General in Ireland at 5s. 0d. per day. William Smith
was appointed as a Provost Marshal on 13 September 1728,
having previously held similar office in England since
17 April that year. The mid-1700s saw a rash of criminal
gangs operating, all under a convenient cloak of patriotism.
They were mainly sectarian in composition, but murder,
rape, robbery, arson and cattle maiming were common
accomplishments. Variously known as Whiteboys, Liberty-
boys, Oakboys, Steelboys, Defenders, and Peep-o-day boys,
they have their emulators to this day. Their activities usually
involved attacks on isolated houses or small bodies of
soldiers. In September 1764 Whiteboys left for dead a J.P.
who tried to do his duty when money was demanded from
the Mayor of Dungannon. On the arrival of troops the
ensuing battle saw 18 terrorists killed and 25 captured. On
the 29 September a body of the same organisation attacked
20 cavalrymen escorting four of their members to Kilkenny
gaol. The sergeant and corporal were killed and several
soldiers wounded. Seven Whiteboys died and many were
hurt, but they rescued their friends.

A Captain Reid became Provost Marshal General in Dublin
in 1792 and held the appointment, which his father had
previously enjoyed, for over eight years. It was not unusual
at one time for offices to remain in one family. In 1794
the Sheriff's marshalsea moved from the old *Black Dog* inn
in Dublin to new premises in Green Street, but retained its

old name. The new accommodation was spacious, having 12 rooms for the prisoners' accommodation. During the final years of the century Provost Marshals were relegated to their proper role, answerable for the conduct of troops in the field and in garrison. Military magistrates operated where martial law was in force, otherwise Justices of the Peace enforced the law. This is not to say that cases did not occur in Ireland, as elsewhere, where a military magistrate was also the Provost Marshal. The day when a Provost Marshal could sell his office had gone for ever in Ireland.

Major Charles Henry Sirr became Town Major of Dublin and Assistant Provost Marshal, and as such was responsible for policing Dublin. His father, who lay in St. Werburgh's cemetery, had previously held the offices. He lived in the Provost Marshal's house in Dublin Castle and had an important collection of works of art there. Allegedly he and his staff were very efficient, but corrupt. On 4 December 1797 Brigadier John Moore, soon to gain immortality at Coruna, joined the Dublin garrison, and General Sir Ralph Abercrombie, soon to die in Alexandria, became Commander in Ireland.

Major Sirr arrested Peter Finerty, editor of the United Irish Society's paper *Press*, by warrant. He was interrogated in the Castle before being handed to the civil authorities. On 22 December 1797 he received two years for libel, but had merely published an unbiased political summary.

The Fitzgerald uprising of 1798 was the worst for 100 years, although the capture of its leaders in the early stages reduced the chances of success. Nevertheless, many innocent people, mainly Protestants, lost their lives. Sirr and his men captured the ringleader, Lord Edward Fitzgerald, after a struggle, but Fitzgerald succumbed soon after from his injuries. Possibly the more notorious leader was Theobald Wolfe Tone, who was captured on board a French ship laden with weapons and stores for the insurgents. He was wearing a green uniform in the French style, and refused to take it off when capture was certain. He was lodged in the Provost prison in charge of the Provost Marshal, Major Sandys.

The Provost prison consisted of two 24ft. by 20ft. cells, half below ground level, dark and damp. The medical officer stated, early in 1798, that no more than 25 men should be held in each cell, but by July both held a total of 150 souls. Later prisoners were moved to prison hulks in Dublin Harbour.

Wexford fell to the rebels on 26 June 1798 after the Battle of Vinegar Hill. One hundred and ninety-seven Protestant prisoners were taken to Wexford Bridge and most killed individually by jamming pikes into their chests and tossing them over the parapet into the river, like so many sheaves of corn. The arrival of troops under Moore saved a few fortunate survivors, and a woman and child whom, though wounded, had hidden under the bridge. The Wexford atrocities were committed by insurgents led by Father Murphy, who had commenced his insurgency by killing a soldier whom he caught stealing. He led under a banner bearing the letters M.W.S., meaning 'Murder without sin'. He was eventually caught and tried, a formality denied many of his defenceless victims, and then executed. A statue commemorates his deeds in his hometown today.

Major Sirr and the Dublin Yeomanry occupied the Royal Exchange, which became an interrogation centre. One famous prisoner was Hugh Ware, who later became a Colonel in Napoleon's army, and fought against his countrymen in the Peninsula. A contemporary writer, Dr. R. Madden, writing of the actions of Sirr and Sandys said, 'There is no redress for these acts, the man who might be fool enough to seek it would become a marked man, subject to be taken up, sworn against, as in Hevey's case, and perhaps hanged'.

The Hevey case referred to occurred in 1798, and was a *cause célèbre* at the time. Apparently the gentleman had annoyed Major Sirr who lodged him in the Provost prison under Major Sandys. After seven weeks he was prepared to agree to anything, and agreed to make over to Major Sandys a mare that he coveted. Once this was done the Provost Marshal bought Hevey before a court martial in Kilkenny, where he was convicted on the word of a condemned man who had been promised reprieve if he testified. Hevey was sentenced to death. The commander, then Lord Cornwallis, quashed the sentence and set Hevey free. Sandys wisely returned the mare as Hevey prepared to bring a civil action against him to obtain possession of it.

Major Sirr pounced on 8 September 1802 and in no time Hevey was back in Major Sandy's care lodged in a cell with prisoners suffering from loathsome diseases. Complaint to the Provost Marshal only brought abuse in reply. An application for a Writ of Habeas Corpus was refused as the judge was told that Hevey was held on warrant for treason. Hevey was eventually released and then started action for false imprisonment. He was represented by Mr. J. P. Curran, later Master of the Rolls, a noted judicial wit. Once when threatened with committal for contempt he flashed back at the irate judge, 'That will be the best thing your Lordship has committed this week'.

Let us return to the main story. During part of the rebellion the 100th Regiment was in Gorey. Daily court martials were held and those rebels convicted hanged by a Provost Marshal. The troops were incensed at the rebels' practice of piking to death captured soldiers who refused to change sides, yet when they left the area their regiment received a written testimony from the local priest and his church-wardens, testifying to the humanity of the Marquis of Huntly, who commanded, and his men.

Major Sandys' character is illustrated by the following story. Learning that a Mr. McNally possessed a silver cup inscribed 'Erin go Brach' (Ireland for ever), he coveted it. He sent a sergeant to collect it armed with a confiscation order on the grounds that the inscription was seditious. The owner refused to hand it over and the sergeant pointed out the inadvisability of provoking the Provost Marshal; McNally still refused. The sergeant was given a file of men and sent back; this time he got the article. The owner, a barrister, promptly obtained a court order for its restitution. Major Sandys reluctantly returned it, but with the offending inscription erased.

The 8 p.m. curfew imposed in Dublin had a disastrous effect on night life. The owners of Crow Street Theatre were promised £5,000 compensation, but never received it.

When Lord Cornwallis became commander-in-chief in 1798 he increased the number of troops to 13,700 and made things easier for the population. One reform was the abolition of Major Sirr's department. However, we know from the Hevey case that by 1802 it was back in business.

Having been found in uniform Wolfe Tone had no choice but to plead guilty at his court martial in Dublin Castle on 10 November 1798. He was lodged in the Provost prison for execution and from there petitioned that he be shot. This was refused and his execution set for 10 a.m. the next day outside the *Black Dog* prison. Unbeknown to him, Mr. Curran lodged an objection before the courts alleging in effect that martial law could not, in this case, usurp the function of the civil courts. The motion was held before the Lord Justice of Ireland, Lord Kilwarden, and as the background of the case could be duplicated in Ireland today, the proceedings are reproduced in full thus:

> The Lord Chief Justice answered Mr. Curran, 'Have a writ instantly prepared'.
>
> Who replied, 'My client may die while this writ is preparing'.
>
> Lord Kilwarden then spoke to the Sheriff, 'Mr. Sheriff, proceed to the barracks and acquaint the Provost Marshal that a writ is preparing to suspend Mr. Tone's execution, and see that he is not executed'.
>
> The Court waited on tenter-hooks for the return of the Sheriff, who soon returned and addressed the court, 'My Lords, I have been to the barracks in pursuance of your order. The Provost Marshal, Major Sandys says he must obey Lord Cornwallis'.
>
> Mr. Curran immediately rose, saying, 'Mr. Tone's father, my Lords, returns after serving the Habeas Corpus, he says General Craig will not obey it'.
>
> At this the Lord Chief Justice addressed the Sheriff, 'Mr. Sheriff, take the body of Tone into your custody. Take the Provost Marshal into custody, and show the order of the Court to General Craig'.
>
> The Sheriff left and shortly afterwards returned saying that he had failed to gain admission to the barracks, adding: 'Mr. Tone, having cut his throat last night, is not in a condition to be removed. As to the second part of your order, I could not meet the parties'.
>
> The Lord Chief Justice then ordered, 'Let a rule be made for suspending the execution of Theobald Wolfe Tone, and let it be served on the proper authorities'.

Wolfe Tone died of his injuries. There is no doubt that had he not taken the action he did he would have hanged unless reprieved by Lord Cornwallis. Provided martial law had been invoked within constitutional requirements it would appear to be paramount. Lord Cornwallis, a humane man, obviously had no compunction respecting the legality of the court, or its verdict.

A Court of Enquiry sat on 25 June 1800 to establish how 46 prisoners managed to tunnel out of the Provost prison. At this time the Deputy Provost Marshal of Dublin was a William Blair. At 9.30 p.m. on 9 September 1803 Major Sirr and his men raided 28 Parliament Street, Dublin, arresting 'General' Thomas Russell who had a price of £5,000 on his head. He had returned from exile with Robert Emmett, who also has his niche in Irish revolutionary history.

Sir Arthur Wellesley had, you may recall, been summoned from Ireland for service in the Peninsula. He obviously had a high opinion of Major Sirr, for he wrote from Villa Fermosa on 14 April 1811 recommending that he investigate certain forgeries that had accompanied application for commissions in his army.

Insurrection broke out in Western Ireland, where a gang of terrorists known as 'Capt. Rook's men' caused considerable trouble. Their depredations followed the pattern that had been held as normal in Ireland for over three hundred years. By 1822 they reached a new low when three carts carrying wives of the Rifle Brigade were ambushed. The women were raped again and again before release, by which time one was incurably insane.

Major Sirr died in 1841 and was buried beside his father in St. Werburgh's churchyard. In 1844 his collection of antiques and curiosities were sold to the Irish Academy, and now form part of a national collection.

Elsewhere in this account we learn of the formation of a Military Police Corps in England during 1855. The actual date of the arrival in Ireland is not known, but they were certainly in the Curragh on 1 August 1877. During 1881 recently commissioned Lieutenant Quartermaster C. Broakes became Assistant Provost Marshal at the Curragh. He went off to the Egyptian campaign but returned to his Irish appointment in 1883. Military police were used with other soldiers to police Dublin during the civil police strike there in 1882.

Military police were also stationed in Dublin, Cork and Belfast from 1888, for which purpose the Corps strength was increased. These remained permanent stations until the partition of Ireland in 1922. It seems that it was not unusual for police sergeant-majors to be appointed A.P.M.s in Irish garrisons. This is believed to be the last occasion that soldiers were appointed to these posts that they once dominated. There were isolated cases in more recent years, though appointments were for trooping purposes. The writer, then a warrant officer, was appointed A.P.M. on His Majesty's transport *Circassia* in March 1947, and as the appointment carried an individual cabin as a perk it was gratefully undertaken.

The precedent sent by Lieutenant (Q.M.) Broakes was followed in 1889 when Sergeant-Major J. L. Emerson was commissioned as a Lieutenant (Q.M.) and appointed A.P.M. The Curragh.

So the 19th century and the period covered by this work drew to a close. The hated Provost Marshal no longer stalked the land, but the new military police were firmly in control, but only in matters concerning the forces of the Crown, civilians having nothing to fear from them, except in a few stated circumstances.

CHAPTER VII

EARLY STUART TO THE RESTORATION

PROVOST MARSHALS and their men were responsible for crowd control during the coronation of James I (1603–1625). The Provost Marshal and R.M.P. similarly assisted during the coronation of Queen Elizabeth II on 2 June 1953. It was in James's coronation year that the City of London drew up instructions for their Provost Marshals. Many nominated tasks are today those of local government offices and included control of hawkers, street cleaning, supervising night watchmen, market arrangements, sanitary precautions in times of plague, weights and measures inspection, regulation and control of eating houses, and many other duties in addition to their peace-keeping functions.

The right to appoint Provost Marshals in London and the seven Home Counties was reaffirmed by a Proclamation of 23 July 1616, being renewed on 17 July the following year, during which time Justices asked that Provost Marshals be replaced by Head Constables. They were told that the Office of Head Constable had never been abolished and they should still be appointed. In both 1623 and 1624 Lords Lieutenant were again reminded of their obligations to appoint Head Constables and Provost Marshals. The continued opposition to the latter was one of the various causes of the coming Civil War, yet when that was successfully concluded Provost Marshals were more in evidence than ever, as we shall see.

Sir Walter Raleigh, writing to his wife from the West Indies on 14 November 1617, reported the death from fever of his Provost Marshal, Mr. W. Steed. As is well known, Raleigh returned empty-handed from his attempt to find

El Dorado, and was executed for treason in Old Palace Yard, Westminster, on 7 November 1618.

Having referred to the New World it will be as well if we here cover all references to it in the period under review. Virginia had a Provost Marshal from an early date, and in a disciplinary code published on 22 June 1611 the following provision was made for his protection: 'He that shall abuse and injure the Sergeant Major, the Provost Marshal, either by word or deed, if he be a Captain he shall be cashiered, if a soldier he shall pass the pikes. No soldier shall withstand or hinder the Provost Marshal or his men in the execution of their Office, upon pain of death'.

It is, of course, still an offence to obstruct a Provost Marshal, but the penalty has been reduced! Earlier in this account we have seen how in 1513 the Provost Marshal ranked as a sergeant-major (major) in action. In the code referred to above the rank appears to have been regularised. Of 'Passing the Pikes', otherwise known as 'Running the Gauntlet' we shall read more later.

The Virginian Provost Marshal was able to commit prisoners to the galleys, a hitherto unencountered military punishment. This was, of course, in addition to the normal range of punishments and detention in the marshalsea.

In Georgia during 1773 the Provost Marshal functioned on similar lines to those in the West Indies and was a chief of police with local government duties.

General George Washington's army of the United Colonies had Captain Bartholomew Von Heer as Provost Marshal in 1776. During September of that year the British executed an American spy, Nathan Hale, who died very bravely, a fact commented on by Mr. Cunningham, our Provost Marshal. Apparently the callous treatment of the condemned man by Cunningham was behind Washington's later refusal to reprieve Major John Andre, a British spy. Both victims were cast in the same mould, and their memory should be kept green in the countries for which they died so resolutely.

The first privately published details of a Provost Marshal's duties appear to be those reproduced in *Five Decades of Epistles of Warre*, by Francis Markham in 1622. These are of great importance to the serious student and the relevant paragraphs are therefore given in full:

2. This office I have seen in mine experience to carry a double and two-fold estimation—men judging of the good or evil thereof according to the worthiness or unworthiness of the party which held it, the honest, wise and understanding men swaying it with Reputation and Renown. The foolish, base, and contemptible person ordering it with a regard of as much or more Imputation. But all this is fault in election, not in place: for it is certain, the office in itself is both worthy, necessary, and good, a calling fit for a gentleman of blood and quality, and a degree wherein a man may express any virtue to the life, both with applause and admiration.

3. It is also of great profit and advancement; which infers merit; and there is knit into it a singular trust, which must ever allow of much Faith and Wisdom; I cannot compare it in our civil government to any office nearer than that of under Sheriff's which however the proverb is:

    'Twice an under Sheriff, ever a knave'—yet it is but corruption that makes good the adage: for I know of many honest men that many years have had the place, yet many times better than a world of those which condemn it.

4. But to proceed, the gentleman which should be elected to this place of Provost Marshal, would be a man of great judgement and experience in all Martial Discipline, well seen in the laws and ordinances of the camp, and such a one as knew well the use, benefit and necessity of all things belonging either to Food or Raiment. He should be a lover of justice, impartial in his dealings, and free from the transportation of passions: he should have an ear that could contemptuously beat back, not furiously drink in, slander and railing languages: he should have an eye that could gaze on all objects without winking; and a heart full of discreet compassion, but not touched with foolish or melting pity.

5. In brief he ought to be only the Law's Servant, and indeed to challenge no more in himself, than so much as expressed to her his obedience.

6. For the nature of his office—he is first the greatest and principal gaoler of the Army, having power to detain and keep prisoner whosoever shall be committed unto him by lawful authority, and though some contemptuously call him the Hangman or Executioner of the Army, yet it is not so, but as our Sheriffs of Counties are bound to find slaves for such needful uses: so he by his place is obliged to find men and other implements for all such occasions, and to that end hath

allowances for any attendants to dispatch any execution how suddenly soever commanded, and to that end it is not lawful for the Under Provosts to go at any time without Halters, Withs or Strangling cords of March, ever about them.

7.   The Provost Marshal hath the charge of all manner of Tortures, as Gyves, Shackles, Bolts, Chains, Belbowes, Manacles, Whips and the like and may by his ministers use them, either in case of Judgement or commandment from a Marshal Court or otherwise upon unruliness at his own discretion: he is by his Officers to see all the places of execution prepared and furnished with engines fitting to the judgement, whether it be Gallows, Gibbets, Scaffolds, Pillories, Stocks or Strappadoes, or any other engine which is set up for terror and affright to such as behold it.

8.   This Officer hath the guard and keeping of all such prisoners as are taken in the wars, till they be either ransomed, exchanged or by the General otherwise disposed: and in this case the nobler his usage is, the greater will the praise be of his humanity and virtue.

9.   If any drums or trumpets shall happen to come from the enemy, they are by the Provost Marshal to be entertained, accommodated and provided, unless it please the Lord Marshal himself otherwise to dispose of them. And that all these duties beforesaid may with more efficiency and luster be performed, he shall have his Quarter in the strongest and most securest part of all the Army, and in all marches he is also to have the place of greatest safety for the assurance of his prisoners.

10. Moreover, it is the office of the Provost Marshal, by authority of the Lord Marshal, to guard with a good convoy of men, both to the camp and in the camp, and from the camp, all manner of victuallers, viandors, merchants and others which bring any provisions to the camp, and as soon as they are entered, he shall rate and set price; in a reasonable and indifferent manner; upon all their goods, and secure them from the insolence of the soldier, providing that no man take anything from them without payment; he also looks to the proportions of the true weights and measures, and reconciles any difference in buying and selling, for which labour he hath of the Providers or Merchants, the hides and tongues of all manner of cattle that are killed, and every week sixpence apiece in money numbered for their stalls, which sixpence a week he is accountable for unto the Lord Marshal, for to him that fee is belonging.

11. It is likewise the office of the Provost Marshals, to see that the Market Place of the camp be once in two days swept and kept sweet and clean, that all garbage and filthiness be burnt

and consumed and that no man do the office of nature but in places convenient, and that in the whole camp or garrison there may not be anything which may turn to a general nuisance.

12. The Provost Marshal must have an especial care to the keeping of the peace, and to apprehend the least occasion which may tend to breach of the same, he must prevent all mutinies, quarrels and disorders, and that no uncivil discussion may have strength to out-face or withstand the power of his command, he shall ever have about him a guard of his Under Provosts and servants, who with short truncheons in their hands, according to Military form, shall enforce obedience to any lawful commandment which proceedeth from him, and having taken them in their actual transgressions, to commit them to prison, or the bolts, as the nature or evil example of the crime deserveth, for it is a duty expected at this Officer's hands, to be a ready suppressor of vice and disorder, and to be a maintenance and advancer of all those which have any semblance or likeness with an honest, sober and civil inclination: whence it behoveth him to have a ready and quick judging eye between the good and the bad, so that he may in an early hour restrain all immoderate and unlawful gain, and rather to compel the cut-throat to kill himself with envy, than to consume others with the rust and cankor of his unsatisfied covetousness. It is also a main point in this Officer's duty to discover the lurking subtilities of treacherous spies, and by learning the true interpretations of men's words, looks, manners, forms and habits of apparel, to be able to turn the insides of the hearts outwards, and to pull out that little devil of deceit, though he lie hid in never so dark a corner; and truly a better service cannot be done; nor is there any Act sooner learned if a man will apply his knowledge but seriously thereto.

13. To conclude the last duty of the Provost Marshal is; after the watch is set at night; to survey the Army, and see if it remain calm and still, and that no disorderly noises or tumults keep any part of it awake and not silent; and in this survey, if he encounter any immoderate fires, or superfluous candle-lights he shall cause them to be put out and extinguished; or if he hear in Sutlers cabins or other harbour any drunkards, tobacco-takers, or other unruly persons, whose noise is both offensive to the camp and giveth to others an evil example, he shall presently suppress them, and make them depart, or else upon grosser disorder, commit them, for besides the undecency and unfitness of the action, such clamours and noises are more than hurtful in a camp, specially being anything near where the sentinel standeth, for it is an interruption and

hindrance through which he cannot possibly discharge his
duty.

A very comprehensive catalogue of responsibilities!

One of our most famous infantry regiments, The Black
Watch, 'Am Freicadam Dubh' was originally raised in
Scotland as a military police organisation. Disbanded by
George I (1714–1727) in 1717 they were re-raised in 1725
for use 'in disarming the people, *bringing criminals to justice*
and to hinder rebels, etc., etc.'.

The force was under military law and it operated from
Inverness and Fort William. In 1739 they were mustered
into the regular army as the 43rd Foot, but today rank as
the 42nd The Black Watch, Royal Highland regiment. The
regiment celebrates 1739 as its foundation date and makes
no claim to be the first military police corps. However, they
deserve a mention here as 107 years of military police service
should not be lightly written off.

Another step forward came in Articles of War of 1625
when this clause appeared:

> That there be a Provost Marshal appointed in every Regiment,
> when the Regiment be full, and a prison ordained soldiers apart
> from any other.

Here we have the creation of a Regimental Provost Marshal,
whose office is still with us as the Regimental Provost
Sergeant.

One clause in these Articles is today reproduced in military
police offices on both sides of the Atlantic, usually in an
imagined vellum reproduction of the original—

> The Provost must have a horse allowed him and some soldiers
> to attend him, and all the rest commanded to obey and assist
> him, otherwise the service will suffer, for he is but one man and
> must correct many and cannot therefore be beloved.
> And he must be riding from one Garrison to another, to see
> that the soldiers do no outrage, nor scathe about the country.

It is interesting to note that the need for mobility, long
appreciated by civilian Provost Marshals, had not been
overlooked by the military!

By June 1642 Charles I (1625–1649) and his parliament, whilst hoping for peace, prepared for war. When the break came the king invoked 22 Henry IV Cap. 5 and issued Commissions of Array, whilst parliament mobilised by issuing Military Ordinances, each side vehemently proclaiming the other's illegality. All six London Train Bands declared for parliament, and so many recruits came forward that they divided in two, making 12 regiments, and these halted the royalist advance at Brentford on 25 October 1642.

The Earl of Essex as Captain General of the parliamentary forces commissioned Captain James Seigneur as Provost Marshal and Sir Samuel Luke as Scoutmaster-General, and once the king's headquarters had settled in at Oxford little that went on there remained hidden from Sir Samuel.

A Military Code promulgated by Essex on 6 September 1642 formed the basis of similar Codes for many years to come. There were over forty capital offences, and boring through the tongue for certain lesser crimes. During the autumn the king overhauled his administration and produced his own Code. The king's units were 1,000 strong, parliament's about 1,200, with a Regimental Provost Marshal in each regiment. The later addition of a quartermaster relieved Provost Marshals of much of their regimental support duties. Known parliamentary Regimental Provost Marshals in this period were:

Sir John Merrick's regiment: John Theme.
Earl of Stanhope's regiment: Robert Powell.
Lord Wharton's regiment: George Higham.
Lord Rochfort's regiment: John Burbeck.
Lord St. John's regiment: Robert Lucas.
Lord Brook's regiment: William Coleman.
Lord Manderville's regiment: John Turner.
Lord Robert's regiment: Humphrey Franouth.
Colonel Sir Henry Cholmlie's regiment: Nicholas Garth.
Colonel Sir William Bamfield's regiment: Richard Gray.
Colonel Sir William Constable's regiment: John Yarner.
Colonel Thomas Grantham's regiment: Robert Gibbons.
Colonel Sir William Fairfaxe's regiment: Henry Fisher.
Colonel Thomas Ballard's regiment: Benjamin Ludlow.
Colonel Charles Essex's regiment: Martin Benthim.

Parliamentary soldiers led by their Provost Marshal looted Chichester cathedral when that city fell to Sir William Waller on 29 December 1642.

Early the following year the royal army created the Provost Marshal General for its chief Provost officer. The first to be so nominated was Captain William Smith, who was responsible for Oxford, where he amassed a fortune at the expense of his prisoners. Parliament also adopted the new designation, and the first holders were:

Provost Marshal General of Foot: Captain James Seigneur.
Provost Marshal General of Horse: John Baldwine.
Provost Marshal General of Artillery: Christopher Troughton.
Provost Marshal General of Dragoons: Daniel Lyon.

When Oliver Cromwell was on his way to London on 14 January 1643 he called at St. Albans, where he found the High Sheriff reading the Royal Commission of Array in the market. He arrested the Sheriff and sent him to be detained by the Provost Marshal in Ely House, High Holborn.

John Lilbourne, a prominent parliamentarian, was able to escape from Oxford by bribing Captain Smith, who was an expert in getting prisoners to change sides—he simply starved them until they agreed. He forbade doctors to heal sick prisoners, and would only feed those who volunteered to work on Oxford's defences. In Oxford Castle, where many were kept, water was so scarce that prisoners fought each other to get at puddles. Many prisoners starved to death rather than be false to their beliefs. According to Henry Connington—one of Sir Samuel Luke's best agents—there was an unsuccessful attempt on Smith's life on 21 March. There is little doubt that this evil Provost Marshal General did much that harmed the king's cause.

After the betrayal of Reading by its commander, Colonel Fielding, the Scoutmaster, Captain Whitehead escaped to Oxford where he was able to reveal the treachery to Charles. At the same time one of Luke's agents escaped from Oxford and gave a harrowing description of his sufferings after capture and of the inhumanity of Smith. During that August Smith executed one of the king's soldiers who had refused to march from Oxford until he received his back pay. The conduct of royalist soldiers, forced to live off the land through lack of pay, and of drunken royalist gallants in Oxford, alienated many who otherwise would have supported the king.

A series of parliamentary pamphlets attacking Smith caused the king to sack him on 22 January 1644. An officer named Thorpe was appointed to succeed him. In the matter of Smith as in so many matters, Charles had consistently refused advice, proving once again that he was his own worst enemy.

By this time Cromwell's regiment, the Ironsides, was the pride of parliament, and from it sprang the New Model Army and the king's defeat. In Lieutenant-Colonel Whalley's troop in the regiment, which today corresponds with an H.Q. Squadron, there were 97 men, including a Provost Marshal.

Before the Battle of Cheriton Sir William Waller proclaimed that all prisoners were to be handed to the Provost Marshal General within 12 hours of capture, on pain of cashiering or imprisonment, according to the rank of the offender.

Drunkenness plagued the parliamentary forces in Farnham, and on 24 April 1644 the Provost Marshal was authorised to draw drunks up on their toes, suspended from a chain, with a jug round the neck, and to leave them as long as he wished.

Under Article 7 of the parliamentary Articles of War soldiers resisting a Provost Marshal or his men could suffer death. On 26 April a soldier was acquitted on this charge at Farnham, but on 7 June one Robert Halifax was executed at Stow-on-the-Wold. On 8 July it was necessary to remind Provost Marshals that prisoners committed to their custody must be brought to trial, and on the 17 July Provost Marshal Thomas Williams was sentenced to be suspended, as just described, and cashiered for drunkenness and other offences.

The king's efficient Scoutmaster-General, Sir Charles Blount, was killed by a drunken officer in Oxford in late

May. Later the conduct of royalist troops caused the local inhabitants to form a Vigilante organisation to defend themselves. Known as 'Clubmen' they soon deteriorated into bandit gangs, robbing and murdering both soldiers and civilians alike. Their activities and the operations to suppress them are a story in their own right.

By late summer the king had advanced into Cornwall where, on 8 August, in sight of both armies his Provost Marshal General and Under Provost Tom Elyott arrested the king's General Lord Wilmott for treason. The king exercised leniency because of his excellent former service and exiled him to France.

On losing Lostwithiel Lord Essex deserted his army, which surrendered to the king on 2 September. This was possibly the high point of the royalist cause; after this things began to disintegrate. The Cornish levies deserted in droves as they had no wish to serve outside their home county. John Tavernor was appointed Provost Marshal for East Cornwall and Captain David Hawes for the West. They were very successful in rounding up deserters, but nothing could make the men remain with the Colours if they did not wish to do so.

At one time Hawes ran the king's mint in Exeter and was extremely well thought of. In 1650 parliament fined him £60 for his support of Charles, this representing a sixth part of his estate.

The effect of the New Model Army on the civilians, in contrast with the ill-disciplined royalists, was very good. There were many Provost Marshals on establishment, each with a body known as 'Mounted Police' in support. Provost Marshals had the power of summary execution, which was rarely exercised, and their men could inflict 60 lashes, which they often did. Each army had Provost Marshal Generals of the four arms, and a Judge Advocate at headquarters. At the same time the king was belatedly endeavouring to improve discipline in his forces, one step being to close Oxford's inns at 9 p.m. in an effort to control excessive drinking.

Meanwhile a commander in Exeter had become a local tyrant. He was Sir Richard Grenville—bearer of a famous name. Much of his soldiers' pay found its way into his pockets. He would often imprison prominent local royalists, holding them until a fine was delivered to his Provost Marshal.

Parliament grudgingly accepted the arrival of a Scottish army in Newcastle during 1645, where any royalist fugitive apprehended was promptly handed to the parliamentary Provost Marshal, who rivalled Captain Smith in brutality.

Captain Richard Lawrence became parliamentary Provost Marshal General of Horse that year, and both sides went into winter quarters after Devizes fell to Cromwell on 23 September. The following January the son of Bodmin's mayor complained to the king's cavalry commander, Prince Rupert, that Sir Richard Grenville had arrested his father and was demanding £50 for his release. When ordered by the prince to let the mayor go Sir Richard promptly arrested the son also. On the Provost Marshal being instructed to release father and son Sir Richard told him that if he did so he would be liable for the mayor's fine. Prince Rupert then freed the victims and locked Sir Richard in his own gaol.

The king surrendered to the Scots on 5 May and the war ended with the surrender of Pendennis Castle on 17 August. Parliament governed by dividing the country into Districts ruled by a Major General, each with a Provost Marshal as Chief Constable, who thus returned to the pre-eminence of Elizabethan times. One such was Thomas Tyack, Provost Marshal for Cornwall, whose pay was 30s. (150p) weekly, with 4d. (1.4p) for each prisoner. When eventually discharged on economic grounds he was fortunate in being paid up to date. The Somerset Provost Marshal, David Barrett, had previously been a shoemaker in Wells. His prison at Banwell was in the house of the former Bishop of Wells. He was a monster and among those who died at his hands was the Dean of Wells, Doctor Walter Raleigh, nephew of the great adventurer.

The Scottish army returned home in 1647, after first handing the king to his enemies. Parliamentary soldiers, now generally known as Commonwealth troops, settled down to garrison life, with its usual pettiness. During May in Saffron Walden a Captain White complained of being

locked up by the Provost Marshal after an argument with
his colonel. Passive resistance was encountered in Oxford
when the university was reorganised. On one occasion the
Provost Marshal and his men had to break in and forcibly
evict the dean's wife, who had refused to leave when her
husband was dismissed.

What in effect was a second civil war occurred during
1648, and dissension arose among the ruling party. On one
occasion Cromwell personally intervened to talk a wavering
unit into adhering to its allegiance, ordering one man to be
shot on the spot, and handing 11 more over to his Provost
Marshal. By this time it was acknowledged that peace could
never be guaranteed whilst Charles lived, and his trial was
arranged. Captain Pitson, Scoutmaster-General to Sir William
Waller's army, so impressed Cromwell with his report on
the Battle of Preston that he was rewarded with £100, and
his back pay of over £450. On 12 December Cromwell
ordered his Provost Marshal General of Horse to arrest
Sir William Waller and others for plotting against him.

The execution of the king in January 1649 coincided
with the murder in Holland of Dr. Isaac Dorsila, former
Advocate General who framed the king's Indictment.
Prisoners from an unsuccessful royalist uprising were sent
as slaves to the West Indies. One of the leaders, Sir Richard
Mauleverer, whose father was one of the signatories of
the king's death warrant, was committed to the charge of
the Provost Marshal in the Tower of London.

Cromwell's later campaign in Ireland resulted in a flood
of transportations to the Caribbean, where the garrisons
were consequently increased. In Jamaica during 1656 the
famous Throgmorton court martial occurred. Major Throgmorton had contested the court's authority to try him for
mutiny, so the President ordered him thrown out of the
court. Outside, when the Provost Marshal went to hit the
accused on the head with his sword, Throgmorton raised
his hands to protect himself. He was immediately charged
with resisting the Provost Marshal, convicted, and shot.

Sir John Reynolds was commissioned on 25 April 1657
to command an army in the Lowlands, with authority 'to

assign and appoint one or more Provost Marshals for the execution of his commands, according to the terror thereof'.

Cromwell was not the sort of man to let a little thing like a Commission worry him, and personally appointed Colonel Roger Alsop as the expedition's Provost Marshal, with authority to appoint a deputy when required. Sir John did not enjoy his command long, for shortly afterwards he was shipwrecked and drowned.

CHAPTER VIII

RESTORATION TO LATE GUELPH

THE DEATH OF CROMWELL on 3 September 1658
heralded the end of the Commonwealth, for only pygmies
remained to replace the giant. General George Monck's
southward march ensured the Restoration, and Charles II
(1649-1684) entered London on 29 May 1660. Monck
became Captain-General of a newly-raised army with
authority for appointing as many Provost Marshals as
required. It became customary for regiments to decide
whether to have a Quartermaster and a Provost Marshal, or
have a dual appointment; for example:

1664 John Simmonds held both offices in the Maritime Regiment
of Foot from 11 November.
1665 Patrick Vaux assumed both offices in the Holland Regiment
on 23 June.
1684 Peter Smith became Provost Marshal and Henry Hawker
Quartermaster of the Royal Dragoons. Thomas Jones held
both appointments in the 1st Regiment of Guards, but the
2nd Guards had Mathew Ingram as Quartermaster, but no
Provost Marshal.

John Evelyn, the diarist, as a Commissioner for Kent and
Sussex, was empowered to appoint Provost Marshals to
control Dutch prisoners. He visited Chelsea hospital on
8 February 1665 to inspect prisoners and the Provost Marshal
there. The only complaint he received was that the bread
was too fine.

When Henry Morgan (the only pirate to be knighted, and
to become a colonial governor), was operating out of Jamaica
in 1670 the governor, Modyford, commissioned him to raise
a force to attack Panama. Here is part of the commission.

Remember this was issued to a pirate in the name of King Charles II:

> . . . further ordained that there is no pay for the encourage-
> ment of the said fleet, that they shall have all the goods, mer-
> chandise, etc. that can be got in their expedition, to be divided
> among them according to their usual rules, and for their better
> encouragement to engage in this so necessary service it is further
> ordained that no person really belonging to the fleet shall be
> molested for his debts, but hereby protected until further
> orders, of which the Provost Marshal is to take notice at his
> peril.

Thus the king was authorising pirates to loot, to exist under their own rules, and to be exempt from action for debt. Provost Marshals in the Caribbean at this time were civilian officials, and had many civic administrative tasks to perform in addition to their peace-keeping responsibilities.

In 1672 John Evelyn appointed a Provost Marshal for the town of Rochester, and it was in this year that the Duke of Norfolk became hereditary Earl Marshal.

Sir James Turner's 'Pallas Arnata' records military punish-ments in vogue during 1683. These included 'Running the Gauntlet', originally called 'Passing the Pikes'. In this prisoners were beaten as they ran between two lines of soldiers. This was used in Palestine as late as 1946 after a particularly revolting bomb outrage. Disciplinary action followed, for no matter how great the provocation nothing could excuse descent to the level of the criminal gang responsible.

A Provost Marshal was sent to Wigan in 1685 when Clifton's regiment mutinied, and it was in that year that James II (1685–1689), a staunch Catholic, came to the throne. Shortly afterwards Monmouth's Rebellion caused 13 new regiments to be raised. At this time the Articles of War contained many references to a Provost Marshal. Article 49 authorised Regimental Provost Marshals the same fees as their army counterparts. Under Article 50 courts martial were authorised to raise warrants for Provost Marshals to execute their sentences, and under the following Article the Court could vary a Provost Marshal General's fees as they thought fit. Perhaps it was realised that he was not catered for under Article 49.

Death was the punishment for hindering a Provost Marshal or his assistants, under Article 55, which also ruled that if a prisoner escaped, after a person called on to assist a Provost Marshal or his assistants failed to respond, that person could suffer the punishment the prisoner would have received. This created, for the first time, an obligation for officers to assist when the prisoner was accused of a capital offence.

It became an offence under Article 56 for a sword to be drawn while a court martial was in session; the offender could be arrested by the Provost Marshal and punished at the court's discretion. Presumably previous disorders in court prompted this Article, which did not apply to Regimental Provost Marshals. These officials were also excluded from Article 57, which authorised Provost Marshals to apprehend and execute prison breakers.

If a Provost Marshal refused to accept a prisoner, or released one without authority, he could be punished, even executed, if the prisoner had been on a capital charge—such were the provisions of Article 62. Today, of course, military prisons are the concern of the Military Provost Staff Corps, who must accept prisoners unless the establishment is full or has infectious disease present.

Article 63 permitted a Provost Marshal to release a person handed to him by some other authority who did not furnish a charge within 24 hours. This is still the law, and for that reason military police carry a form, Army Form A.6009. This is both a receipt for the prisoner and a holding charge for the guard commander.

There was a Provost Marshal in the island of St. Helena during the years 1687–8. On 25 August 1688 Sir Henry Morgan, ex-pirate and colonial administrator, died in Jamaica, at which time Provost Marshals had become powerful men in our Caribbean possessions. Usually governors and senior officials were appointed from England, but their deputies were supporters of the local paramount political party. Apart from the governor most chief officials, including the Provost Marshal, stayed at home, leaving their office in the hands of local deputies, and this gave rise to widespread corruption and maladministration. It had been stipulated after the Restoration that locally-passed laws must be approved by the home government, but governors got round this ruling through Decrees and Proclamations. As the Militia was officered by local political appointees life for Opposition members could be very hard. The various deputies levied fees for their services, remitting an annual tribute to their principal at home. These colonial Provost Marshals also arranged elections, issued writs, ran prisons, licensed traders, collected taxes and executed warrants. Their presence was felt at every level in the community and almost without exception they were cruel, tyrannical and corrupt.

William of Orange, soon to be William III (1689-1702), landed in England on 15 November 1688. His invasion plans were meticulous, and his military budget indicated his priorities, allocating £420 for engineer services, £815 for medical matters, but £1,164 for Provost—possibly the only occasion when Provost got the lion's share of the funds.

Within a year William had sent an army to the Continent, but en route the 1st Foot Regiment mutinied at Ipswich, and, although put down, it resulted in mass desertion later in Holland. An indirect result of this was the first Mutiny Act.

Colonel Cadwallader Jones became governor of the Bahamas in 1690, assuming the office of Provost Marshal among others. He became a complete despot, introducing censorship and imprisonment without trial for opponents; finally on 24 January 1692 the citizens rebelled and locked him in his own gaol. A counter coup was successful and the leader of the revolt, Thomas Bulkley, was arrested and later sentenced to a prison term. Among the members of the jury hearing his case were six pirates, two alcoholics, and a man waiting trial for buggery!

On 7 June 1692 much of Port Royal, capital of Jamaica, vanished into the sea during an earthquake, and Sir Henry Morgan's grave was engulfed. Over 8,000 died, including Captain Molesworth the Provost Marshal, brother of the governor.

There was a Provost Marshal with the artillery train at the
battles of Steinkirk and Landen; he was paid 3s. (15p)
daily and his two assistants 2s. 6d. (12½p) each. A matross
in the train, Ben Blackbourne, was caught stealing powder
at Ghent in June 1693. After court martial he was discharged, but not before being flogged and branded on the
head by the Provost Marshal. It was also in 1693 that the
home government sacked Colonel Cadwallader Jones, and he
vanished from the scene. Bulkley hurried to London to
obtain redress if possible. By the time his case came
up in 1697 he was hopelessly insane and an inmate of
Bedlam.

During 1696 in Ghent a court martial sentenced a soldier
to 14 days bread and water, to be kept in irons, and dis-
played by the Provost Marshal for one hour daily. Shortly
after this his allowances for prisoners were set at 10 stivers
for the first day and two thereafter for each cavalry corporal
and trooper, and five stivers with two daily afterwards for
Dragoon corporals and troopers.

By 1706 musters were controlled by the Judge Advocate,
and when overseas he was responsible to the home government, which greatly reduced the chances of peculation
among local officials. Army administration was improving
all the time; the introduction of the post of Quartermaster
General, equating with today's Chief of Staff, permitted
more centralised direction, with Provost Marshal General,
Scoutmaster-General, Wagon Master General, and another
newcomer, Commissary General, all directing branches
of the Service, and absorbing much that historically was
the lot of a Provost Marshal. Orders were disseminated
through a horde of aides-de-camp. Military punishments
were still brutal, with boring through the tongue for
blasphemy, a task the Provost Marshal superintended, and
which was abolished in 1710.

The Bahamas became a Crown Colony on 6 February
1718, with Captain Noodes Rogers as governor. All officials,
including the Provost Marshal, were appointed by the first
Council, but thereafter home government endorsement for
appointments was required.

John Martyn became Provost Marshal General in England on 25 December 1719, and four years later was followed by Joseph Garston, who was also Provost Marshal to the three regiments of Guards in the Lowlands. This is the first recorded appointment of one individual to what amounted to a Brigade, and equates with today's Brigade Provost Officer. When Garston returned on 20 July 1726 James Howard took over.

The appointment on 16 January 1724 of Joseph Tipping as Provost Marshal for the garrison and town of Gibraltar was another milestone in our story, for here was a dual civilian and military commitment, probably due to the unusual situation and circumstances pertaining to our occupation of the Rock.

Between 1727 and 1728 the 7th Foot were employed on police duties in the West Country, and on the night of 17/18th May 1743 the Black Watch mutinied at Finchley, North London. They were on their way overseas, and wrongly believed they had enlisted for home service only, as had been the case in their military police days. According to later Depositions only two of the mutineers had been members of the earlier force. These men, Thomas Stewart and Duncan McIntyre were later sentenced to death, but on reprieve were transported for continuous service in the colonies, being held pending passage under the care of Provost Marshal Dodd at the Savoy military prison, London. This officer was charged, under a warrant of 2 June 1743, with arranging the various mutiny trials and for the attendance of witnesses. Later a corporal and two privates were executed by shooting in the Tower, and many more transported for life. Mr. Dodd was famous in his day, and his name features on many documents dealing with desertion in that period. The Provost Marshal General in Westminster then received 5s. (25p) per day; yet the Provost Marshal to the Horse Guard regiment enjoyed 7s. (35p), plus 5s. 6d. (27½p) subsistence allowance daily. Provost Marshals in Minorca and Gibraltar each received 4s. (20p) daily, and one with an army in the field £17 12s. 10d. (£17.14p) for a 200-day period, plus three rations a day. This suggests that rations were more valuable than money, for his pay was only 8½p per day.

One result of moving the Black Watch from Scotland was an upsurge in robbery and extortion. The custom of farmers buying protection with cereals, known as 'blackmeal', gave rise to the modern 'blackmail'. Many felt that had the Black Watch been on hand the rebellion of 1745 would never have got off the ground; but it did, and Sir John Cope's troops suffered a humiliating defeat at Falkirk on 20 August. Among English prisoners taken that day were the Provost Marshal's clergyman and hangman, both of whom were eventually released unharmed. Later our artillery commander at the battle, Captain Archibald Cunningham, was cashiered with ignominy for cowardice, paraded in front of the troops, and after his sword had been broken over his head, physically kicked out of camp by the Provost Marshal.

Captain Stratford Eyre, 62nd Regiment, had been present at the battle and was later appointed Provost Marshal to the Duke of Cumberland's army, and as pacification of Scotland progressed other Provost Marshals, with responsibility for civil law enforcement, were appointed to Forts Augustus, George, and William, each receiving 2s. 6d. (12½p) per day. Some time after this Provost Marshal Stratford Eyre had the task of interrogating Scottish prisoners held in Tilbury Fort, Essex; a task he performed efficiently but harshly.

Throughout the Seven Years War the Allied Continental army had a well-ordered Provost Service, with a Provost Marshal, Deputy Provost Marshal, and Constables, the latter being something entirely new—at least not encountered in the army since the Middle Ages. Thus the terms Provost and Constable were still interchangeable after 600 years; small wonder that the story gets confusing at times! The English Provost Marshal with this army received 4s. (20p) daily, and one with the Hanoverian Horse Guards in our Service 2s. 6d. (12½p).

Strict rules on the treatment of prisoners were agreed under the Treaty of Ecluse in 1759, and Provost Marshals together with their Constables, if taken, were to be exchanged at the first opportunity—perhaps both sides appreciated their services! Unfortunately, prisoners taken in Canada more often than not were scalped by 'friendly' Indians— 'friendly' to the other party of course! Early in 1761 the Allied army under the Duke of Brunswick was faced with an enemy numerically far superior, and his logistical support failed almost completely. Normally well-behaved British soldiers soon became as expert as their Continental comrades in foraging. The Duke on the 16 June ordered the Provost Marshal to be severe, but found time to rile against prostitutes, directing—'Brothels will absolutely not be tolerated and prostitutes or *fillies de joie* are to be arrested and chased from the camp with ignominy. The Provost Marshal will inflict a withering punishment on them'!

In 1763 England withdrew from the Continent, leaving the contestants to their own devices. Six years earlier the commander-in-chief moved into the new Horse Guards in Whitehall, thus giving the army its first permanent home, and it was about then that Newberry's *Military Dictionary* defined a Provost Marshal as:

> An Officer appointed to seize deserters and other criminals, and also to set the rates on provisions in the Army.

Many of the extraneous duties had obviously been shed by then, but his powers clearly still applied to soldiers and civilians alike.

Things started moving towards a conclusion in our long-drawn-out campaign in Canada after General Jeffrey Amherst became commander-in-chief. He used his Provost Marshals to bring plundering under control, for the looting by our troops had turned many of the local inhabitants against us in the past. He also insisted that officers behaved as such at all times. After a Captain Thornton lost his ship by attacking Fort Levis on the River St. Lawrence against orders he was court martialled. During the proceedings the Provost Guard gained notoriety through never neglecting to exhibit their prisoner to the public gaze whenever escorting him to or from the court.

That a Provost Marshal was very necessary in London is apparent if the contribution to crime by the army in London was not. If one reads J. Lindsay's excellent book, *1764*, published by Muller in 1959, one will see a variety of offences. In April a pay sergeant absconded with the pay of 150 recruits. In early June three soldiers were arrested when 16 of them were caught committing unnatural offences in a room. A guardsman was sent for trial on 7 July for attempting a similar offence on a waiter near the Horse Guards; and in August a girl was robbed by a soldier in Grays Inn Road and afterwards thrown into a pond. Possibly the action of the pay sergeant was the cause of an order later in the year that in future his office was to rotate among the Regiments of Guards as a precaution against fraud.

It was during the 1770s that the cumbersome procedure for dealing with recovered deserters was tidied up. Henceforth magistrates were authorised to pay out bounties for apprehensions, on the production of a certificate from the Provost Marshal at the Savoy military prison that the man concerned was now in his custody.

After being recruited in Germany for the British Service the 3rd Waldeck regiment arrived in New York on 20 October 1776 for service against the Colonial rebels. On the strength of the regiment was a Provost Marshal and his servant. Unfortunately half the unit was captured at Baton Rouge in 1779 and the remainder later in Pensacola. After eventual release the regiment was repatriated to their homeland where they were disbanded in 1783.

During the American War of Independence our Provost Marshals appear to have been very active. Perhaps one day someone will find time to make a study of that period, the results of which should make a valuable contribution to the history of Provost.

There had been naval Provost Marshals for many years. Indeed they no doubt descended from the Ships' Constables referred to earlier. With the passing of time R.A.F. Provost Marshals appeared on the scene. However, as they are extraneous to the development of our story there will be few references to them. One story should be told as it illustrates that, like their military and civilian counterparts, naval Provost Marshals numbered humane men among their ranks, for a letter of 17 May 1780 shows that two mutinous sailors were excused 500 lashes apiece through the intercession of a naval Provost Marshal.

Popular Major Burke was Provost Marshal and Town Major of Gibraltar in 1781, until he died from wounds caused by a Spanish shell. On 12 April that year discipline broke down when the men's scanty rations were reduced. This was during one of the many sieges of the Rock, and the soldiers were incensed on discovering that the inhabitants had hoarded stocks of food and were making no attempt to share them with the garrison. Major Burke and his men went round destroying all stocks of alcohol, and ensuring that women were not molested.

Mr. John Baker, Provost Marshal of the Bahamas, and the entire Legislative Assembly was sacked by the governor in 1784. He had learned that during recent elections Baker had substituted the names of the unsuccessful candidates for those who had been elected.

Grose's *Military Antiquities,* published during 1786, had a very good description of a Provost Marshal's duties. It contains all the details of which we are familiar, with the added task of ensuring butchers buried the offal. Apparently the Provost Marshal could, if necessary, rank as a captain to increase his authority, and he was permitted a sergeant assistant.

Captain Horatio Nelson took his ship H.M.S. *Albemarle* into Quebec during 1795 when scurvy attacked the crew, but he fell in love with Mary Simpson, 16-year-old daughter of the Provost Marshal, and planned to desert and elope with her. His officers heard of this, and, despite protests, forcibly carried him on board and sailed, thus preserving him to become our premier naval hero!

One way that soldier convicts could escape from the Savoy military prison was by volunteering for service in the New South Wales Corps, the infamous 'Rum Corps'. One batch that did so mutinied on the voyage out in 1797, taking their transport, *The Lady Shore,* into Montevideo, not realising that Britain and Spain were at war, and were promptly made prisoners-of-war. H.M.S. *Tremendous* later recaptured them, and in due course they were back in the Savoy, in the care of its most famous Provost Marshal, Mr. Thomas Bass.

Repeated complaints against Brigadier Thomas Picton, governor of Trinidad, led to his replacement by three Commissioners, of whom he was one, in 1803. The senior Commissioner, Colonel William Fullerton, M.P., brought an able team with him from England, and appointed one of them Provost Marshal. He found that the prison was being used by landowners as a means of controlling their slaves. Reforms were instituted and these upset William Payne, the executioner, who foresaw a big drop in earnings. He therefore promptly submitted his bill for outstanding charges; examples of his services being:

Flogged under gallows	1 man
Mulatto man and one negro flogged through town	2 men
Hanged and burned and head cut off	1 man
Ears Clipt	1 man

Colonel Fullerton raised many charges against Picton. These included illegally hanging four sappers for rape, and burning a man at the stake. The Legislative Assembly deposed Fullerton on a technicality, but he had already sent his Provost Marshal home to report. Picton was later proceeded against in London on 37 counts, but was convicted on one charge only, that of torturing a woman, and this was later set aside. The Provost Marshal was sacked, thus losing his £200 a year income. His assistant, who had been with him in London, had his allowances stopped and eventually arrived back in Trinidad destitute. Picton, who had very little experience of active service, became a Major General, and died a hero's death at Waterloo. The battered top hat that he wore during the battle is still in existence. Paradoxically he was popular with his men, but nevertheless had few claims to being a gentleman.

There is a macabre story concerning a civilian Provost Marshal in Sydney, Australia. Apparently on 20 September

1803 the rope broke when he hanged one Joseph Samuels. The victim was then again strung up, but as the rope was too long he fell on his feet, and on a third attempt the rope snapped off at the knot. The distraught Provost Marshal reported back to the governor, who promptly reprieved the much-hung Samuels!

These were cruel years no matter where a man served. Things were particularly bad for soldiers in the West Indies where diseases that had yet to be understood decimated units, and harsh discipline often completed the deterioration commenced by nature. A dreaded station was Fort Charles, one of the Jamaica garrisons, where three sides of the cantonment was fronted by sea, and the fourth by a pestilential swamp. It was under these conditions that in two years flogging averaged 180 lashes for each member of the garrison.

It was on 25 October 1810 that King George III (1760–1820) became ill for the third and last time. From that point onwards the Prince Regent virtually ruled the country, finally assuming the throne as George IV (1820–1830) on 29 January 1820.

The year 1813 brought an improvement in the Military Code when 53 Geo. III, Ch. 17 was passed into law. This authorised the continuance of Articles of War in peace-time and owed much to its introduction to representations from our commander in the Peninsula. Henceforth a permanent Military Code existed, and although it was not the final answer, together with the Mutiny Act it was a step forward. Much remained to be done before military law was satisfactorily codified, and the soldier given the same protection from legal abuse as that afforded to his civilian countrymen.

We will now leave the general story and turn to the Indian sub-continent. There a fascinating period of this account will unfold, much of which will not be to our credit. The same can be said for the other side in the main feature: the Indian Mutiny. But one should not forget that wickedness and cruelty are no more the prerogative of any race or breed than are honesty and gentleness, both of which were encountered in equal measure throughout the tragedy in men and women of goodwill on both sides.

CHAPTER IX

INDIA BEFORE THE SIEGE OF DELHI

INCLUDED IN THIS ACCOUNT will be a little of what is known of the early Indian Military Police, a para-military corps more akin to today's gendarmes than to the popular concept of a military policeman.

When Thomas Lott, eldest (senior) sergeant of Fort St. George garrison, Madras, was appointed Provost Marshal on 24 October 1678, the details of penal instruments to be maintained were identical to those enumerated in Markham's *Five Decades of Epistles of Warre,* reproduced in Chapter VII. This coincidence suggests that Markham's work had become a military textbook within a space of 50 years. Four months after appointment Sergeant Lott was commissioned as an ensign and succeeded by Isaac Abraham. An example of punishments he had to superintend can be seen in the Fort's records for 5 May 1679, which read:

> Giles Scudamore, Elias Loyd, Henry Salter, Frederick Perdue, Charles Lacon, John Goldsby, and Thomas Arnold, who ran away from this garrison the 3rd April, and were taken at Trivelcore, and returned by force the 10th of the same month, being called before the Councell and examined concerning the said fact, the Commission Officers being present, were sentenced to ride the wooden Horse for three daies, three hours at a time, and to serve five years de Novo, the first two yeares at 81 fanams per Mensem, and the last three yeares at the usual pay for the garrison. And Giles Scudamore, Corporal, and Elias Loyd, Rounder ['N.C.O. Marching Reliefs' in modern parlance], being upon guard and having received the Word that night before running away, besides the said punishment of rideing the Horse, shall be confined a month in irons, with allowance of rice and water, and forfeit that month's pay to the Honourable Company.

And Henry Salter and Frederick Perdue, Private Sentinells, and John Goldsby, Gunners Mate, alsoe running away from their guard, beside the punishment of rideing the Horse, shall each of them forfeit one month's pay to the use of the poore, excepting 40 fanams apeece for Dyett Money.

Provost Marshal Abraham handed over to Tillman Holt on 21 July 1679. He was permitted to run his house as 'a house of entertainment'. Presumably Mrs. Holt was not among the proferred attractions? Holt had a good run and Wheatley Garhorn took over on 29 July 1703, but he died after four years, and Ephraim Goss became Provost Marshal in his stead.

In 1773 there is reference to a long defunct judicial panel, 'The Jury of Matrons'. These ladies were assembled to examine Gunda, a condemned woman who pleaded pregnancy. They disagreed with her, and the Provost Marshal in due course reported:

Golam Ali, a blackman, and Gunda, a blackwoman, were hanged this morning at eight o'clock in the centre of the Grand Bazaar.

An early instance of the Duke of Wellington's faith in Provost appears in his letter to Lieutenant-General Harrison, when, as Arthur Wellesley, commander of the force that captured Seringapatam, he wrote on 4 May 1799:

I wish you would send the Provost here, and put him under my orders. Until some of the plunderers are hanged it is vain to expect to stop the plunder.

The following day he repeated his request, but later wrote: 'Plunder is stopped, the fires are all out and the inhabitants are returning to their homes. I am now employed in burying the dead'. Which suggests the Provost Marshal had arrived and given satisfaction!

Serving as Deputy Provost Marshal with the Bombay Column of the army of the Indus from December 1838 until February 1840 was Sergeant John Hill, 4th Light Dragoons. He was at the storming of Ghuznee, for which he received the Ghuznee medal.

During his Sind campaign Major-General Charles Napier constantly reminded all ranks of the need to respect the local inhabitants. He issued a long Order of the subject on 18 January 1843, in which he referred to his Provost Marshal by name, thus: 'The Major General calls the attention of all in the camp to the orders of Lt. Col. Wallace 18th Ultimo, and begs to add that he has placed a detachment of Horse at Capt Pope's orders, who will arrest any offender, and Capt Pope shall inflict such fine or other punishment as the Bazaar Regulations permit'. He added the profound observation: 'without obedience any Army becomes a mob, a Cantoment a bear garden. The enforcement of discipline is like physic, not agreeable, but at times necessary!'

Later the hostile *Bombay Times* castigated the General for having his Provost Marshal flog an Anglo-Indian clerk who had run down a native by galloping furiously; the paper actually incited his men to mutiny. He was not impressed and let it be known that he had no intention of abolishing flogging, as Lord William Bentinck had earlier done. Napier had been schooled by Wellington in the Peninsula years before, and held that on campaign flogging was essential if discipline was to be preserved.

When General Lord Gough defeated Chuttar Singh at Gojerat on 21 February 1849 the only staff casualty was Mr. S. Budd, his Provost Marshal. In his despatch the General commended the Provost Marshal and the Judge Advocat General, Lieutenant-Colonel Birch, for their work during the engagement. The presence of his law-enforcement officers suggest that, like Waterloo, it was a 'near run thing'!

Sir Charles Napier, in November 1849, suggested raising 150,000 military police in the Punjab for policing, escorts and guards. In an emergency they would be available as troops. Lord Dalhousie, who would never believe anything suggested by Napier was good, vetoed the idea. After Dalhousie ceased to be Governor General some military police were raised, although comparatively few in number; they were of immense assistance during the post Mutiny period.

In the early 1800s the 'Cachar Levy' was raised in Nowgong, Assam. Commonly called the Assam Military

Police, from 1852 they became the Frontier Police. As military police they watched over the eastern frontier, and undertook internal security operations when required. During 1852 Lieutenant-Colonel Fytche raised the 1st Burma Military Police. He only recruited men of previous bad characters, proving the truth of the old adage. Later the force was renamed the Barsein Police Corps. In Bengal three years later Captain Rattray raised a military police unit, eventually nine being created in that province. The unfortunate practice of submerging unit designations under a commander's surname causes errors of identity as time passes. During the hectic times following the Mutiny, Rattray's Sikhs are often read of, but not, however, as being a military police unit. In consequence the contribution of military police in pacification operations is often unappreciated by the reader. One such corps surviving is the 17th Cavalry, originally raised in 1857 as the Multra Police Corps, a military police unit. Later their name was changed to the Rohilkand Auxiliary Police Levy or Robarts Horse, under which name they mainly featured in contemporary accounts.

The tragedy that was the Sepoy Mutiny became inevitable on 4 February 1856. On that day Lord Dalhousie annexed the Kingdom of Oudh. Within a short time ancient ruling families had been reduced to impotency, insulted or deposed. This, together with the insufferable attitude adopted by most Europeans towards the natives, which in due course drove many of the ordinary peasants to rebel and join the mutineers, added to the well-known case of the objectionable cartridge grease provided by the Ordnance at Dum-Dum arsenal, bringing the Bengal army's cocktail of discontent to its terrible maturity that Sunday morning in Meerut on the 10 May 1857.

Our aged senior officer at the scene was incapable of the resolute action that could have restored the situation. Nothing was done to prevent the mutineers streaming to Delhi, where their arrival set Bengal ablaze. It is fair to mention that advanced age was commonplace among officers in the Honourable East India Company's service. Captains of fifty, Colonels of sixty-five, Brigadier-Generals of seventy, and eighty-five-year-old Generals were to be expected; nor was H.M. Army in much better case.

There had been previous mutinies. Those of 1806 and 1824 were vigorously suppressed, but after a third mutiny in 1844 Lord Gough reprieved most of those convicted, and we can be sure that this was not forgotten in 1857!

So whoever made the suggestion that Sir Henry Lawrence be appointed Chief Commissioner for Lucknow must get the credit for creating the rock on which the uprising foundered. He set to work to undo the harm that had been done since annexation, and in this he was greatly assisted by the new Governor General, Lord Canning. At best, however, they could only localise the horrors that were to come.

Sir Henry encouraged recruitment into the recently-raised Oudh Military Police. This force, commanded by Captain Gould Weston, consisted of 2,000 mounted military police under his direct control, and three regiments of military foot police:

1. Regt. O.M.P. with its headquarters at Sultanapore and under the command of Captain Bunbary.
2. Regt. O.M.P. located in Sitapore and commanded by Captain John Hearsey.
3. Regt. O.M.P. stationed in Lucknow with Captain Adolphus Orr in command.

The force headquarters and that of the mounted military police were also in Lucknow area. Detachments of M.M.P. were spread throughout the district with some co-located with each M.F.P. regiment. The M.M.P. wore uniforms of French grey and M.F.P. dress was modelled on that of the French Zouaves.

When Captain Herbert Bruce of 2nd Bombay European Light Infantry assisted in the amputation of several fingers of the Captain of the S.S. Pioneer, injured on passage from Persia to Bombay on 6 May 1857, he could never have dreamed that shortly he would be the most important military police officer on the sub-continent—but we are getting ahead of our story.

On learning of events in Meerut Sir Henry Lawrence lost no time. Selecting the Residency as offering the best position for defence he armed and provisioned it from available resources. Lieutenant Thomas of the Madras artillery was put in charge of the guns, Lieutenant Jones became responsible for supplies, and Captain J. W. Carnegie, 15th Bengal Infantry, organised defence measures and was appointed Chief of Intelligence and Provost Marshal. A proposal to raise Sepoys pay was dropped as it was thought that although the irregulars merited a raise, the regulars did not.

After an unsuccessful attempt on Ferozepore arsenal by Sepoys of the 45th and 57th Bengal infantry regiments on 13 May, 100 were court martialled. Two were hanged and 12 were blown from guns in executions organised by a Provost Marshal. By late May garrisons all over Bengal were rising, with local Europeans being murdered or put to flight. Thousands of mutineers converged on Delhi where the decrepit old king was proclaimed emperor. Although he was too senile really to comprehend what was happening, his sons were not, and in due course several paid dearly for their part in the rebellion, as the Munity had become.

Troops rushed to Bengal from all over India and from outside the country, but in the meantime surviving Europeans had to trust to themselves and loyal elements of the Indian army. From Bombay came the 1st European Fusiliers (Neill's Bluecaps), to form the nucleus of a force that under Brigadier Henry Havelock would try to relieve Lucknow. Young Lieutenant William Cleland, on active service with Neill's for the first time, no doubt learned much that served him in good stead years later as Provost Marshal in Egypt.

Fires broke out in the lines of 2 O.M.P. during the night of 27 May. Sepoys of units in Sitapore garrison helped extinguish the fires, but the European officers would not accept that incendiarism was the forerunner of mutiny. That same day Captain Weston, accompanied by Lieutenant Mecham and a detachment of 7th Oudh irregular cavalry, visited Maliabad, but as they withdrew the town erupted behind them. On 30 May all dependents, European and Indian, moved into the dubious safety of Lucknow

Residency. Officers slept there but returned to their units during the day, never knowing if they would survive to make the return journey that night.

Two companies of M.F.P. and 50 M.M.P. were among those who received refugees in Mulhamdi on 1 June. The following day Sitapore garrison, including their military police, mutinied. An M.P. detachment of 20 men who had been guarding the home of Mr. C. J. Christian, the local Commissioner, murdered him and all his family, together with the children's nurse. It is ironic that earlier he had assured Sir Henry Lawrence that his military police and irregular cavalry were sufficient to keep the remainder of the garrison in check. Captain Hearsey, the O.M.P. commander, escaped, but most other Europeans, service and civilian, were slaughtered that day. In Mulhamdi the recently-arrived refugees recommenced their journey on 4 June, but were murdered by the escort. In the town very few Europeans got away, and it is recorded that Oudh military police were foremost among their murderers.

On 9 June the 1st O.M.P. mutinied, and when Colonel S. Fisher of the 15th Irregular Cavalry went to reason with them a military policeman shot him in the back. The M.P. commanding officer, Captain Bunbary, and three others were hidden by a loyal Hindu, and after incredible adventures all reached safety in Benares, but, as was the usual pattern, all other Europeans in Sultanapore died.

With the mutiny of the M.M.P. in Lucknow on 11 June the end of O.M.P. was in sight. Captain Weston boldly faced his men, but was ignored, though no attempt was made to harm him. The 3rd O.M.P. rose the following day at Moti Mahal, thus completing the disintegration of the force. Their O.C., Captain Orr, rode after them and caught them up on the Cawnpore road. The mutineers were so struck by his bravery that they promised he would not be harmed, but refused to return to duty. Orr's efforts were not entirely wasted, as several members of the 2nd O.M.P. who had been guarding Weston's house and had thrown in their lot with the mutineers, returned to their allegiance and followed Orr back to the Residency, where they served loyally throughout the ensuing siege. It is thought that the 3rd O.M.P. would have remained steadfast but for mishandling by Mr. Gubbins, who had been Acting Chief Commissioner for a short period when Sir Henry was sick.

In the struggle that was to follow the O.M.P. officers played their part. Captain Weston was in charge of a position known to history as 'Fayrers Post'. Captain Orr was one of the defenders of 'Gubbins Post', where he and Lieutenant Mecham emerged unscathed after being blown up by a mine.

We must anticipate a little in order to complete the story of the pre-Mutiny Oudh military police. The Siege of Lucknow lasted from 29 June until 25 September. Sir Henry died of wounds on 2 July after nominating Major Banks as his successor, with Brigadier-General Inglis to conduct the defence. Major Banks was killed on 19th July, and Inglis then assumed the office of Chief Commissioner in addition to his other role. A relief column under Major-General Havelock joined the garrison on 25 September, and in effect became a reinforcement. Final relief was made on 17 November by General Sir Colin Campbell. Within five days the Residency was evacuated. In his last despatch on handing over command Inglis wrote:

> Capt. J. W. Carnegie, the Special Assistant Commissioner, whose valuable services prior to the commencement of the Siege I have frequently heard warmly dilated on, both by Sir H. Lawrence and Major Banks, and whose services will probably be more amply brought to notice by the Civil Authorities on some future occasion, has conducted the Office of Provost Marshal to my satisfaction.

The Provost Marshal ended the Siege as a Brevet Major and was twice wounded. He received the Mutiny medal with clasps 'Lucknow' and 'Defence of Lucknow'. In the *London Gazette* of 18 May 1860 a belated award of the C.B. was announced. There was no mention of the gallant Captain Gould Weston in the despatch, but this omission was righted in Governor General's Order No. 1546, which directed that his name be added to those recorded as commanding outposts. The few Oudh military policemen who served throughout the Siege were awarded the medal with clasps and, in common with other surviving loyal Indian soldiers, the Indian Order of Merit.

Part of the punitive measures ordered once the extent of the Mutiny was realised was the passing, on 31 May, of Act XIV of 1857. This suspended due process of law where insurgents, military or civilian, were concerned. District Commissioners were authorised to impose death sentences without the presence of a legal officer. This received Assent on 8 June, and a subsequent amendment authorised courts martial of at least five officers to inflict the ultimate award. Appeals were not permitted, and sentences were effective immediately. There is no doubt that many were executed without trial, as is evidenced by the award of two days confinement to barracks on a soldier of Neill's Bluecaps at Cawnpore, for the offence of 'hanging a native without permission'. The atrocities perpetuated on women and children in Cawnpore were such that God-fearing men became obsessed with vengeance. One should bear in mind in mitigation that throughout the uprising thousands were tortured and murdered in the most horrible circumstances. No form of trials were conducted, and their only crime was that of having a white skin or being of mixed blood. Among the murderers at Cawnpore must have been men of the 3rd O.M.P. who made their way there after rising at Lucknow. Space does not permit re-telling the Cawnpore story here, but of all who have gone down in history as depraved monsters, the Nana Sahib, the petty noble responsible for the holocaust, must surely rank as one of the most despicable creatures ever born of woman.

Neill's Bluecaps formed the nucleus of a force commanded by Brigadier-General Henry Havelock that hurried to the relief of Lucknow. Colonel Neill took a small detachment and recaptured Allahabad on 7 July. Every captured rebel was hanged immediately after trial. Captain Drummond Hay was left to hold the town when Neill pushed on; his written instructions to Hay included this sentence, 'I have always tried by G.C.M. any prisoner connected with the Garrison, the Provost hanging those so sentenced'. Many captured mutineers from other garrisons stood a better

chance under Hay--they certainly had none when Neill was
in command!

Havelock captured Futtehpore, Pandoo Nuddi and
Maharajpore all within six days, and by 17 July neared
Cawnpore. It was then that the Nana Sahib ordered the
murder of over 300 women and children. These unfortunate
prisoners had been confined to the Bibighar, or women's
house, and they were slaughtered by butchers from Cawnpore bazaar, assisted by such mutineers who had stomach
for the work. The poor wretches died under circumstances
of obscene cruelty. Blood was splashed three feet high on
the walls and eventually congealed three inches deep on
the floor. The bodies and odd heads and limbs were thrown
down the well, and when that was full piled in a disgusting
tangle on top. The Nana Sahib then blew up the magazine
and retreated. On seeing the explosion Havelock moved in.
The reputation of Neill had preceded him and many
inhabitants had left the town. Those remaining had little
chance of survival once the troops saw the horrors of the
Bibighar. Their reactions disgusted the intensely religious
Havelock, and he issued the following order:

> The marauding in this camp exceeds the disorders which
> supervened on the short lived triumph of the Nana Sahib.
> A Provost Marshal has been appointed with special instructions
> to hang up, in their uniform, all British soldiers that plunder.
> This shall not be an idle threat. Commanding Officers have
> received the most distinct orders on the subject.

Thus only 122 years ago, when recaptured mutineers
were entitled to a trial, British soldiers could be executed
by a Provost Marshal who was not required to report his
intentions to higher authority, but could, if the order is
interpreted literally, execute on sight!

The Provost Marshal was also instructed to flog any
soldiers caught out of camp without permission. An Indian
soldier caught looting was hanged when the Provost Marshal
assured Havelock that the facts were true, Havelock saying,
'Then that shall be my justification before God'. Neill, now
a Brigadier-General, was put in military charge of the city,

but Havelock, who detested his subordinate's merciless
outlook, told him, 'Now General Neill, let us understand
each other; you have no power or authority whilst I am
here; you are not to issue a single order'.

Havelock marched for Lucknow on 25 July and Neill,
now solely in command, promptly issued the following
Orders:

1. The well in which are the remains of the poor women and
   children so brutally murdered by that miscreant, the Nana,
   will be filled up.
2. The house in which they were butchered, and which is stained
   with their blood, will not be washed or cleaned by their
   countrymen. Brigadier General Neill has determined that every
   stain of innocent blood shall be cleaned up and wiped out
   previous to their execution by such of the miscreants as may
   hereafter be apprehended, who took an active part in the
   Mutiny, to be selected according to their rank, caste and degree
   of guilt.
3. Each miscreant will be taken to the house in question and will
   be forced into cleaning up a small portion of the blood stains,
   the task will be made as revolting to his feelings as possible,
   and the Provost Marshal will use the lash in forcing anyone
   objecting to complete his task.
4. After properly cleaning up his portion, the culprit is to be
   immediately hanged, and for this purpose a gallows will be
   erected close at hand.

Later, in a letter home Neill described how the first
prisoner, a former Subhadar of the 6th Bengal native
infantry regiment, had been punished under this order. He
was of high caste and objected when a sweeper, who as an
untouchable was the lowest of the low in the eyes of the
culprit, gave him a brush and orders to clean a square foot
of floor. He was flogged by the Provost Marshal until
the task was properly completed, and then hanged. Neill
described another occasion when a former official was forced
to lick his portion clean, adding: 'no doubt this is a strange
law, but it suits the occasion well, and I hope I shall not be
interfered with until this room is thoroughly cleansed in
this way. I will hold my own with the blessing and help
of God. I cannot help seeing His finger in all this, we have
been false to ourselves so often'.

Thanks to Sir John Lawrence, brother of Sir Henry, trouble in the Punjab was nipped in the bud. On 6 July at Rawalpindi disaffected units were disarmed, and when 30 Sepoys bolted with their arms they were chased and killed or captured by Punjab military police. A mutiny by the 14th N.I. regiment of Jhelum the following day was successful and the mutineers captured a number of guns. A charge by members of the 7th Punjab military mounted police, led by Lieutenant Battye, recovered two of the guns. By 25 July a large band of mutineers were trapped at Phillour when a party of the 7th P.M.M.P. cut adrift a floating bridge. A force under Brigadier-General John Nicholson then annihilated the encircled enemy. Nicholson then, in an epic march, took his men, including the 7th P.M.M.P., to join the army assembling outside Delhi, fighting many successful actions on the way.

When Havelock had first arrived in Cawnpore he put Mr. Sherer, former magistrate of Futtehpore, in charge of the civil administration. One day Sherer found an unknown officer awaiting him in his quarters. 'I am Herbert Bruce', said the stranger, 'I hope we shall be friends and work together cordially'. Thus began an unbeatable partnership. Bruce had been ordered to raise a military police to control the lines of communication, and Sherer was tasked with administrative and logistical support. Bruce jokingly called his men the 'Sweeper Police', for he recruited untouchables, and surrendered mutineers against whom no crimes could be laid. It must be remembered that many Sepoys had to pay lip service to the Mutiny in order to stay alive, but who rejoined the Colours as soon as they could do so with safety. The police wore distinctive red turbans, and these were still being worn by the West Bengal armed police, lineal descendants of Bruce's police, as late as 1959. In all, five mounted and 14 foot units were raised, and much of the credit for maintaining the rule of law in pacified areas must go to them. Tragedy resulted from the first attempt to use the new force in an outstation; a post was opened in Bithor, the Nana Sahib's home town, but the sergeant in charge threw a party and they were all drunk when a band of mutineers surprised .them. All were killed, and the sergeant's body thrown into the street for the jackals.

With the aid of captured documents Bruce was able to apprehend prominent supporters of the Nana Sahib. However, he met the occasional setback: once his most trusted informer was informed against, and a search of his kit revealed items that could only have come from the Bibighar. In due course he was hanged by his erstwhile colleagues.

Provostwise the rising in Delhi has little to interest us. On 11 May the mutineers there did a most unwise thing when they burned the house of Sir Theophilus Metcalfe, the chief magistrate, as we shall learn later. From late May our troops began concentrating outside Delhi, but continued attacks on them and sickness were a constant drain on their strength. The Provost Marshal carried out daily executions of captured insurgents; usually this was in the evening of capture, as there were no men to spare for guards.

A spirited action on 30 July enhanced the reputation of the new military police. A unit of them under the command of Captain Dawson was part of a small force that recaptured Maliabad, which was then given a military police post and henceforth remained in our hands. On another occasion 50 military police and 16 Europeans defended a house in Arrah against constant assault, until a force led by Major Vincent Eyre, relieved them. Another bridge incident occurred at Mohan, when a government official, Mr. Pat Carnegie, with a force of military police, beat off constant attacks by a large band of enemy who wanted to cross. They held them off until an English contingent commanded by Colonel Evelegh came up and destroyed the attackers, very few of whom escaped.

Captain G. St. P. Lawrence, commanding a body of Punjab military police, anticipated a mutiny in Ajmir prison, and when it came he and his men were waiting. They gave immediate pursuit to escaping prisoners, all of whom were killed or recaptured. Meanwhile Havelock had found that he had insufficient strength to attempt to relieve Lucknow, particularly as constant fighting and cholera had reduced his available force considerably. By 13 August, then a

Major-General, he was back in Cawnpore, to gather reinforcements.

Before Delhi a force of 10,000 had assembled by 14 August. Brigadier-General Archdale Wilson took over command from Major-General Reed, who was a sick old man. Energetic action by the new commander restored flagging morale and steps were also taken to restore personal turnout which had deteriorated under the former ailing commander. Back in Cawnpore, Havelock had made a spirited dash and retaken Bithor, which rebels had held since they annihilated the military police post. This action is believed to be the last in which a British unit, Neill's Bluecaps, carried their colours in action. Young Lieutenant Cleland was the bearer, and he was wounded during the action.

Mr. Sherer had started to reform the original police force for use when normality returned. Brigadier-General Neill confused them with Bruce's military police, and felt they were being used beyond their capacity. The extent of his misapprehension is apparent from a letter sent to Mr. Sherer on 27 August, part of which reads, 'I may say, attempting to establish your Police is not only useless, but risking the lives of men well disposed to the state to no purpose. The murders and capture of your men at Bithor prove this'. It was Bruce's sweeper police who suffered there, of course, not the new civil police. The Brigadier appears to have been completely out of touch with the police situation in his area.

The Siege of Delhi can be said to have commenced in earnest on 8 September, by which date there had been further changes in command, which finally was again assumed by Archdale Wilson, promoted Major-General for the purpose. His army totalled 12,588 all ranks, of whom only 3,766 were Europeans. Among those joining as reinforcenemts was the Rajah of Jhind with his Sikh horsemen. It is of great interest that the impending battle was to be fought with a British army in which Indian and other local troops outnumbered their British comrades in arms by three to one.

Detailed Orders for the conduct of the operations were issued, No. 4 of which directed that all plunder was to be handed over to appointed prize agents, and ruled that anyone found in possession of plunder would be handed over to the Provost Marshal for punishment.

Whether the staff officer who drafted the Order believed that it would be obeyed we shall never know. If he did he was naive to say the least and could have had no experience of the aftermath of the fall of a city. However, the fall and sack of Delhi lay in the future. This chapter therefore closes with the storm of retribution about to break, and the future of the British Raj hanging on the outcome of the operations!

CHAPTER X

INDIA–AFTER DELHI

THE ASSAULT ON DELHI commenced on 14 September
and cost us 1,200 casualties, with a further 200 by the
completion of operations six days later. The final loss from
all causes since the operation began was 5,090 all ranks.
Brigadier-General Nicholson was one of those killed. The
old emperor and two of his sons were captured by the
famous Hodgson, who executed the sons. His own death
a few days later effectively prevented possible disciplinary
action being taken against him. The scenes of violence and
depravity following the fall of the city rivalled Badahoz.
Operational Order No. 4 was forgotten—if it was ever read,
and fear of the Provost Marshal and Prize Agent was not
evident on this occasion. Few officers were seen looting, but
there were many happy to purchase from soldiers the
results of their plundering. Fighting between various factions
over the division of spoils was often settled by shot or
bayonet. Force had eventually to be used to drive the
looters from Delhi, the gates of which were then strongly
guarded. Trials of mutineers commenced immediately; it is
said that of 3,306 prisoners over 400 were executed, though
some sources insist that thousands suffered the extreme
penalty. In addition to courts martial the chief magistrate,
Sir Theophilus Metcalfe, opened his court, sanctioning executions on a Sunday morning. Many were hanged from the
charred timbers of his destroyed house. Disguised mutineers
or armed civilians were shown no mercy. The Assistant
Provost Marshal at Delhi was an N.C.O. of advanced years,
and he complained bitterly of overwork, on one occasion
having to hang 10 men together. Two more sons of the

117

emperor were captured and, as it was proved they had assisted in the murder of Europeans, they were shot, but neither died outright and the overworked A.P.M. had to despatch them.

One form of punishment common at this time, and which was used against convicted mutineers, was that of blowing away from guns. Three sides of a square were formed by troops told off to witness the execution. In the unoccupied side of the square the gun or guns would be sited, facing outwards. The condemned were marched on parade, escorted, if one was available, by a Provost Marshal—or in his absence by an officer detailed for the task. The prisoner would be lashed to a gun with the small of his back across the muzzle, his body arched backwards because of the shortness of straps from his wrists and ankles to spokes of the wheels. The charge, verdict and sentence would be read out while the gunners kept their eyes on the Provost Marshal, who, as soon as he had finished reading, drew his sword, looked at the gunners, and when satisfied that all was as it should be, swept down his arm. The gunners touched their smouldering portfires to the touchholes of the guns and in a flash the execution was over! Sometimes, particularly if the usual charge of two pounds of gunpowder had been exceeded, they would be bespattered. The head usually shot up into the air, falling back to earth like a spinning football. The band would strike up a rousing march and the troops marched off; once the guns had been limbered up and driven off it was all over. Then, and only then, down would come the kitehawks, the street-cleaners of India, in their dozens.

Let us now return to Cawnpore where Lieutenant-General Sir James Outram had arrived on 16 September with considerable reinforcements. All available forces marched out the following day for Lucknow. Outram generously left Havelock in command, but in fact soon became commander in all but name. Neill commanded a Brigade, but did not live to see the Residency relieved, being shot just outside Lucknow, which was entered on 25 September. Outram assumed command from Inglis and his force became, as explained earlier, part of the garrison. On learning the details

1. Sir Henry Guyldford—first identifiable Provost Marshal, appointed in 1511.

here lyeth the bodie of Thomas Nevynson of Estrye Esquier who died y
ffln day of July 1590 beynge att the tyme of his death provost marshall
& Scoutmaster of y Est partes of kent & Captayne of y lyghte horses of the
lathe of S augustines who had to wife Anne the daughter of Richarde
Æ holde Esquier deceased by whom he had issue 6 sonnes & 4 daughters

2. Tomb of Thomas Nevison, Provost Marshal, in Eastry church, Kent.

3. Provost Marshal's house, Edinburgh Castle.

4. Major George Scovell, 57th Foot.

5. Trooper, Mounted Staff Corps, formed for the Crimean War.

6. (*right*) Trooper, Staff Corps of Cavalry, the first established Military Police.

7. (*opposite above*) Mounted Policemen of the Crimea—soldiers dragging stores to the camp.

8. (*opposite below*) 'Blowing from the Guns', from a painting by Orlando Norie.

IN MEMORY OF
MAJOR THOMAS TROUT
WHO SERVED IN SPAIN THROUGH THE CAMPAIGNS
OF 1836-7 WITH THE BRITISH LEGION UNDER
SIR DE LACY EVANS, AND IN THE 7TH HUSSARS
DURING THE CANADIAN REBELLION 1838.
AND WAS FOR MORE THAN 20 YEARS
PROVOST MARSHAL AT ALDERSHOT.
BORN 26 AUGUST 1817. DIED 13 FEBRUARY 1881.

ERECTED BY HIS BROTHER OFFICERS.

(*opposite above*) Major Thomas Trout, Provost Marshal Aldershot, and father ₊e Military Police.

(*opposite below*) Memorial tablet to ₊r Thomas Trout.

(*above*) Lt. Col. William Cleland, ₊ost Marshal at the Battle of Tel el ₊r, 1882.

(*above right*) Lieut. C. F. N. Macready, ₊on Highlanders, Staff Capt. Provost at ₊andria, 1884.

(*right*) Major H. F. Coleridge, DSO, ₊ls, first Provost Officer to be so decor- ₊A.P.M. Klerksdorp, South Africa, 1901.

14. Mounted Military Police, Aldershot, 1898.

15. Military Foot Police, Aldershot, 1898.

of the supply position he wrote to the commander at the Alambagh, an outpost of the garrison, ordering the Provost Marshal there to flog anyone caught stealing stores. He was to award 50 lashes, but if thefts occurred after the first flogging future offenders were to be hanged.

Back in Cawnpore Bruce was constantly in trouble with the commander, Colonel Wilson, a martinet. Fortunately, Sherer was an able diplomat and managed to keep the peace. When a rebel force cut the Delhi road two marches away Colonel Wilson led his troops, plus a battalion of military police under Bruce, to attack them. They were put to flight and the road re-opened, and there was no further interference with travel to or from the town.

Both sides took advantage of the immobility imposed by monsoon rains, but on 4 October a rebel leader, Harichand, led a dash with 12,000 men and attacked Sandela. There Captain Dawson with his 12th Battalion Bengal military police, and other locally-raised elements, held them off until relieved on 8 October by Major Maynard, with a force in which were 600 military police infantry and 250 military mounted police. The two forces combined and drove the rebels back to Panii. Brigadier-General Barber then arrived with a force in which there was a 900-strong battalion of Bengal military police. He attacked Harichand the day after arrival and completely defeated him for a loss of only 82, which, unfortunately, included Major Maynard who was gravely wounded.

By then there were several field forces operating in Bengal, possibly the most important of which was the Central India field force, commanded by Major-General Sir Hugh Rose. His Provost Marshal was Conductor D. Buchanan, whose Mutiny medal is a highly-prized exhibit in the R.M.P. museum. Troops of Brigadier-General C. S. Stuart's Mhow field force ran amok after the recapture of Dhar on 23 October. Soldiers from the 86th regiment, some gunners and Indian troops lost their senses after sacking native grog shops, destroying men, women and children wherever found. The Force Provost Marshal assisted by the soldiers' own officers had to use violence to restore order. Another of the pacification units, the Oudh field force, was under the command of Brigadier-General Hope Grant and had two battalions of military police with it, each 400 strong. Maybe their prisoners were sent back to Cawnpore where, during the first four days of October, the Provost Marshal was particularly busy ordering executions, working from sunrise to sunset, sometimes even later, and using gallows accommodating six at a time. It is more likely, however, that the O.F.F. acted the same as the other forces, and executed prisoners on the day they were captured.

General Sir Colin Campbell arrived in Cawnpore on 3 November as overall commander of our forces. He travelled as fast as possible with his entire staff crammed into three horse-drawn gharries, and was unescorted until a few marches from the town, when an N.C.O. and two men of Bruce's military police came out to meet him. Leaving Major-General C. A. Windham to command the garrison he pushed on with the troops assembled there and relieved Lucknow on the night of 25/26 November. Poor Havelock, now Sir Henry, died of dysentery in the closing moments of our occupation and was buried within sight of the city that had dominated the last months of his life. That same night a resurgent Tantia Topee closed in on Cawnpore and Windham was forced to withdraw to a prepared entrenchment leaving the town, which had been set on fire, to burn. An urgent appeal for help was sent to Sir Colin for assistance. Windham had been let down by one of his officers who had retreated without authority, and then some of the men broke into the liquor stores and ugly scenes ensued. Bruce and his military police manned their section of the defences and, though hard pressed, the rebels were kept out. Luckily attempts to destroy a vital bridge over the Ganges were left until it was too late and it was secured by Sir Colin who relieved the entrenchment. Tantia's army of over 25,000 men withdrew a few miles, and our forces reorganised themselves.

A period of adjustment was then embarked on in the devastated town. Police cover was assumed by the newly-raised civil police, and the military police were dispersed among the various field forces, apart from the headquarters staff, who were located in *Duncan's* hotel, then utilised as the military headquarters, a role it had recently played for the insurgents. Bruce handed over command of his military police to Major Mowbray Thompson, one of the few survivors of the Cawnpore massacre, and then joined Sir Colin Campbell's headquarters. Henceforth whenever Sherer moved about in the pacified areas he took 100 military police with him as an escort. He also established posts manned by them at every Ganges crossing point, and, together with Mowbray Thompson, installed military police to cover the whole of the old Futtehgahr Magistry District, once it had been cleared.

Meanwhile the Oudh field force was being particularly successful. The soldiery attributed this to the accompanying magistrate, Mr. Powell, known as 'Hanging Powell'. He made no distinction between mutineers and rebels, as some others did. Such was his reputation that when the force approached Farrukabad the villagers opened the gates and surrendered Najir Khan, a leading rebel who had been hiding there. Leaving a small detachment of military police the force moved on to re-occupy Mhow on 8 January. There Powell condemned nearly 100 in one day, and by evening all were hanging from the branches of a great pipal tree that stood in the main square. He would commence trials as soon as camp was pitched at night, the Provost Marshal hanging those so sentenced immediately.

After re-occupying Futtehgahr Sir Colin Campbell moved out on 1 February 1858, leaving behind a force which included 350 military mounted police. They liaised with those previously dropped off by Sherer in the rural areas, and kept watch on a roving band of some 1,500 insurgents. Sir Colin proceeded to the recapture of Lucknow, which was achieved by 21 March for a loss of only 119 fatal casualties, only one-seventh of those inflicted on the rebels. Strict measures were taken to prevent looting once the first flush of victory had passed. Guards were posted at all gates and the roll called hourly in all units. Any camp follower found armed was hanged immediately by the Provost Marshal. Triangles were set up in the main street for the immediate flogging of offenders. However, it was some days before the inhabitants felt safe enough to attempt to return to normal life, so great had been the effect of the first few days disorders. The war correspondent, W. H. Russell, was attached to Sir Colin's headquarters, and he wrote an excellent account of the recapture of the city and records meeting Sergeant Gillespie of the 93rd Highlanders, whom he last met as an A.P.M. in charge of Russian prisoners of war during the Crimean War.

Brigadier Sir Hope Grant, recently knighted for his services, recaptured Jalalabad with his Oudh field force and moved on in pursuit of an insurgent body led by Beni Medhu. A military police unit commanded by Captain Hill formed part of the O.F.F. at this time. Of 11 units in the force six are identified by the commander's surname, which illustrates the point made earlier that recognition of units is often obscured by personal designations. Beni Medhu was decisively beaten, leaving over 600 dead on the field. Our losses were 67 killed in action and 33 dead from heat exhaustion. Barki Fort was captured in June by the Hawoh military police battalion led by Lieutenant Lachan Forbes. This fort stood at the junction of two rivers and controlled the country for miles around. The rebel defeat was complete, their leader Rup Singh barely escaping with his life. Following the usual practice a holding force of military police was left in the fort and the battalion moved on. At Suhajnee on 27 September a unit of Bengal military police led by Lieutenant Charles George Baker routed over 1,000 rebels at extremely low cost. For his conduct in this operation Lieutenant Baker was awarded the Victoria Cross.

Mr. Russell tells of an incident at Cawnpore that October when he met a former grass-cutter employed by Bruce's military police at Sechendi. His head was completely wrapped in a turban, leaving only his eyes visible, and his arms ended in stumps wrapped in dirty rags. The M.P. post there had been attacked by men of the Rajah of Gwailor's army. The military police, all former members of a cavalry regiment that had been disarmed when suspected of disloyalty, fought until all were killed. Because the grass-cutter was so low in the caste scale the rebels deigned to kill him, so they chopped off both his hands and ears, slit open his nose and then released him. When met by Russell he was making his way home to Amritsar. That same day Russell saw four men brought into Cawnpore by Mowbray Thompson's men; three prisoners had been caught trying to cross the Ganges on inflated skins, the fourth was the headman of a nearby village, who had offered the M.P.s 25 rupees to let their prisoners go.

By late October even the most vocal of Bruce's critics were admitting that his tactics were right. Spread as they were all over the pacified areas the military police were able to shadow dissidents while a galloper summoned the nearest field force. The enemy found they could not shake off the red turbans, and that once spotted retribution was sure to follow.

Lord Canning, the Governor General, arrived in Allahabad on 1 December on a tour of the troubled areas in an attempt to convince the inhabitants that the government was in full control again. At a reception for the local notables the path to the dais was lined by infantry and military police, the latter specially selected by Lord Clyde, as Sir Colin Campbell had become, in recognition of their outstanding contribution towards restoring order. Shortly before this Beni Medhu appeared on the scene again in the little town of Poorwa, which was defended by a detachment of H.M. 23rd Regiment and a unit of military police, all under command of Major Bulwar. The attack was beaten off and the rebels fled, leaving many dead behind. In December another benefit from establishing military police control of the area became apparent: revenue started to come in for the first time since the Mutiny broke out, and this eased a growing cash crisis.

Not long afterwards Lord Clyde was on operations near Beyramghat, accompanied only by his cavalry and a detachment of the newly-reformed Oudh military police, having left the infantry behind in attempting to head off a large body of insurgents. His staff officers became apprehensive when a large body of horsemen came into view, but soon their red turbans identified them as Captain Hill's

regiment of military police. They joined Lord Clyde's cavalry
and later took part in a successful action against the insurgents whom the commander-in-chief had been seeking. The
last recorded engagement by the C.I.F.F. occurred at Koli
in the Oudh on 23 November. Lieutenant William Cleland
was badly wounded in this affair.

When Lord Clyde approached Deriabad on 7 December
swarms of camp followers started stripping the fields. Lord
Clyde led his officers and military police among the looters,
beating them with sticks and the flats of swords, but all to
no avail. They completely devastated the fields, and compensation had to be paid to the enraged farmers. The Chief of
Staff, Colonel Metcalf, was described on this occasion as
'displaying immense vigour in executing the duties of Provost
Marshal'!

One of the final actions of the Great Mutiny, as it is now
remembered, occurred at Burbeach on 17 December when
a small force of military police encountered a body of insurgents in the town. When the policemen later rejoined their
comrades their lances and swords were bloodstained, and
they were driving 20 prisoners before them, having met and
defeated the enemy in the main square. By the end of the
year all surviving rebel leaders had been driven into Nepal,
and Bengal was being effectively controlled by the military
police. The end of the campaign came officially on 22 January
1859 and within a year a revitalised civilian police force controlled all towns and the civil administration was again fully
effective throughout the Province. Thus ended 21 months of
brutal insurrection, rumblings from which are felt to this day;
at the same time the many instances of sacrifice and kindness
encountered during this awful period were not the prerogative of any particular race, colour or creed.

A force called the Baghalkund military police was raised
in 1859 for service in that part of India. At full strength
it consisted of three risaladars (squadrons) of cavalry, and
nine infantry companies. The uniform of the force was
modelled on that of the French Zouaves.

When honours and awards flowed after the campaign
Mr. Sherer was overlooked. All he ever received was a

letter from Sir James Outram acknowledging his immense contribution and apologising for the fact that he had been forgotten. This was a very poor substitute for public recognition, and even for that he had to wait until leaving India in April 1860.

The success of the military police suggested to the authorities that a similar organisation could be employed to advantage on the North East Frontier. A Frontier military police battalion was therefore raised at Sylhet in 1863. During 1882 it was reorganised with greater emphasis on the military role, and finally in 1917 all police connections were severed when it became The Assam Rifles.

One of the pre-Mutiny regiments of Bengal military police (Rattray's Sikhs) was part of a force sent to put down the Jaintia Hills rebellion of 1862, the operations being successfully concluded in four months. At the conclusion of the small Jowakhi campaign in 1878 the commander, Brigadier-General J. Ross, complimented his Provost Marshal, Captain C. S. Morrison, 14th Bengal cavalry, for his efficiency. Unfortunately, within two years Captain Morrison was dead of cholera contacted during the Second Afghan War. That war, 1878–80, was probably the most overt manifestation of India's fear of Russia, a stage of which Kipling termed *The Great Game,* but with the benefit of hindsight more aptly could be termed *Much Ado about Nothing,* with apologies to the Bard.

An unusual feature of the Second Afghan War was that it consisted of two stages. The first campaign lasted from 22 November 1878, and ended with the Treaty of Gandamack on 26 May the following year. The second campaign commenced with the murder of Sir Louis Cavagnari, our ambassador to Kabul, on 3 September 1879 and terminated in Northern Afghanistan on 15 August 1880, and on 20 September in the Kandahar region. When first constituted the army was known as the Khyber field force, but components broke away to become the Peshawar Valley field force under Lieutenant-General Sir Sam Browne, V.C., the overall commander. The Provost Marshal until 15 November 1879 was Major R. B. McEwen, 92nd Highlanders. In the

2nd Brigade of 2nd Division, Lieutenant G. Frend, 5th
Fusiliers was Provost Marshal, a position equating with the
Brigade Provost Officer of today, and for four months of
1879 the Provost Marshal at 2nd Division headquarters was
Captain W. F. Longbourne. Other elements of the original
army became the Kurram Valley field force, commanded by
Major-General F. S. Roberts, V.C., and for most of the
force's existence Major W. V. Ellis, 25th Bengal Native
Infantry was the Provost Marshal. He was in Kabul during
our first occupation and earned a Brevet Majority and two
Mentions in Despatches for his services. The third component
from the original body was the Kandahar field force led by
Lieutenant-General D. M. Stewart. Major W. C. Harrison,
30th Bombay Native Infantry, was Provost Marshal, and he
also earned a Brevet Majority and a Mention. In the second
campaign he served in a non-Provost capacity. This force
in its turn threw off a small independent body, the Thal-
Chotial field force, whose claim to fame is that it pioneered
a new route through the hills back to India. During the time
this small body existed its Provost Marshal was Lieutenant
J. Nagle, 70th Regiment.

When the first campaign ended, after little serious fighting,
the P.V.F.F. headquarters was at Gandamack, where the
Treaty was signed. The K.F.F. was in the Ghilzai area, and
after the peace became responsible for Southern Afghanistan,
the other forces returning to India. An ambassador was
installed in Kabul, and his subsequent murder and that of
his staff by Afghanistan army mutineers on 3 September
1879 gave rise to the second campaign. The field forces
were hastily re-formed and a line of garrisoned posts
established throughout the tribal areas, the most important
having a Provost Marshal on the staff. One such appointment
was held by Major J. T. Whish, 16th Bengal Native Infantry
at Ali Masjid. Until April 1880 Major W. C. Ormond, 5th
Fusiliers, was Provost Marshal at Landi Kotal, his successor
being Lieutenant C. M. Lester, 2nd Battalion P.W.O. These
lines-of-communications posts were known as the Khyber
Line Force, and later the most advanced positions became
the 2nd Division Khyber field force under Major-General

R. O. Bright. Troops assembled on the Kurram Valley line became the 1st Division of the force and were commanded by Major-General F. S. Roberts, V.C. The divisions joined up at Kota Seng and advanced on Kabul. The Provost Marshal of the K.F.F. was Major M. C. Seton, 67th Regiment, until succeeded by Captain (Q.M.) J. Walsh, 72nd Highlanders, who remained with Roberts until the end of the war, participating in the epic Kabul to Kandahar march and subsequent battle, earning two Mentions in the process. Provost Marshal and officer in charge of the Field Treasure Chest, today's Field Cashier, of 1st Division was Captain J. C. T. Humfrey of the Army Pay Department. Another A.P.D. officer, Captain R. O. S. Brooke, was Provost Marshal of 2nd Division. Certain units of the force were formed into a mobile column with Lieutenant A. Weston, 6th Dragoon Guards as Provost Marshal. The troops that had remained in Southern Afghanistan were reconstituted as the Kandahar field force for the second campaign, with Lieutenant-Colonel G. F. Belville, Bombay Staff Corps, as Provost Marshal, and Deputy Judge Advocate, a sinister combination if there ever was one! (Perhaps this explains why flogging of military offenders was commonly resorted to during this war, seven years after the official abolition of its use as a military punishment.) An officer later recorded that he had seen the same man flogged on three separate occasions during three months in 1880. Lieutenant-Colonel Belville was present during the siege and battle of Kandabai, in due course receiving a Mention. The Kandahar field force threw off the small Ghazim field force which marched to Zaiabad, where it met up with the 1st Division of the Khyber field force, then marched hurriedly back via Ghazin to the assistance of its parent force, which had been further weakened by the creation of the Pesh Bolak field force, which during the whole period of the war had Captain C. S. Gordon, 2nd Battalion P.W.O. as its Provost Marshal. From September 1880 Lieutenant E. Hanstock was Provost Marshal of the Kandahar field force's 2nd Division. Other Provost officers during this period were Major V. W. Tregear, 41st Bengal Native Infantry, who was for a time Provost Marshal to the

3rd Brigade of the Reserve Division, and a fellow unit officer, Captain B. Wemyss, held a similar position in a brigade on the Khyber line. Captain J. E. Baines, Royal Warwicks, for a time was Provost Marshal on the Kurram lines of communications.

Unlike the earlier campaign the second saw much bitter fighting before Major-General Roberts took Kabul and hanged 11 of the mutineer murderers, including their general. News then came of the reverse suffered by the Kandahar field force on 28 July 1880, and their subsequent retreat into the city of Kandahar. Beset by hordes of fanatical tribesmen they faced annihilation if relief did not soon come. Roberts rose to the occasion and his march from Kabul to Kandahar was a military achievement that still excites admiration. 'Bobs Bahadur', as he was known to his India troops, relieved Kandahar and his troops won a resounding victory on 20 September 1880. Forces engaged in this war received the appropriate medal and clasps, but for the epic march a special star in bronze was struck, which in appearance is not unlike the Khedive Star struck for Egyptian service a few years later. So ended one of our little wars, unique in many respects, the most important of which, as far as we are concerned, is that it was extremely well documented respecting Provost appointments.

Mention Kohima to any soldier and he will conjure up visions of Japanese attacks on that town in World War Two. Few know of the earlier siege of the town from 13 to 26 October 1879 during the Naga rebellion. After murdering a British political officer and most of his Gurkha escort, thousands of Nagas converged on Kohima police post, where 78 Gurkhas and 40 Assam military police under Captain D. G. Reid fought them off until relieved by a force under Brigadier-General Nation. In the final assault 27 Assam military police took part. The Indian General Service medal with clasp 'Naga 1879–80' was awarded for this spirited little action. Another affair occurred in December of that year when a force, of which three-quarters were Assam military police, went to Saduja to punish the rebellious Abhor tribe, the only serious fighting occurring in Dambuk where six of the A.M.P. were killed. It was two years later that A.M.P. were reorganised into three military police battalions, known as the Surma Valley, Lakhimpur, and Naga Hills battalions respectively. Later still they were re-named the 1st, 2nd and 3rd Battalions Assam Military Police. Across on the North West Frontier a military police battalion was raised in 1885, but it was not popular, and in two years only 512 men had enlisted. During the Burma campaign of 1885–87 a battalion of Burma military police served with our army from the outset, and during 1886 two further battalions were raised. Eventually the B.M.P. totalled five battalions, with Mandalay and Rangoon each having a resident battalion, the others serving where required.

Throughout the Black Mountain Expedition of 1888 Captain W. Lambert, 3rd Punjab Cavalry, a veteran of Roberts' march, served as the Force Provost Marshal. In the Lashai campaign, which lasted for over three-and-a-half years, from 1889, a military police battalion formed part of the available troops, and in the six weeks' long Samana operation conducted by Brigadier-General Sir W. S. A. Lockhart in early in 1891 a military police battalion was in the forefront of the action. Another short campaign was undertaken in the Kachin Hills for three months in the following year. The Chin Hills military police battalion served throughout the operation. Present at the Relief of Chitral in 1895 was the Kurram and Border battalion of military police. In all these colonial wars the indigenous military police proved their worth over and over again, and the brief mention given here will bring them to the notice of today's military policemen, and in a small way perpetuate their various names.

At the time of the Boer War it was suggested that Indian military police could hold the lines of communication, just as they had done in the days of Herbert Bruce. It was reported that there were 30,284 military police available in India, but the idea was never implemented. This was a pity, for the system pioneered by Bruce was, in fact, eventually used in South Africa, but without utilising military police battalions.

On 3 June 1907 a Levee was held in Buckingham Palace for the surviving officers of the Mutiny, and on 23 December the *Daily Telegraph* gave a dinner in the Albert Hall for survivors of all ranks. The events of those fateful days of 1857 have now been permanently recorded on the tapes of historical fact and fiction. Alas! even as I write this in 1979 police units in India are mutinying. Ah well, I long ago learned that nothing is new!

CHAPTER XI

EUPOPE – 1808-1812

DURING THIS PERIOD three ancillary Corps came into prominence in contemporary writings. They also appear from time to time in more recent publications and as all have been linked with Provost to some degree it is important that the reader acknowledges from the start the role of each. Armed with this knowledge references to these three Corps in future will be readily understood and interpreted.

First comes the Royal Staff Corps, a body whose nearest relative today would be the Royal Pioneer Corps. They were employed on works services, but only on fortifications when under Royal Engineers' supervision. They were not always on the best of terms with their sister Corps, but, nevertheless, have left their mark for us to see today in the shape of the Royal Military Canal behind the Kent coast. In the Peninsula they were occasionally used for traffic control, but have no more claim to being called military police than have the 4th Battalion The Border Regiment, who, during our final advance in Burma during the Second World War, were brought out of the line to control traffic and to police centres of habitation.

Second in our trio of confusing Corps is the Corps of Mounted Guides, also called the Corps of Guides. Originally formed from French deserters and local inhabitants they were used for collecting intelligence, both topographical and strategical, interpreting, traffic control, and at times to assist local A.P.M.s, but this duty was merely complementary to their main role, and at no time a compelling reason for their existence. Officers for this Corps often came from the Royal Staff Corps, and this connection between the

Corps adds to the confusion met in certain accounts. If any Corps can claim these men as their military forebears it is the Intelligence Corps to whom the right must go, but after accepting this it must be admitted that Wellington was inclined to look on them as a form of police, as we shall see later in this story.

The last Corps was the Cavalry Staff Corps, also known as the Mounted Staff Corps. This was raised as a military police force, and is, as will be shown, the true origin of the Royal Military Police. Officers from the R.S.C. also served in the C.S.C.; in fact some officers served in all three Corps at various stages. To add to the confusion each Corps was colloquially known as 'The Staff Corps', and all-in-all the records are very confusing. The effect of this is similar to that caused by the indiscriminate description 'Marshal' used in ancient times. Nevertheless, if we have learned that only the Cavalry Staff Corps were military policemen then we are equipped to follow the story on.

Our tale starts in the Peninsula soon after the arrival of Wellesley in late 1808. Realising the need for guides speaking the local language, he raised the Corps of Mounted Guides from French deserters and local inhabitants. The first Commandant of the new Corps was Captain George Scovell of the 57th Regiment, but serving with the Royal Staff Corps, and the strength was established as one sergeant, one corporal, and 16 privates. Their worth was rapidly apparent, and they were eagerly sought after by commanders.

After the Convention of Cintra the main British army left the Peninsula, leaving a force under Sir John Moore, who, when the French army marched on Madrid, was obliged to go to the aid of the city instead of wintering in Portugal, as had been his intention. Madrid fell on 3rd December, but Moore did not learn this until seven days later, and this delay was to prove his undoing. At Salamanca on 6 December Moore received, from the hands of a French renegade, Colonel Charmilly, a letter from the British ambassador to Spain. The letter was an attempt to usurp Moore's authority, and when he learned that not only was the Frenchman aware of its contents, but actually wished to speak to the staff to insist that the commander followed the ambassador's wishes, Moore became enraged and had his Provost Marshal throw the man out of the headquarters.

The long fighting retreat to Coruna then followed with scenes of disorder and drunkenness common in every village the troops passed through. On one occasion over a thousand men, all too drunk to stand, had to be abandoned to the French after liberal use of the rearguards' bayonets failed to rouse them. The Corps of Mounted Guides proved their worth over and over again, and on 16 December they were increased by a further seven men. Our sharp little victory at Sahagun five days later gave the French cavalry a bloody nose and enabled our retreat to continue for some time unmolested. At Cacabelos, where the army halted on 2 January, General Paget ordered the flogging of two men caught plundering by the Provost. Two others, condemned to death, were lifted on the shoulders of members of the Provost staff, ropes thrown over convenient boughs, and at a signal the Provostmen ducked and launched their burdens into eternity.

Our evacuation of Coruna was marred by the death of Moore, and of the C.M.G. only 12 men and Captain Scovell got safely away to fight another day.

By 22 April 1809 another British army under Wellesley was back in the Peninsula, and on 23 May in Oporto authority was given for re-raising the C.M.G. Scovell was selected again by the Q.M.G., Sir John Murray, to command, the strength of this Corps to be:

4 Lieutenants	4 Cornets
6 Sergeants	6 Corporals
20 Privates	2 Farriers

The Corps were to receive pay and allowances as cavalry and were to be mounted at public expense.

A General Order of 3 May authorised the continuance of an Order of Moore's permitting Assistant Provost Marshals (or, as they were more generally called, assistant Provosts), who were staff sergeants or sergeants, the pay and allowances of Ensigns.

The first of Wellesley's many letters deploring the conduct of his troops was written from Coimbra to our representative with the Portuguese government, the Hon. John Villiers, on 30 May. The relevant extract reading:

> . . . They have plundered the country most terribly, which has given me the greatest concern. The Town Major of Lisbon, if he has the orders, will show you if you wish to read them, those I have given out on this subject.
>
> They have plundered the people of bullocks, among other property, for what reason I am sure I do not know, except it be, as I understand it, their practice, to sell them back to the people again. I shall be very much obliged to you if you will mention this practice to the Ministers of the Regency, and beg them to issue a proclamation forbidding the people, in the most positive terms, to purchase anything from soldiers of the British Army.
>
> etc., etc.

After the battle of Oporto the General Orders made it an offence for soldiers to buy bread before the Commissariat had made an offer. This order was rarely obeyed by the soldiers and never by their wives, who were also given to looting the regimental clothing carts whenever an opportunity to do so was presented. Wellesley was particularly pleased, however, with a corporal of the 71st Regiment who not only refrained from robbing a French general whom he had taken prisoner, but prevented others from doing so. He promoted the man to sergeant, and, on learning that he had been a Sergeant Assistant Provost under Moore, but had lost his appointment after the evacuation, wrote to Horse Guards about the case.

Wellesley wrote to Marshal Beresford, the British commander of the Portuguese, on the subject of the C.M.G. on 2 June, saying:

> I have been endeavouring to form a Corps of Guides—that is to say one of officers and non-commissioned officers, who should be interpreters between our people and those of the country who must show them the roads. We have got some officers but we want non-commissioned officers. I will be very pleased if you will allow us to have Jose Bannas, Corporal in the 2nd Company of Grenadiers, and eight or ten other Sgts, Cpls or

steady soldiers, men of good character, who can speak either English or French, to make them Sgts or Cpls of Guides. They will have with us the pay and allowances of British Cavalry.

Much of Wellesley's valuable time in the early days was devoted to improving discipline of all ranks. He appreciated that he could not defeat the French unless the local inhabitants were on his side. It was neglect of this so obvious precaution by the French that eventually helped Wellington, as he became, bring about their downfall.

Writing from Abrantes on 16 June he had this to say to one of his subordinate commanders:

> I now trouble you upon a subject which has given me greatest pain. I mean the accounts which I receive from all quarters of the disorders committed by, and the greatest irregularity of the XXX and XXX regiments. I have ordered a Provost to Castello Branco to put himself under your orders, and I hope you will not fail to make use of him.

He ordered that the units concerned should be hutted in woods outside the above town, specifying that they must not be under fruit trees, and that the roll must be called hourly during day and all, including officers, must answer their names. By preventing the opportunity to straggle he hoped to reduce looting.

The following day he sent his famous letter, which called for a regular Provost establishment, to the Horse Guards. This document is a milestone in army law enforcement and is therefore reproduced in its entirety.

To Viscount Castlereagh,

My Dear Lord,

I cannot, with propriety, omit to draw your attention again to the state of discipline of the Army, which is a subject of serious concern to me, and well deserves the consideration of His Majesty's Ministers.

It is impossible to describe to you the irregularities and outrages committed by the troops. They are never out of sight of their officers, I may almost say out of sight of the Commanding Officers of their regiments and the General Officers of the Army, that outrages are not committed, and notwithstanding the pains which I take, of which there will be ample evidence in my Order Books, not a post or a courier comes in, not an Officer arrives from the rear of the Army, that does not bring me accounts of outrages committed by the soldiers who have been left behind on the march, having been sick, or having straggled from the regiments, or who have been left in hospitals.

We have a Provost Marshal and no less than four assistants. I never allow a man to march with the baggage. I never leave a hospital without a number of officers and non-commissioned officers proportionable to the number of soldiers; and never allow a detachment to march, unless under the command of an officer, and yet there is not an outrage of any description that has not been committed on the people who have universally received us as friends, by soldiers who never yet, for one moment, suffered the slightest want, or the smallest privation. In the first place I am convinced that the law is not strong enough to maintain an army upon service. It is most difficult to convict any prisoner before a Regimental Court Martial, for I am sorry to say that the soldiers have little regard to the oath administered to them, and the officers are all sworn to 'well and truly to try and determine, according to the evidence, the matter before them', have too much regard to that administered to them. This oath to the members of a Regimental Court Martial has altered the principle of the proceedings of that tribunal. It is no longer a Court of Honour, at the hands of which a soldier was certain of receiving punishment if he deserved it, but it is a Court of Law, whose decisions are to be formed according to the evidence, particularly of those on whose actions it is constituted as a restraint. But, admitting the Regimental or Detachment Court Martial, as now constituted to be a control on the soldiers equally efficient with that which existed under the old constitution of a Court Martial, which my experience tells me it is not, I should wish to know whether any British Army (this Army is composed of second Battalions, and therefore but ill provided with officers) can afford to leave with every hospital, or every detachment, 2 Captains and 4 subalterns, in order to be enabled to hold a Detachment Court Martial. The law in this respect ought to be amended, and when the Army is on service in a foreign country, any one, two or three officers, ought to have the power of trying criminals, and punishing them instanter, taking down all proceedings in writing and reporting them for the information of the Commander in Chief on their joining the Army. Besides this improvement of the law, there ought to be in the British Army a regular Provost establishment, of which a proportion should be attached to every Army sent abroad. All the foreign armies have such an establishment; the French 'Gendarmerie Nationale', to the amount of 30 or 40 with each of their Corps, the Spaniards their 'Policia Militar' to a still larger amount; while we, who require such an aid more, I am sorry to say, than any of the other nations of Europe, have nothing of the kind, excepting a few Sergeants—who are all taken from the line for the occasion—and who are probably not very fit for the duties which they are to perform.

The authority and duties of the Provost ought, in some manner, to be recognised by law. By the custom of British Armies the Provost has been in the habit of punishing on the spot (Even with death, under the orders of the Commander in Chief) soldiers found in the act of disobedience of orders of plunder, or of outrage. There is no authority for this practice excepting customs which I conceive would hardly warrant it; and yet I declare that I do not know in what manner the Army is to be commanded at all, unless the practice is not only continued, but an additional number of Provosts appointed.

There is another branch of this subject which deserves serious consideration. We all know that the discipline and regularity of all armies must depend upon the diligence of the regimental officers, particularly the subalterns. I may order what I please, but if they do not execute what I order, or if they execute it with negligence, I cannot expect that British soldiers will be orderly or regular.

There are two incitements to men of this description to do their duty as they ought; the fear of punishment, and the hope of reward. As for the first, it cannot be given individually; for I believe that I should find it difficult to convict any officer of doing this description of duty with negligence, or more particularly as he is to be tried by others probably guilty of the same offence. But these evils of which I complain are committed by whole Corps, and the only way in which they can be punished is by disgracing them, by sending them into Garrisons and reporting them to His Majesty. I may and shall do this by one or two battalions, but I cannot venture to do it by more, and then there is an end to the fear of this punishment, even if those who receive it were considered in England as disgraced persons rather than martyrs.

As for the other incitement to officers to do their duty zealously, there is no such thing. We who command the Armies of the country, and who are expected to make exertions greater than those made by the French Armies, to march, to fight, and to keep our troops in health and discipline, have not the power of rewarding, or promising a reward, for a single officer of the Army; and we deceive ourselves and those who are placed under us, if we imagine that we have the power or if we hold out to them that they shall derive any advantage from the exertions of it in their favour.

You will say, probably, in answer to all this, that British Armies have been in the field before, and that these complaints, at least to the same extent, have not existed, to which I answer, first, that the Armies are now larger, their operations more extended, and the exertions required greater than they were in former periods; and that the mode of carrying on war is different from what it was. Secondly, that our law, instead of being strong in proportion to the temptation and means for indiscipline and irregularity, has been weakened, and that we have not adopted the additional means of restraint and punishment practised by other nations, and our enemies, although we have imitated them in these particulars which have increased and aggravated our irregularities.

And, finally, that it is only within late years that the Commanders in Chief abroad have been deprived of all patronage, and of course, of all power of incitement to the officers under their command.

It may be supposed that I wish this patronage to gratify my own favourites, but I declare most solemnly that, if I had it tomorrow, there is not a soul in the Army whom I should wish to promote, excepting for services rendered.

I have thought it proper to draw your attention to these subjects, which I assure you deserve the attention of the King's Ministers. We are an excellent Army on parade, an excellent one to fight, but we are worse than an enemy in a country, and take my word for it, that either defeat or success would desolve us.

Believe me, my dear Lord,
Ever yours most sincerely,
Arthur Wellesley.

In this excellent account Wellesley has recorded for all time the conditions of his soldiers and their officers, so devastatingly disparaging that comment would be superfluous.

The reasons for establishing the C.M.G. were touched on in a letter from Castello Branco to the Military Secretary on 1 July. The letter also referred to A.P.M.s' pay and allowances, the relevant paragraphs reading:

7. The Appointment of Assistant Provost Marshals, I am sorry to say, is but too necessary, and I trust that the allowance granted to them by the late Commander of the Forces in Portugal, viz—Ensigns' Pay and Allowances, by his Order of the 14th April, and the allowance to purchase a mule, given to me, will be approved of by the Commander-in-Chief.

9. The Order of 7th May, attaching Mr. Cussan and Mr. Androde to the office of the QMG was issued with a view to the formation of the Corps of Guides, respecting which the Order was finally issued on the 23rd May 1809. This Corps is essentially necessary in all operations in Portugal. It is most difficult to

obtain any information respecting roads, or any of the local circumstances which must be considered in the decisions to be formed respecting the march of troops, and this difficulty obliged me last year, and all those who have since conducted operations in this country, to form a Corps of this description.

Thus we have confirmation that the C.M.G. was the brain-child of Wellesley in the first instance, but to return to the extract:

The object is not only to have a Corps whose particular duty will be to make enquiries, and have a knowledge of the roads, but to have a class of persons in the Army who shall march with the heads of columns, and to interpret between the Officers Commanding them, and the people of the country guiding them, or others from who they may wish to make enquiries.

One question continued to vex the commander and his Provost throughout the campaign—the conduct of soldiers' wives. Instances will be given in this story from time to time of their misbehaviour. On 4 July at Zarzor Maior, General Lord Hill, on receiving a complaint against wives of the 29th Regiment alleging that they had been stealing crops, had them rounded up, and certain ladies whipped by the A.P.M. on his orders. Later in the campaign a common law wife of a 7th Regiment sergeant was flogged on the behind by an A.P.M. for stealing. She promptly ran off to the enemy and was later heard of living happily with a French colonel.

Although the Portuguese were quick to complain at the conduct of our troops they would rarely attend to give evidence when culprits were brought to trial. Writing to our representative with the Portuguese government, John Villiers, from Plascenia on 9 July, Wellesley said:

. . . The artilleryman who has committed the murder at Cascaes must be tried according to the laws of the country, or for a military offence under the Articles of War. My opinion is that he ought—and all guilty of similar offences—ought to be tried (I mean tried in earnest, and not as the Officers of the ----th were tried) according to the laws of the country, but if the Government prefer that we should take cognaisance of these offences, as being of a military nature, we will do so at once in every case, but they must assist in obliging the witnesses to come forward and give their testimony on oath, to which I find they have great objection.

Growing resistance by Portuguese guerrillas provoked cruel retaliation by the French, who could ill afford the large numbers of men required to keep open their lines of communication. When the French Provost Marshal was captured by guerrillas Marshal Massena ordered savage reprisals, including the execution as bandits of captured Portuguese Ordenanza (militia) personnel. From that point on guerrillas tortured all French prisoners before executing them.

After the battle of Talavera on 28 July there were occasions when our troops became difficult to control. According to George Napier, writing years later, wives were harder to prevent from plundering than the men, and he recommended that—'the only way to control them is to have plenty of Provosts to flog them and hang them without mercy'. There is no official record of women being hanged for plundering, although several soldiers were. Wellesley was particularly disgusted on several occasions when, following victories, he saw wives engaged in what were called their 'sports', which was what the looting of wine cellars was known as. In this they were often worse than the uncouth Irish former militia-men who predominated in our regiments. Casks would be broken open and women, often with babies at their breasts, would fight with men, up to their knees in wine, to get at the best vintages. When the A.P.M.s arrived on the scene more often than not the women were caught while the soberest men got away. The women would be flogged before being released. These were the incidents that gave rise to the nickname 'Bloody Provost' during this period. Floggings and summary executions were the Provost hallmark and proof of passage.

Further annoyance was caused by the practice of the women buying up the available bread in villages before the Commissariat officers arrived on the scene, and this resulted in the following General Order being published at Medellin on 24 August:

The women of the Army must be prevented from purchasing bread in the villages within two leagues of the station of any Division of the Army; when any woman wishes to purchase bread, she must ask the officer of the Company to which she belongs for a passport, which must be counter-signed by the Commanding Officer of the Regiment.

Any woman found with bread in her possession, purchased at a place nearer than two leagues, will be deprived of the bread by the Provosts or his assistants; as will any woman who goes out of camp to purchase bread without a Passport. Women who have been discovered disobeying this Order will not be allowed to receive rations.   Arthur Wellesley

Wellesley again wrote to Villiers from the neighbourhood of Badahoz on 8 September, complaining of the unwillingness of the inhabitants to prosecute after having complained against soldiers, and telling· of his own efforts to maintain discipline, one sentence reading:

It is a curious circumstance, that notwithstanding I have been aware of the necessity and have determined to execute any man found guilty of plunder, I have not executed one, although I really believe that more plunder and outrage have been committed by this Army than by any other that was ever in the field, to this end I have not less than seven or eight Provosts, other Armies having usually two.

During the retreat back into Portugal which ended on 8 October our troops were better behaved than they had previously been under similar circumstances. Nevertheless, drunkenness and plundering did occur, and at Leira two soldiers caught by Provost robbing a church were hanged from a wayside olive tree on the orders of Wellesley. This could well have been the first occasion on which he personally ordered the extreme penalty on this campaign, but his Provost had long used it as a matter of course for those apprehended in the act of plundering, and, of course, not all such incidents occurred near the commander's location.

From late in October until the close of the campaign the Town Major of our Lisbon base was Major W. Geddes, who ranked as an A.Q.M.G. in the Q.M.G.'s department. He worked closely with the Provost and proved of great assistance to them during his term of office.

While Wellesley was endeavouring to carry out his role in the Peninsula another British army was operating in the Lowlands under command of the Earl of Chatham. Our early successes there were made worthless by the terrible sickness rate, and by 23 December our army had returned home. Six months later 11,000 of the original force of 40,000 were still suffering from what was called Walcheren Fever, but which was, in fact, malaria. The Provost Marshal and his Provost Guard had been quartered during the campaign at East Zuburgh, near Flushing.

A contemporary account of life in Wellesley's army during this period tells that the soldiers who had been flogged referred to themselves as having been 'Provosted'. However, in the King's German Legion component of our army flogging was not common, as the following story illustrates. On one occasion a party of 300 convalescents were marching to rejoin their units under command of a K.G.L. officer. The march had been marred along the route by a series of robberies and drunken outrages. A quick appraisal of the situation was made, and a dependable corporal was then put in the rear to hurry along the stragglers, but, on reaching Viseu, where Wellington, as he then was, had his head-quarters, the corporal accepted a drink of looted wine. At that moment the owner arrived with a file of soldiers to arrest the looters. The corporal and others were put in arrest and eventually taken before Captain Edward Pakenham of the A.G.s department, who told them that they were lucky not to be executed. This they knew was no idle threat, for a short time before a Private Maguire of the 27th Regiment had been hanged for theft of only a few shillingsworth of property. The K.G.L. officer was ordered to continue the march and get an A.P.M. to give the men 24 lashes each morning until they rejoined their respective units. These men were lucky, for the first morning the officer sent for them and said that he would not flog them as it was not a practice carried out in his country.

It was from Viseu that Wellington wrote to Major-General the Hon. W. Stewart, commanding a force holding Cadiz, on 27 February 1810. Stewart had apparently requested authority to appoint his own Provost Marshal. The answer reveals the authority given Wellington in these matters under his own Warrant.

> . . . I send herewith a Warrant authorising you to convene General Court Martial, and the Warrant for the appointment of a Deputy Judge Advocate, which you will fill with the name of the officer you think proper to appoint to that office.
>
> The Warrant under His Majesty's Sign Manual does not authorise me to depute the power of confirming the sentences of General Courts Martial.
>
> In respect of a Provost, I am authorised by the King's Warrant to appoint only one Provost Marshal, but I have appointed several Assistant Provosts, who have the same authority, and you will appoint one under your command.
>
> I enclose a copy of the orders which have been issued upon this subject, and I shall further desire the Adjutant General to send you a copy of all the General Orders which have been issued in this army.

The General Order referred to had been issued a few days earlier and is very comprehensive, leaving commanders in no doubt as to the powers enjoyed by Provost, and also making it quite clear that punishment by a Provost must follow crimes he had personally witnessed and that officers could not order Provost to inflict punishments for crimes committed out of their sight.

Here is the Order:

> The Commander of the Forces is concerned to observe that the power of the assistants of the Provost Marshal of the Army has, in more than one instance, been abused; and that officers have thought themselves authorised to send orders to the Assistant Provosts, under which orders abuses have been committed, contrary to the established usages and rules of the service, and the intentions and orders of the Commander of the Forces.
>
> 2. The office of Provost Marshal has existed in all British armies in the field. His particular duties are to take charge of the prisoners confined for offences of a general description; to preserve good order and discipline; to prevent breaches of both by the soldiers and followers of the army, by his presence at those places in which either are likely to be committed, and, if necessary, he has, by constant usage in all armies, the power

to punish those whom he may find in the act of committing breaches of order and discipline.

3. The authority of the Provost Marshal to punish must be limited by the necessity of the case; and whatever may be the crime of which a soldier may be guilty, the Provost Marshal has not the power of inflicting summary punishment unless he should see him in the act of committing it. If he should not see the soldier in the act of committing the offence of which he may have been found guilty, a report must be made to the Commander-in-Chief of the army, who would give such orders as might be deemed expedient, either for further enquiry, for the trial of the soldier, or for the infliction of summary punishment, according to the nature of the case, the degree of evidence of the soldier's guilt, and the existing necessity for an immediate example.

4. The duties and authorities of the assistants of the Provost Marshal attached to the several divisions and stations of the army are the same as those of the Provost; but the conduct of those officers and the exertion of their authority require the constant and watchful attention of the General Officers commanding divisions, and of the Staff officers attached to them, as that of the Provost Marshal does of the Commander of the Forces and of the officers of the General Staff.

5. They should attend particularly to the nature of the offences against good order and military discipline, of which the soldiers and followers of the army may be guilty at different times and under different circumstances, and to allow the Assistant Provosts to punish them in a summary manner, only when committed under those circumstances when summary punishment may be necessary for the sake of example, and in which the prevalent and continual commission of the particular crime may be injurious to the public service.

6. The Commander of the Forces desires that it may be clearly understood that no officer whatever has a right to order the Provost Marshal or his assistants to exercise the authority entrusted to them; nor can the Provost Marshal or his assistants inflict corporal punishment on any man, excepting they should see him in the act of committing a breach of order and discipline. Their duty is, by vigilance and activity, to prevent those breaches which the Commander of the Forces is sorry to observe are too common, and to punish those they catch in the act.

That there was no improvement in the position regarding the attendance of civilian witnesses at British courts, is evident from a letter from the commander to Mr. C. Stuart, Villier's successor, on 6 March:

. . . I am concerned to add that I know of no means which have not already been adopted to keep British soldiers in order. Detachments are never allowed to march, excepting under command of an officer, and the most strict orders have been given for the regulation of the conduct of soldiers when so employed, and an officer of the Provost Marshal's establishment is employed whenever the numbers of any detachment will justify such an appointment.

But all has hitherto been in vain, the outrages complained of are still perpetrated, and they will continue until the government and people see the necessity of doing their utmost to convict, before a Court Martial, those soldiers of the crimes of which I am sorry to say I am too well convinced they have reason to complain.

Proof that Wellington was well versed in the requirements of policing is evident from the text of another letter to Stuart on 24 March. Written from our headquarters in Viseu:

. . . Till I received Dom M de Forjaz's letter I admit that I did not contemplate the probable insurrections in the town which, whether on the right or wrong side would be equally fatal to us, and probably oblige me to withdraw, even though pressed by no other military necessity. Thus the people would be the immediate cause of their own subjection. I conceive, however, that it will be possible to establish in the town a very vigorous system of Police, to be well weighed, considered, and arranged beforehand, to be carried into execution at the critical moment. The foundation of this system should be in the existing Police, which, I believe, is very good. The town, if not already divided, might be divided into districts. In each district there should be a person employed under the Lieutenant de Police. A certain number of married inhabitants of each district, not already belonging to any military establishments, should be enrolled to be Police Constables or soldiers, under the direction of their Magistrate or Officer, to keep the Peace in their own district, in case there should be any disturbances in the town.

These persons should be armed but not paid, unless actually called out and employed under a proclamation by the Government. They might then, by patrolling the streets of their district constantly, at all hours of the day and night, prevent assemblies of the people in the streets or coffee houses, where all mischief commences. This is the outline upon which Dom M de Forjaz, who has more local knowledge and ability, might work, and bring out a perfect and, I hope, a simple and practicable system.

The town, of course, was Lisbon, the security of which was vital to our army. A few days later, on 6 April, in fact, Wellington sent the Adjutant-General a long complaint respecting the quality of his troops, explaining:

> . . . The orders of the Army, and the Provost's establishment, which is larger than was ever known with any British Army, will show the pains which the General Officers, the Commanding Officers of Regiments, and I have taken to prevent the commission of these crimes.

He concluded by saying:

> I am concerned to be obliged to make the Commander-in-Chief so unfavourable a report of an Army which has shown that it possesses many excellent qualities, but it contains facts which ought not be concealed from his knowledge.

Yet in the midst of all his vast worries and responsibilities Wellington was able to find time to put in a good word for a bad soldier in whom he had faith. Writing to Vice-Admiral the Hon. C. Berkeley on 17 April, he said:

> There is a man by the name of Stephen Bromley, now in charge of the Provost Marshal in Lisbon and I should be very obliged if you will let me know whether you will receive him into one of HM Ships if he should be discharged from the service. He is a stout man and has not been guilty of any crime that renders him infamous.

After our successful engagement at Busaco on 27 September, Wellington was forced to withdraw into Portugal, behind the secretly-prepared defences of Torres Vedras. By coincidence Provost hanged two of our men, one British and one Portuguese, outside Leiria exactly one year to the day after two others had been hanged there for looting.

On 19 October he again wrote to Admiral Berkeley, this time over the transport of French prisoners to England. He expressed concern over their treatment, as this extract confirms:

> . . . I confess, however, that as the French treat well the prisoners whom they take from us, and the Portuguese treat their prisoners exceedingly ill, particularly in point of food,

I should prefer any arrangements by which prisoners who have once come into the hands of the Provost Marshal of the British Army, should avoid falling under the care of any officer of the Portuguese Government.

One A.P.M. caught a soldier coming out of the town of Coimbra on 27 October, carrying a large gilt mirror. He promptly tied the mirror round the man's neck and hanged him, leaving him as a warning to others. Several other soldiers later caught looting were saved by the timely arrival of Wellington who, on hearing the story, pardoned them because their unit had fought with great gallantry at Busaco. According to Commissary August Schumann, of the K.G.L., it was on the retreat to Portugal that Provost hanged a woman. Although this does not reflect in the records, much must have gone on out of his sight that Wellington's headquarters never heard of.

Prisoners taken at Busaco marched before the rearguard and it is said that their astonishment on seeing for the first time the defences of Torres Vedras was equalled by that of the Provost Guard escorting them. For a year thousands of Portuguese, directed by officers of the Royal Staff Corps, had worked in secret on fortifications that surprised both friend and foe when their existence finally became known.

During the period that our army wintered behind Torres Vedras the establishment of the C.M.G. was increased so that, besides the commandant, there were 72 other members of the Corps, viz.: six lieutenants, six cornets, eight sergeants, 50 privates, and two trumpeters; the two farriers appear to have been deleted from the establishment. It was also ruled that local inhabitants should be hired through the magistrates as guides in their own area, thus releasing C.M.G. personnel for more important tasks.

That the Provost Marshal was not to be considered omnipotent in matters of law was a point made by the commander to Major-General the Hon. C. Colville, President of a General Court Marshal, in a letter of 27 December. Wellington objected to the results of the trial of a surgeon and, referring to a witness's evidence, said:

. . . and, secondly that, 'he considered himself justified by the
opinion given and presence of the Provost Marshal'. I have to
observe in respect of the second plea that the officer styled
'Provost Marshal' in the sentence of the Court is the Assistant
Provost attacked to the Division. (Whose evidence, by the bye,
Surgeon —— might have produced to the Court, preferably to
that of his trumpeter), whose business it is to enforce the orders
of the Army and to preserve discipline among the soldiers and
their followers and not to administer justice between the officers
of the Army and the individuals of the country, nor to act as
counsel to the officers of the Army.

   The Assistant Provosts are not Commissioned Officers, and
the General Court Martial will, by the point of their sentence,
give them an authority in the concerns of the Officers of the
Army which they certainly do not otherwise possess.

The findings were sent back to the Court for reconsideration. From this we learn that an A.P.M., although an N.C.O.,
had his own trumpeter; presumably there were occasions when
the trumpet was the only method of communicating with a
mob of unruly soldiers. Perhaps one day someone will unearth
the Provost call used to identify an A.P.M. on these occasions,
recent attempts to trace it having been unsuccessful.

A combination of the Torres Vedras defences and the
introduction of a scorched-earth policy during our retreat
eventually forced Massena to withdraw. He crossed into
Spain on 5 April 1811, with 33,000 men out of his original
74,000. Only 2,000 men were battle casualties, the remaining
38,000 vanished by starvation, disease, desertion, and under
the cruel knives of the guerrillas. Our army finally advanced
300 miles in 28 days, such were the fruits of Torres Vedras!

In April Captain Scovell was made responsible for all
military communications and for the military post office.
Detachments of C.M.G., each under an officer, were established at Castello Bronco, Niza Portalegre, Lisbon, and with
Wellington's headquarters, and thus an efficient courier and
road patrol service was maintained. On 30 May Scovell was
promoted to major, and one would think that his appointment was of such importance that recognition was belated
and insufficient. At this time the headquarters was described
as being unpretentious, with little to denote its presence
apart from a guard of R.S.C. soldiers.

Our base commander in Lisbon, Major-General Peacocke, was a man whose latent talents were greatly developed by Wellington, and he became very good at his job. On 13 July the commander wrote him a letter on the subject of a suspected spy; yet another instance of his concern with every aspect of his command. The letter concerned an Englishman who had been arrested when acting suspiciously in Lisbon. Part of it reads:

> . . . The phraseology of his letter to you is evidently that of a person who has been in the service of the French, and I beg you to communicate with Mr. Stuart in order to have him released from confinement in gaol, and sent him to Headquarters under charge of an Assistant Provost and a guard, but let his reasonable conveniences be provided for.
>
> I beg you also to sent me any letters or papers, or the memorandum of any interrogation of them, which can throw light upon his conduct or intentions.

As a result of the conduct of an officer in a certain village his court martial was ordered. It appears he took reprisals after one of his men had been robbed. The following extract of a letter from Wellington to Stuart on 13 July shows that the commander had come to realise that the inhabitants were not backward whenever opportunity was offered to benefit at the cost of the British soldier. It is included here to refute the impression the correspondence has so far created that our soldiers were in a 'friendly' country.

> . . . that although Capt —— will be brought to trial for having taken it upon himself to do justice, I am not astonished when an officer of the British Army is guilty of this conduct.
>
> They scarcely ever enter a village in which they or their men are not robbed, and can get no redress on the spot, and as for punishment for any crime committed, I regret that since I have been in Portugal, I have not known any man punished, except those suspected of being French partizans.
>
> But whatever may be the conduct of the Portuguese Government, I shall not allow the British Army to commit irregularities with impunity and Captain —— shall certainly be tried, if within a month, any evidence should be produced against him.

The letter ended on a somewhat plaintive note:

> It is useless to inquire whether any steps have been taken against the criminal confined for the robbery?

Wellington's continued determination to ensure that local inhabitants' rights were respected is reflected in his letter to the magistrates of Borba on 23 July:

> I send herewith a soldier of the British Army, who was lately concerned in committing a robbery at Elvas in the house of Joana Euphema Rita Silveria; and he sold some of the articles stolen, viz—sheets and a table cloth for 5 dollars, to a woman at Borba, whom he will point out to you. I beg you to attend and see this person, and that you will recover the sheets and send them to Elvas to the woman. I likewise request you to carry into execution the law against the woman who purchased the sheets, etc., as she must have known them to be stolen.

There seems little doubt the Provost ran a military prison of some sort in Lisbon; we have had references to men being held there by Provost, and the following extract of a letter to Admiral Berkeley on 29 July gives another instance of this, and of the general's concern for the common soldiery.

> Lord Blantyre has written to me to propose transfer to the Navy of a boy by the name of John Fraser, who is so prone to desertion that they cannot keep him with the 42nd Regt.
>
> I have sent him to the Provost at Lisbon, and if you have no objection to taking him, I request you desire General Peacocke to send him on board any ship you please, and I will discharge him from the 42nd. He will not be at Lisbon for some days.

The English civilian whom Wellington, in his letter of 13 July to Peacocke, requested be sent to his headquarters, was eventually repatriated to England. The letter of explanation sent to the Secretary of State for War on 21 August told the whole story, and an interesting one it was:

> I received information from Major General Peacocke some time ago, that a British subject, by name of —— was confined at Lisbon by order of the Portuguese Government, on suspicion of being a spy; and upon perusal of the report of his examination, and of the letters he had written, having been of opinion that there was some foundation for the suspicion, I requested the

Portuguese Government to deliver this person over to me, in order that I might examine him. They readily complied with this request and —— was brought to this Headquarters in charge of the Provost Marshal, and having had two conversations with him he appears to me to be able to give but a very unsatisfactory account of the motives for which he came to this country, where he knows nobody, and his account of his former life in England is by no means consistent. I have therefore deemed it expedient to send him back to Lisbon, and to direct Major General Peacocke to send him to England by the first opportunity that will offer after he shall reach Lisbon.

Since the works between the Tagus and the sea were commenced, I have directed that they should not be inspected by anybody, from a desire to prevent not only a description, but a plan of them from being given to the public and to the enemy. —— was found near the works at Alhamdra, and had questioned the peasants in the neighbourhood respecting the make and calibre of the guns in them, and the number of men, etc., etc., and he was arrested by the guards of the Ordenanza stationed in the works. I have his examination before the magistrates of Lisbon, and by me, he stated that he had come to Portugal with a view to serving in the German Hussars, and it appeared that the ship in which he said he had come had returned to England, and he knew nobody in Lisbon.

From the terms in which he addressed Major General Peacocke I was inclined to believe that he had been in the French Service, and that he intended to enlist into the Hussars, in the belief that he would be able to desert from the Corps with the intelligence which he should have procured, more easily than from a British Regiment, but on examining him I did not find any cause to confirm the suspicion that he had been a soldier. But as he had no business in Portugal, and cannot give a satisfactory account of himself, I thought it best to send him to England.

The reference to the German Hussars touches on one of the worries that plagued Wellington. Men of the K.G.L. had little in common with their British comrades in arms; indeed, they often had relatives serving in opposing French forces, and there is at least one case on record of brothers meeting in close combat. The Duke of Brunswick's Oels regiment was particularly prone to desertion, many of its men having been recruited direct from prisons. An account of the execution of two of these men for desertion at Villa Mayor on 5 September has survived. The division concerned was

drawn up to form three sides of a square, the condemned
men standing with their backs to the open side. The firing
party, drawn from their own comrades in the regiment,
faced them. The sentences were read out and the chaplain
performed his office; then the prisoners were made to kneel
down and their eyes were covered. The Provost Marshal
raised his handkerchief and the firing party, who were so
near that they could not miss, fired as the cloth fell. The
Provost Marshal then fired one shot into the head of each
man as he lay on the ground. Troops were then marched off,
being given 'eyes right (or left)' as they passed to ensure
that the lesson was not lost on any of them. It was usual to
have six riflemen for every one person to be executed on
these occasions.

Authority to increase the number of privates in the
C.M.G. was given on 6 September, there being a further
recruitment of 30 men permitted from that date.

Major-General Peacocke received a letter from Wellington
written from Frenada on 1 November, in which future
moves were discussed. The letter ended with reference to
an incident in which the authority of an Assistant Provost
Marshal had been concerned; the extract reads:

> I was sorry to hear of Captain ——'s conduct. I had intended
> to delay to make any general rule on the subject of the authority
> of the Provost till Captain —— should be tried, who has been in
> arrest above three months for conduct of the same description.
> But I find that Captain ——'s is not the only instance that has
> occurred of similar misconduct and abuse of authority, not-
> withstanding the conversations which took place on this subject
> in the Army generally at the time of Captain ——'s arrest, showed
> that the authority and duties of the Provost were well under-
> stood, and rendered it probable that a similar abuse would not
> take place. Indeed this conviction, not less than the desire to
> leave the whole subject open for Captain ——'s defence, induced
> me to delay laying down any general principle upon it.

On the same day Wellington re-published his General Order
for the office and duties of the Provost Marshal and his
Assistant Provost Marshals, prompted no doubt by increasing
instances of officers instructing A.P.M.s to act in contravention of the General Order.

The battle of Ciudad Rodrigo on 19 January 1812 was followed by scenes in the town in which the British army thoroughly disgraced itself, the town being given over to looting, rapine and drunkenness. The A.P.M.s of the 1st, 2nd and 3rd Divisions, assisted by their Provost Guards, and possibly the C.M.G., were unable to restore order until the following day. It was said that the incident was the worst case of indiscipline since Civil War days, but, unfortunately, within a few weeks, even worse was to come.

At Itusia on 23 January a mass execution of 11 men, some of whom were our deserters found in Ciudad Rodrigo, took place. It appears that the Provost Marshal had not briefed the firing party correctly on which man each six was to aim at. Not all the soldiers were killed. One, a soldier of the 52nd Regiment, called out to an officer spectator by name to put him out of his misery. The men were finally despatched by a second volley from the distraught firing party, the Provost Marshal administering the *coupe-de-grâce.*

We know that at this time there was a Provost Marshal at headquarters, and A.P.M.s at Lisbon, Cadiz, Tarifa, one with each Divisional headquarters, a total of 10 A.P.M.s in all.

The siege of Badahoz commenced on 17 March, an auspicious day as many of our troops were Irish Catholics. At 10 a.m. on 5 April a deserter named Arnal was executed. He appears to have been a quiet man, and the previous day's orderly officer, on going to inspect the prisoner, was taken aback to find him unconcernedly playing cards with the Provost guard. At his execution he declined the offer of a blindfold and went stoically to his death.

Badahoz fell the following day and for two days it underwent the horrors of sack. Our soldiers, ably assisted by Spanish, Portuguese, camp followers, and the dregs from the gaols, looted and raped their way from street to street. The memory of this stayed with Wellington till the end of his days. It was there that he saw soldiers dead drunk laying on cellar floors with wine flowing out of their mouths. In the confusion surviving enemy forces were able to escape and retreat to San Cristobel. On the third day Wellington marched a fresh Portuguese brigade into the town and had a gallows erected in the Plaza next to the cathedral. The Provost Marshal and A.P.M.s of the three divisions there set to work with their respective Provost guards and gradually restored order to the devastated town.

Whether the inability of our Provost service to control the troops influenced the decision we shall never know, but within six days of the fall of Badahoz, Wellington increased the establishment of the C.M.G. again so that it now had 150 privates. A captain, sergeant-major and quartermaster-sergeant were also provided, and the energetic Major Scovell promoted to Lieutenant-Colonel. There can be little doubt but that this was a period when the use of the C.M.G. to assist Provost was most frequently resorted to; certainly it was very necessary.

Writing from Fuente Guinalda on 14 May, Wellington requested that Major-General Cooke appoint a Provost for Carthagena, his letter reading:

> I beg that Sergeant James Johnson may be appointed Assistant at Carthagena to the Deputy Provost at Cadiz. His pay will be Ensign's pay and Allowances under the General Order of the Army of 3rd May 1809.

There is a nice little story of about this time. General Sir Lowry Cole, with an escort of C.M.G., rode up to a party of our light infantry who were defending themselves from robbery by a larger party of Spanish soldiers. Misreading the situation the general thought that the Spaniards were trying to arrest our men for looting, and called on them to submit, but they plunged into an adjacent river to escape. The general called on them to come back, for the river was deep and fast running, promising that he would not punish them. The soldiers thought otherwise and safely swam to the further bank. It is not without interest that the soldier who recorded this tale described the C.M.G. as 'the police of the Army'—evidence indeed of what the contemporary soldier considered to be their role!

Wellington wrote to the Secretary of State on 10 June, complaining further of indiscipline and the ineffectiveness of the Articles of War and courts martial as the rules then stood. He referred to his intention to advance further into Spain, but dreaded the possible consequences if his men did not behave themselves.

After the battle of Salamanca on 22 June, Scovell was particularly mentioned in despatches.

Madrid fell on the 12/13 August and from there a Captain Mackenzie of the 77th Regiment was sent back to Lisbon to take up the new appointment of Commissary of Prisoners, a post that relieved the Provost Marshal of a considerable administrative burden.

While we were in Salamanca an A.P.M. named Mackay got into trouble for exceeding his duty. Wellington, in a letter to Beresford on 8 September, shows appreciation of the dilemma in which Mackay had found himself. Here is the relevant extract:

> . . . I shall be very much obliged to you if you will let me know what you wish done with Assistant Provost Mackay, who is in confinement at Salamanca. It is very clear to me that he knew the Portuguese Sergeant was a Sergeant of the Guard, and he had no right to confine him, and for this, if you wish it, he shall be dismissed from his station.
>
> But what is to be done with the Portuguese Sergeant of the Guard, who resisted the Provost and protected depredators?
>
> As for Mackay's releasing the Sergeant, I believe he had a right to do so, and probably the confinement of the Sergeant will be deemed a sufficient punishment for his offence.
>
> The office of Provost is not adverted to in the Mutiny Act and Articles of War, and the application of the British Provost to the Portuguese Sergeant is quite irregular. But I believe if we do not so apply it, the unfortunate inhabitants of the country would derive but little advantage from its establishment.

Today, of course, whenever our forces and those of allies operate together reciprocal powers of arrest are negotiated, and in Germany these powers have existed between us and the Bundeswehr, etc., since 5 May 1955, the day West Germany emerged from the wrack of war as a new nation.

We commenced to withdraw from our advanced positions to the area of the Ciudad Rodrigo on 22 October, and though

we were able to do so on our own terms, the enjoyment
of this advantage was often marred by scenes of disorder.
To our soldiers retreat bred drunkenness, and thus dissolution. It was during this period that an Irish soldier's
wife, Mrs. Skiddy, came to the fore. She was a veritable
amazon, and doyenne of the female establishment. Notwithstanding General Orders to the contrary, she regularly
led her women off in advance of the men in order to obtain
provisions, and have a meal ready when the day's stage was
over. The Provost Marshal let it be known that if the
practice did not stop he would shoot the women's donkeys.
Undeterred, Mrs. Skiddy led her convoy on one morning,
and at a bend in the road found the Provost Marshal and
his guard waiting. They opened fire, killing or wounding
several of the animals. 'Bad luck to his ugly face, the spy
of our Camp', Mrs. Skiddy screamed. 'May he never see
home till the vultures pick his eyes out', with which piece
of Irish logic she conceded defeat, but the following
morning her donkey, the 'Queen of Sheba', led the women
in their daily contravention of General Orders.

Another Provost tale of this period concerns Wellington
personally. One evening while dining with some noble
officers the Provost Marshal came to the door and announced
the arrest of three soldiers for looting. He was instructed to
hang them immediately at a point where they could be seen
by the troops as they marched the following morning. The
next morning three bodies hung by the roadside for all
to see. The example had the expected effect and looting
ceased for some time to come. Months later it was learned
that the Provost Marshal had raised no objection when a
doctor proposed that they hang the corpses of three
men who had died in the hospital; this was done, and
thus three men were saved for the service. This story
rather takes the edge off the 'Bloody Provost' image it
may be thought, but how did Wellington react when he
finally learned the truth? 'Were you very angry?' he was
asked. 'Yes, I suppose I was at first', he replied, 'but I
had no wish to take the poor fellows' lives, and as the
example had the desired effect, my rage soon died out,

and I confess to you that I am now very glad that three lives were spared', he concluded.

Years later, when General Sir Harry Smith wrote his memoirs (for as a young, newly-married, officer he had taken part in the retreat as a member of a light division) he recalled the kindness of the Provost Marshal, Mr. Stanway, on one occasion on the line of march. The young Mrs. Smith later gave her name to a town whose name rang round the world during the Boer War—Ladysmith.

The conduct of troops caused Wellington to issue the following General Order from Aldehuela de la Boveda on 16 November:

1. The Commander of the Forces requests the General Officers Commanding divisions will take measures to prevent the shameful and unmilitary practice of soldiers shooting pigs in the woods, so close to the camp and columns of march that two dragoons were shot last night; and the Commander of the Forces was induced to believe this day on the march that the flank patrols were skirmishing with the enemy.

2. He desires that notice may be given to the soldiers that he has this last day ordered two men to be hanged who were caught in the act of shooting pigs; and he now orders the Assistant Provosts may attend their divisions on the march, and that they will do their duty, as well in respect to this as to other offences.

3. The number of soldiers straggling from their regiments for no reason except for plunder is a disgrace to the army, and affords a strong proof of the degree to which discipline of the regiments is relaxed, and of the inattention of the Commanding and other officers to their duty, and to the repeated orders of the army.

Twelve days after this Wellington sent a circular letter to all general and officers commanding on the subject of discipline. The reaction was violent and such was the attitude of the British press that he wrote to the Secretary of State to explain the reasons for his complaints. He blamed current indiscipline on recruits from England and regiments joining from the Cadiz garrison, and listed three recommended urgent reforms, one of which was the need to legalise the powers of Provost Marshals and to increase their authorised establishments.

The offensive letter (offensive only, it should be understood, in the eyes of officers who saw themselves described therein) was of considerable length, but part of it is of interest to Provost:

> . . . The Commanding Officers of regiments must enforce the orders of the Army regarding the constant inspection and superintendence of the officers over the conduct of the men of their companies in their cantonments; and they must endeavour to inspire the non-commissioned officers with a sense of their situation and authority, and the non-commissioned officers must be forced to do their duty by being under the view and superintendence of the officers. By these means the frequent and discreditable recourse to the authority of the Provost, and to punishment by the sentence of Courts Martial will be prevented.

Towards the end of the year, Captain Mackenzie, Commissary of Prisoners, received a very sharp note from Wellington. This was written on 19 December and complained that the commander was still being worried on matters affecting prisons. The officer was told to get on with the job for which he had been appointed.

This brings our story to the end of 1812.

CHAPTER XII

EUROPE – 1813-1818

THE NEW YEAR was almost a fortnight old when events were put in train that ended with the raising of our first military police. No doubt as a result of Wellington's frequent appeals, the Duke of York agreed in a letter to the Secretary of State on 13 January 1813 that a form of military police should be raised.

In a letter from Frenada on 26 January, Wellington replied to a Horse Guards query over the delay in bringing a certain officer to trial. As the case was one in which a Provost's authority had been abused the relevant extract is here reproduced:

> Captain —— was Military Commandant at the Hospital Station of Abrantes, and was put in arrest in the month of August on the complaint of Major General H. Campbell and of Lieut. Col. Lord Blantyre for having ordered the Assistant Provost at Abrantes to inflict a corporal punishment on a soldier of the Guards and one of the 42nd for selling their necessaries.

That it had become necessary to re-issue the orders respecting the authority of the Provost Marshal and his Assistants for the third time in this campaign is evident from another part of this letter:

> I enclose a copy of an order which I issued on the 1st November 1811 defining the duty and authority of the Provost of the Army, and that of officers over the Provost and his Assistants.

On receipt of the Duke of York's letter, referred to above, Bathurst immediately communicated its contents to Wellington, who replied on the 24 February, giving his intention to proceed with the formation of the new corps,

and reasons why retention of the Corps of Mounted Guards
was necessary. Here is this very important document in the
history of The Royal Military Police, reproduced in its
entirety:

> I have the honour of receiving your Lordship's dispatch
> of the 27th January in regard to the formation in this Army
> of a Staff Corps of Cavalry under the Adjutant General for
> the purpose of Police, and although I have not received the
> orders with which His Royal Highness the Commander in
> Chief states in his letter to your Lordship that he intends to
> honour me, I propose to proceed forthwith to form the two
> troops of this Corps which it is intended shall be attached to
> the Army in this Country.
>
> At the time I took command of this Army in April 1809
> I formed a Corps of horsemen, then denominated the Corps
> of Guides, which was placed under the command of the
> Quartermaster General's Department. It consists chiefly of
> foreign deserters from the enemies camp, and is officered by
> Portuguese, generally students of the University of Coimbra.
> The object in this formation of this Corps and its duties, at first,
> were to make enquiries about, and to reconnoitre roads; to
> provide interpreters between the common village guides of
> the country and the leaders of columns of troops on their march;
> and to circulate orders and other communications between the
> different divisions and Headquarters.
>
> In proportion as the numbers of the army have been
> increased, and their operations have been extended, and the
> resources of the country in means of communication have been
> diminished, this Corps has been augmented; and in the late
> campaign all the communications between the army and the
> frontier of Portugal all those with Madrid and General Hill's
> Corps, as well as on the Tagus and while in Estre-madura, were
> carried on by the Corps of Guides placed in stages on the roads.
>
> The nature of the disorders committed by our soldiers, and
> the time of their committing them being generally on their
> removal to or from General Hospitals, suggested to me the
> expediency of using the Corps of Guides in aid of the Police
> under the Provost, on the roads on which they should be
> placed for the communications in the next campaign; and with
> this aspect in view I directed a further increase of the Corps
> at the close of the last campaign.
>
> It is my opinion that these measures will not be the less
> necessary even though the Staff Corps of Cavalry should be
> formed in this Army.
>
> First, our English non-commissioned officers and soldiers
> are not very fit to be trusted alone, and out of the view of their

officers, in detached stations at a distance from the Army—as the soldiers of the Guides are for months together, without occasioning any complaint.

Secondly, when the Staff Corps (of Cavalry) shall have supplied the orderlies for General Officers, and those necessary for the Police of the different Divisions of the Army, and for the principal hospital stations, it will not be sufficiently numerous to perform the duties of Police on the great communications of the Army.

Thus the embryonic Corps was acknowledged as being under-strength for its tasks, and with the imposition of having to provide personal orderlies for general officers. The first impediment is still with us, and the second lasted well into the Great War.

Is it not ironic that in this, the first letter in which his proposed military police were referred to by name, Wellington shortened his reference by calling them the 'Staff Corps', an abbreviation then widely used for the Royal Staff Corps?

On 13 March Lieutenant-Colonel R. H. Sturgeon of the Royal Staff Corps was appointed to replace Lieutenant-Colonel Scovell, who had been nominated to command the new police corps. By this time the C.M.G. stood at the highest establishment it ever reached—14 officers and 1,903 N.C.O.s and men. From Ivenada on 24 March, Wellington wrote what is virtually the birth certificate of R.M.P., and here it is, as it was written to Colonel Torrens at the Horse Guards:

Sir,

Having, in consequence of the directions of the Secretary of State, made arrangements for carrying into execution the wishes of the Commander in Chief, for the formation of a Police Corps of two troops, to be denominated the Cavalry Staff Corps, I have to request that you will submit to His Royal Highness's favourable consideration the names of the undermentioned officers for appointements in the above Corps:

Brevet Lt Col G. Scovell, from the 57th Regt, to be Major Commandant.

To be Captains of Troops:

Lieut Lewis During, from the 15th Lt. Dragoons

Lieut J. Gitterick, from the 12th Lt. Dragoons

To be Cornet:
    James Rooke, gent.
    I shall hereafter transmit my recommendations of Officers
for other Commissions in this Corps.
                    I have the honour to be
                            etc.

No doubt the reader will have noticed how, in only two
letters, the new Corps has been given different titles. That
of Cavalry Staff Corps was used again on 6 April when
Wellington wrote to General Baron Victor Alten, saying
that the order permitting two men from each cavalry
regiment to volunteer for the new police applied to all
such regiments, and that none would be permitted to opt out.

The role of the new corps was promulgated in General
Orders of 13 March and 21 April, and within a few weeks
of raising its strength stood at 11 officers and 180 soldiers,
organised in four troops. It is possible that many men were
found by mass transfer from the C.M.G., for about this time
their strength had dropped to three officers and 75 soldiers.
What is particularly important in our story is the case of
Mr. Rooke, who, a civilian, was commissioned direct into
the military police, something that has never been equalled,
except that many young officers now come into R.M.P.
direct from Sandhurst, but only after undergoing the full
cadet training course.

The Horse Guards were notified on 21 April of the
regiments that had contributed to the S.C.C., and only
the King's German Heavy Dragoons and one unit of English
Hussars failed to provide their quota.

It would appear that Lieutenant-General Sir Thomas
Graham found the S.C.C detachment sent to serve with him
insufficient, for on 8 June Wellington wrote to him from
Amusco, saying:

> . . . I will speak to Lord Aylmer to send a second detachment
> of the Staff Corps to your Headquarters tomorrow in aid of the
> Police.
>   I must refer you to the General Orders for the duties and
> authority of the Provost and his Assistants. I doubt the legality
> of the Provost's authority, and, in my opinion, necessity and

custom are the only foundation for it, but the authority ought not to be extended further than has been customary, unless absolutely necessary.

During July when headquarters was at Iturea, a General Order was published to the effect that, when we occupied enemy territory, the inhabitants were not to be terrorised and all supplies paid for. It was made clear that if this was not done we would unite the civil population against us, just as the French had in Spain and Portugal.

In August an A.P.M. caught a soldier stealing potatoes from a field. He handed the culprit over to a guard of the 51st Regiment, who in turn took the soldier to his own commanding officer. When the A.P.M. later returned to flog the man his commanding officer refused to hand him over, promising to punish the soldier himself. Once the A.P.M. had departed his commanding officer released him on payment of a 'fine' of several potatoes. He was punished for being stupid enough to be apprehended by the A.P.M. In the same month the young military police corps were dealt a blow to their morale when four of their men were convicted by court martial for looting. Wellington ordered that they be sent back to England to the depots of their original regiments.

On 8 September the Provost Marshal himself apprehended three men, on different occasions, for stealing near Wellington's headquarters. One man, who had stolen a goose, was beaten about the head with the bird by the P.M., who then released the man and retained the loot for his own supper!

Our first troops crossed the river Bidassoa into France on 7 October, and the next day Wellington wrote from Lesaca to Lieutenant-General Sir John Hope, thus:

> I have had sad accounts of the plunder of our soldiers yesterday, and I propose again to call the attention of the officers to the subject. I saw yesterday, many men coming from Clague, drunk and loaded with plunder; and it cannot be prevented unless the General and other Officers exert themselves. If we were five times stronger than we are, we could not venture to enter France if we cannot prevent our soldiers from plundering.

> I believe you have a good number of the Cavalry Staff Corps
> at your headquarters, and I shall be obliged if you will order
> them out in order to bring in all soldiers, of all nations, found
> straggling from their Corps.
>   etc., etc.

Wellington then wrote a three-paragraphed General Order
on the subject of outrages by soldiers and the lack of disciplinary action by officers, saying that some officers were being
returned forthwith to England, for disposal as the Duke of
York thought fit. The next morning the commander crossed
into France and there issued a long General Order on the
treatment of the inhabitants.

A few days later he wrote a letter to the Spanish
authorities complaining of the failure of certain magistrates
to provide food and accommodation (even though always
promptly paid for these services) for members of the C.M.G.
employed on courier duties on the long lines of communication.

In France the S.C.C. were instructed to ride up and down
the marching columns to prevent looting. They were often
accompanied by Major-General Sir Edward Pakenham, the
Adjutant General, under whose department they operated,
as, of course, did the Provost Marshal and his assistants.
There are several recorded instances of soldiers being immediately hanged during this phase of the war. The Irish seem
to have been the culprits more often than not on these
occasions, for they were particularly adept at rounding-up
livestock wherever they bivouacked. Early in November, in
an attempt to prevent ill-usage of the French, all Portuguese
and Spanish units, except one, were sent back over the
Spanish frontier.

At this time the strength of the Provost staff at Wellington's headquarters totalled eight, including the Provost
Marshal. The headquarters quartermaster was Lieutenant
W. B. Hooke of the S.C.C. Private James Daniels S.C.C. was
employed as orderly to Sir Edmund Pakenham, and Private
David Fitzpatrick S.C.C. served as orderly to the Quartermaster General. Incidentally, the S.C.C. had no corps
uniform, but wore that of their parent regiments embellished

with a red scarf tied round the right shoulder. Lieutenant-Colonel Scovell was also at headquarters in his role of commandant of the S.C.C. Lieutenant-Colonel Sturgeon, commandant of the C.M.G. completed the establishment of those corps in which we are particularly interested in this account. Presumably both Scovell and Sturgeon had subordinates, but other than that of Hooke, their names have not survived. Sturgeon was also officer in charge of military communications and director of the military post, both organisations that depended on the C.M.G. for their efficient and regular services.

When a British soldier robbed a Frenchman near Artois he was caught, court martialled, and hanged, all within three days. A fortnight later French newspapers made much of the incident and demanded action. Wellington replied to the effect that the soldier concerned had been executed 10 days prior to the articles being published.

Whilst his headquarters was at Vera, Wellington received a complaint about the conduct of his troops when San Sebastian fell on 31 August. As he had been in the town on four occasions in September, and there had been no approaches made to him then, he caused enquiries to be made and then wrote to his brother, Sir Henry Wellesley, our representative with the Spanish government, telling the true story. It appears that the town's inhabitants co-operated with the enemy, many actually fighting alongside them, and, as the town fell, assisted the French in putting it to the torch. Several of our soldiers died fire-fighting, or were shot by French holding out in the castle, who could see them outlined by the flames. These facts were confirmed by a written statement from the French commander, who was a prisoner-of-war. There had, of course, been the usual incidents of rapes and several men had been punished at the time. Wellington did not deny that the town had been plundered, but such was the right when a town is taken by storm, as has been explained in an earlier chapter. His letter concluded:

> . . . I now enclose the report of one of the Assistant Provost Marshals sent into the town to preserve order, which, besides

Major General Hay's report, will show that punishment was not neglected.

The headquarters were in St. Jean de Luz by November, the garrison troops being two brigades of the Guards, and a detachment of S.C.C. It was there on the 28th of that month that Wellington refused to confirm the proceedings of a general court martial and sent them back to the president, Major-General Lambert, for reconsideration. It appears that the court had sentenced to death a soldier for assaulting a sergeant of the S.C.C., but had added a strong recommendation for mercy. This had angered Wellington and caused the proceedings to be returned. Historically this letter is unique, in that it refers to the first known death sentence for an assault, on active service, on a military policeman. The relevant parts of the letter read:

> . . . I beg the Court to consider their recommendation in this light, and to apply it to the existing circumstances and situation of the Army, and to what is notorious in regard to this crime.
>
> The increase in the number and the aggravated nature of the disorders committed by soldiers, and the inadequacy of the ordinary course of the Military law to prevent or restrain them, have induced His Royal Highness, the Commander in Chief, and government, to form two squadrons of the Cavalry Staff Corps, in aid of twenty-five Provost Marshals, to endeavour to effect that object. These endeavours have not yet produced the effect wished for; and there is too much reason to apprehend that the odium attached to the character and office of the person, whose business it is to prevent others from committing profitable crimes, will have the effect of preventing the attainment of the object in view.
>
> But if, besides the odium attached to the Staff Corps, there is to be danger in the execution of the duty required from the persons belonging to it; if a Sergeant can be resisted with impunity when endeavouring to prevent a private soldier from plundering and destroying a house; if such Sergeant, as appears in the proceedings of the Court Martial, is put in fear of his life in the execution of his duty, and is actually obliged to remonstrate with the private to induce him not to shoot him; what can be expected?
>
> I beg to inform the Court Martial that a very common, and a most alarming crime in this Army is that of striking and otherwise resisting, sometimes even by firing at, non-commissioned officers,

and even officers in the execution of their duty. It will not be disputed that there is no crime so fatal to the very existence of the Army, and no crime which Officers, sworn as members of a General Court Martial are, should feel so anxious to punish, as that of which this soldier has been found guilty.

It is very unpleasant for me to be obliged to resist the inclination of a General Court Martial, to save the life of this soldier, but I would wish the Court to observe, that if the impunity with which this offence, clearly proved, shall have been committed, should, as is probable, occasion resistance to authority in other instances, the supposed mercy will turn out to be extreme cruelty, and will occasion the loss of some valuable men to the service.

The character of this soldier does not appear to be quite so good as is stated in the letter from the Court. The officer obviously knew nothing about him, and did not even know his name.

Upon the whole I recommend the Court to withdraw its recommendation, and to allow the law to take its course.

etc., etc.

We meet here, so early in the life of the police corps, reference to the odium attached to the office of a military policeman, a state of affairs that was chronic during the Great War and which still exists today to a minor degree in some quarters. We learn also that the S.C.C. was two squadrons strong, and that the Provost Marshal had 24 assistants. This appears to be the highest establishment during the whole of Wellington's European service. By this time a detachment of S.C.C. served with each division, in much the same way as Provost companies do today.

A little anecdote of this period is found in the diary of a soldier. Wounded, he had sought shelter in a small farm occupied by an old man, who agreed to let him stay until fit, but on the condition that he prevented others from looting the house. This the soldier assured by chalking 'Provost Marshal' on the front door. The whole period of his convalescence was spent in undisturbed rest, and his host showed his gratitude by providing good meals.

On 4 December Wellington referred the proceedings of another court martial to the Horse Guards. The court had persisted in acquitting a soldier of looting, even when ordered not to do so by the commander. The soldier was a member

of the S.C.C., and Wellington ordered his return to England
and re-transfer to his original unit, the Royal Scots Greys.

A soldier hanged for rape about this time pleaded that
as he was now in France he thought that it would be all
right! On 14 January a soldier from the 51st Regiment and
another from the Brunswick Light Infantry together entered
a house and each tried to rape a female occupant. The
screams of the two women were heard by members of the
S.C.C., who arrested the men and took them to a nearby
divisional headquarters, where their arrival coincided with
that of Wellington who, when he heard the story, said he
would pardon the man from the 51st, a Private Higgins,
provided he would hang the Brunswicker immediately;
this Higgins did without turning a hair.

August Schumann, a Commissary serving with the K.G.L.
quotes the case of a Spanish muleteer who was caught inside
a French house stealing apples. The Provost hanged him from
one of the windows of the house with an apple stuck in his
mouth. Stories such as these spread like wildfire among the
French, and this, together with the fact that the British
paid on the spot for supplies, ensured ample food being
delivered daily to the various commissariat depots. Our
treatment of the people of occupied France caused them
to openly admit that our presence was preferred to that
of their own army, who paid for nothing.

Even at this late stage in the war, Wellington still complained bitterly about his men, as this letter from St. Sever
to the Horse Guards on 8 March 1814 shows:

> There is no crime recorded in the Newgate Calendar that is
> not committed by these soldiers, who quit their ranks in search
> of plunder, and if the Staff Corps were three times as numerous
> and active as they are, they would not be sufficient either to
> prevent the mischief or detect those guilty of it.

Following the battle of Orthes on 27 February Wellington
took Lieutenant-Colonel Sturgeon to task for shortcomings
in the communications system during the battle. Sturgeon
took this very much to heart and his death in the action at
Vie-en-Bigoire on 19 March was thought to have been

deliberately sought. Major Colquhoun Grant, 11th Regiment, succeeded him. He became a famous figure almost immediately, and had he lived in recent years no doubt would have served in the Commandos or S.O.E., he being that type of man. Prior to appointment to his new post he had been serving with the Royal Staff Corps, but had on several occasions been engaged on intelligence work.

At Toulouse on 16 April Wellington wrote to a Captain Burdett, believed to be in the Provost Service, thus:

> Upon receipt of this letter you will give directions that the person named Francois La Tour may be hanged, as being chief of a Band of Brigands.

With the capitulation of the enemy during the period 14–18 April came the end of the very long war. Both the S.C.C. and C.M.G. ran down and eventually disbanded, the former later to rise again and serve for a further three years.

During the run-down period General Sir Lowry Cole was appointed president of a court martial to try Lieutenant-General Sir John Murray in Tarragona. Arrangements were made for the court to march to its seat in convoy, the escort being 12 men of the Staff Corps of Cavalry under a sergeant.

Paris was occupied and Napoleon deposed. Our Peninsula army was rapidly disbanded, the cream of the infantry leaving for America or home.

We had a garrison in Antwerp where, during May, an incident occurred that cost the A.P.M. his life. This man, a sergeant, was very harsh, and at night would patrol the streets with two of his Provost guard and a drummer. Anyone caught contravening orders would be tied to the nearest lamp-post and flogged. One night he was at the main guard when the field officer, his own commanding officer, arrived drunk to turn out the guard. The following morning these facts were noted in the A.P.M.s report, after he had ascertained from each of the guard that they would support him— but he neglected to record their evidence. At a subsequent court martial the men supported the colonel, who was honourably acquitted. The A.P.M. was then tried by another court. He was sentenced to be reduced to the ranks,

given 500 lashes, and to undergo six months solitary confinement. He suffered the first two, but died soon after in his
solitary cell.

It was on 11 May that Wellington received the last of his
promotions in the peerage from his grateful nation; on that
date he became a duke.

The British Provost Marshal appointed for Paris was
Captain F. Stanway, whom we have met earlier in our story.
In the *Military Memoirs of Edward Costello—95th Rifles*,
edited by Anthony Brett-James, we have a description of
life in the Paris Provost Guard during July. Here it is:

> Shortly after my arrival I was ordered on the Provost Guard,
> which my readers will better understand is a kind of Military
> Police. We were under the command of the Provost Marshal,
> Capt F. Stanway, whose orders were to take all for maraud-
> ing in Paris to his Guard Room for punishment.
>
> Capt Stanway was a keen fellow and sometimes would arrest
> eighteen to twenty in the course of a morning; these were
> immediately flogged, according to the degree of their offence or
> amount of resistance offered, and then turned free.
>
> The depredations became so bad that complaints to the
> Generals of Divisions resulted in orders to keep a stricter watch
> and to take into custody and flog every man caught plundering.
> Our Guard Room was daily filled by soldiers in every uniform,
> for we made no distinction of sect, country, class or colour, as
> we served them all alike.
>
> We had a deal of trouble with the Belgians especially. These
> fellows would go forth in Sections and lay everything in waste
> before them, and whenever hemmed in by the Provost Guard
> they would pelt us with bricks and stones, and sometimes even
> make a regular attack. But Stanway seldom let any escape him.
>
> One morning we brought in sixteen of them and the Provost,
> as usual, marched them into the yard where the punishments
> were generally inflicted. The triangles stared them in the face
> from the centre of the ground, and the culprits, one and all,
> as soon as they saw them, gave a bellow of horror, fell on their
> knees and commenced praying and crossing themselves. But
> Stanway was inexorable. Our men had the greatest difficulty in
> unbreeching them and getting them tied to the halberts. The
> first stripped was, I recollect, a short, fat desperate looking
> fellow. The first whistle of the cat caused him to roar to such
> a degree that all the others joined in, and this set everyone in the
> vicinity off and this aroused their whole Regiment, which was

quartered nearby, and they flew to arms and surrounded the Guard Room. Stanway determined not to relax his duty and ordered us to load, and then placed us in different parts of the building, barricading the doorways, prepared for every resistance, and during intervals continued the flogging.

The assailants became furious and tried to scale the walls for a rescue, but were kept off by the Guards with fixed bayonets, until a shower of missiles made us retire into the building.

Our lives were now in jeopardy, not a man of us dare stir out, until a signal was given to some passing British soldiers, who carried the alarm to the Division, encamped nearby and our Regt and the 52nd turned out to our assistance. The following day the Belgians were moved to Clichy and we saw no more of them.

In June Wellington returned to England and our run-down was speeded up. Once the old Bourbon regime was restored we withdrew through the channel ports and into the Lowlands.

The escape of Napoleon from Elba and the rapid flight of the French Court caught Europe unawares, and April 1815 saw Wellington in Brussels in command of a hotch-potch international army, bitterly regretting the break-up of his Peninsula veterans. On 2 May he wrote to the Horse Guards agreeing that the Cavalry Staff Corps would be of use in the coming campaign, but nothing was then done to reconstitute it. He wrote again on 4 May, complaining of the Provost Marshal selected for him, saying that in Spain he had been obliged to leave the officer in the rear and would do so again for the coming campaign. Lieutenant-Colonel Scovell was put in charge of communications again, and Major (now Lieutenant-Colonel) Grant, came out to head the intelligence department. The Earl of Uxbridge, cavalry commander, was given instructions on 15 May concerning horses, time expired men, ruptured men, and the disposal of his A.P.M.; presumably he was listed last through being considered least important.

What has gone down in history as the Battle of Waterloo occurred during the period 17/18 June 1815, and the brunt of the fighting was borne by the Prussian and British forces, the latter losing 7,000 men out of the 34 battalions engaged.

The P.M. and his A.P.M.s were involved in their traditional roles only. Traffic control in the rear was chaotic and was not improved by the flight of certain allied units who had not even fired a shot. Much sterling work was done by Lieutenant Basil Jackson of the Royal Staff Corps in keeping the roads open and traffic moving, at times using the flat of his sword to enforce his orders.

The immediate chase of the retreating enemy was taken up by the cavalry, with the infantry following along by forced marches. At night they were usually quartered in fields. One contemporary diarist is very critical of Wellington's practice of having the Provost Guard march at the rear, with orders to flog all soldiers found away from their units without a pass. Such procedure had been, of course, common practice in the Peninsula.

Lieutenant-Colonel Scovell received orders on 18 June to reform the Staff Corps of Cavalry. He was to recruit as many former members of the corps as he could find, and could take three good men from every cavalry regiment, giving preference to French speakers. Extra pay of one franc per day was allowed, and they were to retain the uniforms of parent corps, but were to be distinguished by a scarlet scarf round the right arm. Duties were to be as before, with immediate attention to prevention of disorder during the pursuit and consequent alienation of the inhabitants.

One correspondent of this period has told how, on 3 July, his battery was lost near Paris, and, on coming in sight of a French defensive position, turned into a field where they saw a few men of the S.C.C. who were in advance of our main forces. The S.C.C. occupied the village of Dugny, and one of their officers came out and put the lost battery on to the right road.

When Paris was occupied Provost guard posts were established at all entries. Units were billeted outside the city, access to which was only by pass. There was a large Provost guard in the village of Passe, which was on the main road into the city.

One month after he had authorised the reforming of S.C.C., Wellington wrote to Horse Guards to tell them so, and added that as Rooke (who was commissioned as a civilian into the original S.C.C.) was with the army doing nothing, he had appointed him to the new corps.

Another glimpse of the duties of the S.C.C. comes to us through the journal of the then Captain C. Mercer, of the Horse Artillery, whose *Journal of the Waterloo Campaign* was published in 1929. This is what he had to say of an incident, recorded in Paris on 30 July:

> A few days ago, whilst sitting at dinner, an officer of the Mounted Staff Corps (Gendarmerie Anglaise) was announced. He regretted being the bearer of disagreeable orders, but Colonel Scovell, Commandant of the Mounted Staff Corps, had directed him to show me the paper, which he produced, and to inform me that His Grace was exceedingly angry, and had expressed himself very harshly on the subject; therefore Colonel Scovell recommended me to make no remonstrance, as he could not foresee what might be the consequences. The paper was a petition from a certain M. Fauigny (an Italian) setting forth that he is the proprietor of the Grand chateau which has been miserably plundered; but more particularly that British troops now quartered in the village had stripped lead off the roofs, from the baths, water pipes, etc., etc., and sold it. A note written in pencil by the Duke himself was too brief and pithy not to be remembered, and here is the verbatim:

> > 'Colonel Scovell will find out whose Troop this and they shall pay.   W.'

> I was thunderstruck at the complaint and the decision, the one so unfounded and the other so unjust. I signed an acknowledgement at having seen the order and the officer took his leave, recommending me to try and compromise with M. Fauigny, who stated the damage of 7000 or 9000 francs. On enquiry I found that this worthy was an agent of Jerome Buonaparte to whom the chateau actually belongs, as we were told by the Prussians, who actually plundered it.

Wellington wrote from Paris on 1 August to the Horse Guards on the subject of the S.C.C. The letter is interesting as it suggests the reason for Mercer referring to the police as *Gendarmerie Anglaise,* a title for the corps that we have not previously come across in our journey through the years. His letter ran:

I have received your letter of the 27th instant, regarding the Cavalry Staff Corps.

I called it by the name of Gendarmerie at first, in order to render it more palatable to the Allied troops in this Army; among whose officers the strongest objections are entertained to anything like discipline and order; and they would have made the greatest difficulties upon the subject if I had tried to preserve either by means of a British Corps exclusively. I can call it now, however, by any name I please.

I think it had better continue on the establishment on which I have placed it, sending us the old officers and non-commissioned officers, who would, of course, be placed on full pay. There does not appear to be any reason for altering the clothing, as I have distinguished the Corps by a red scarf round the shoulder.

I would wish to keep among the Corps the men of foreign regiments serving with the Army.

There is another contemporary account of the duties at the Provost Guard at this time, and this is found in the following extract from *The Napoleonic Wars of Thomas Morris,* edited by John Selby. The incident occurred in early September 1815.

For several days I was on that disagreeable duty—a Provost Guard—in the village of Boulogne. One night, when patrolling the streets, we arrested two Hanoverian soldiers who at the Guard Room claimed to be officers' servants. This was not accepted and one was tied to a tree and received three or four dozen lashes, as the other was being tied up his master—who had somehow heard of his arrest—turned up and ordered his release. 'And, pray', said the Provost Marshal, 'who are you, Sir?' 'I am an officer of the Hanoverian Service, bearing His Majesty's Commission. 'Have you got that commission with you?' said the Marshal. 'No, I have not.' 'Then go about your business or I shall flog you too!' The officer, seeming glad to get away, left his servant, who was immediately tied up and received his due allowance.

Of course, these proceedings were in obedience to orders, but they were most disgraceful to the service.

The N.C.O.s who accept the position of Provost Marshal seldom go back to their own Regiments, but generally get promoted in some other Corps, where they take especial care not to mention the particular duty they have been on, or they could be received in the same way Jack Ketch would probably be if he were to force himself into any respectable society.

The witness also describes a military execution where the Provost Guard formed the escort and firing party. The format was as previously described except that, in this case, as the Provost Guard waited to fire, the commanding officer announced what he must have known for some time, that the duke had pardoned the man. This would never be appreciated by the poor wretch, however, as the news unhinged his mind.

Morris's account is interesting in that it gives us a soldiers' opinion of those who became Assistant Provost Marshals, an excellent example of the odium to which Wellington referred in his letter of 28 November 1813.

The last of the Duke's letters concerning the S.C.C. now follows. It is an important document in our history and will therefore be reproduced in full. It will not escape the reader's notice that Lieutenant-Colonel Scovell's sterling work had been rewarded with a knighthood. The letter was written in Paris on 11 October:

> Sir George Scovell has communicated to me your Lordship's letter of the 3rd instant, regarding the formation of the Cavalry Staff Corps with this Army.
> When first a Corps of this description was formed, it was necessary to take for it soldiers of all nations of which the Army is composed; and in order to get good men for it, and to make it in their interest to do their duty, I was under the necessity of issuing the enclosed order, by which one Franc, or ten pence, per diem was allowed to each. I do not think I can now lessen this allowance to them, and, if the Staff Corps should be formed according to the establishment stated in your Lordship's Dispatch of the 3rd, it will be necessary that I should discharge those men now in the Corps, and get others from the British Regiments at the rate of pay fixed in your Lordship's Dispatch.
> As, however, it may be hoped that in a short time the Corps may be dispensed with altogether, your Lordship may probably be induced to be of opinion that it is as well to continue to let it exist as long as it may be necessary upon the footing fixed by the enclosed General Order.

This letter suggests that, but for a pay cut proposal by Lord Palmerston, there was every possibility that the S.C.C. would have remained on permanent establishment. For years the Duke had advocated the formation of a unit of military police and it would be quite out of character for him suddenly to reverse his opinions. He appears to have compromised by accepting the eventual disbandment as the price for continuation of existing rates of pay.

Napoleon arrived in St. Helena for his second period of exile on 15 October 1815, and to ensure that this time there would be no escape a strict guard was maintained, in addition to which Sergeant Jeffries, of the 66th regiment, was appointed to the emperor's household staff as Confidential Assistant Provost Marshal. He was nominated personally by the governor, Sir Hudson Lowe, and lived at Longwood, the emperor's residence. The records do not tell us what his exact duties were, and to date no other examples of a Confidential A.P.M. have come to light, so we must each make our personal interpretations of his role.

As the S.C.C. had been reformed after Waterloo no medals were issued, and when, years later, the General Service Medal with appropriate bars was awarded for Peninsular service for all who cared to apply, 19 went to surviving members of the S.C.C. Sixty bars were awarded as follows: Vittoria, 5; Pyrenees, 12; Nivells, 10; Nive, 8; Orthes, 10; and Toulouse, 15. The actual recipients were:

For Vittoria, Pyrenees, Nivelle, Nive, Orthes and Toulouse: Captain L. T. During, Lieutenant H. Becke, Lieutenant A. Bartley, Sergeant W. Bird, and Sergeant H. Graham; *for Pyrenees, Orthes and Toulouse:* Lieutenant T. McDermott, who as late as 1855 was still on half pay as a member of 7th Veteran Battalion, and a Military Knight of Windsor; *for Nivelle, Nive and Orthes:* Lieutenant J. W. Tipping, who at the time of his death in 1856 was on the half-pay list and was quartermaster at the Royal Military College; *for Pyrenees, Orthes and Toulouse:* Cornet J. Forsey, who retired on 25 October 1814 and was still alive in 1856, Private G. King; *for Pyrenees, Nivelle, Nive, Orthes and Toulouse:* T.S.M. J. Fife; *for Toulouse:* Private D. Smith, Private S. Meanwell, Private T. Woon; *for Nivelle and Toulouse:* Corporal J. Hall, Private R. Stevenson, Private J. Thornton; *for Nivelle and Nive:* Corporal T. Fielder; *for*

Pyrenees and Toulouse: Private J. Poole; *for Vittoria, Pyrenees and Toulouse:* Private J. Mahoney.

Obviously some bars were for service in other corps. Of the many excellent N.C.O.s who served in the Peninsula as an A.P.M., only Sergeant J. Norman of 3rd Dragoon Guards claimed his medal with Clasps for Talevera, Albuhera, Vittoria, Pyrenees and Orthes. The medal bore the inscription 'Provost Marshal' on the rim. What a pity he never left a diary.

Our forces in France were gradually run down and only a skeleton force remained by the time of the Convention of Aix-la-Chapelle on 18 October 1818. The last S.C.C. left on 20 September, and were either discharged, returned to their former corps, or placed on the half-pay list of officers. For nearly half a century S.C.C. remained in the army list, junior to all the cavalry, but senior to the foot, then on the death of the last half-pay officer the S.C.C. sank into the morass of history.

CHAPTER XIII

MISCELLANY–TRAGEDY AND TRIUMPH

REFORMS in our Military Penal Code from 1828 onwards gradually eliminated the savage punishments which from ancient times had been the soldier's lot. The following year Articles of War attempted to give a veneer of authority to Provost Marshals, and in the same year the appointment of Provost Marshal-General was abolished. Henceforth Provost Marshals were answerable only to the local commander. An indication of the state of discipline in 1830 can be gathered from the fact that there were 2,684 court martials, at which 655 sentences of flogging were recorded.

The northern district of England during the Chartist riots was commanded by Major-General C. J. Napier, and he did much to ensure adoption of a report submitted by Colonel Shaw Kennedy on 28 November 1838 dealing with counter insurgency operations. Henceforth the report became a basis for training in the subject. Another of Napier's suggestions resulted in a shake-up of the Judge Advocate General's Department, and the establishment of a rudimentary Army Legal service.

Records suggest that news of the abolition of Provost Marshal's General did not spread as quickly as it ought, for the island of St. Lucia still had one in 1840, part of his duty being to arrange bunkering for steamships, then an up-and-coming mode of transportation. When, three years later, legislation reduced the number of lashes to which a man could be sentenced to 50, there were many who foresaw a complete breakdown in discipline as a result, but that did not happen.

Queen's Regulations of 1844 authorised the rank of captain for a Provost Marshal, and from then on other ranks were appointed only to the office of Assistant Provost Marshal. Today an A.P.M. ranks as a Lieutenant-Colonel, sure evidence that the office is at last considered respectable!

Provost lost a great friend when Wellington died in 1852. A few years before his death he had written to the Marchioness of Salisbury after a controversy arose over the flogging of women during the Peninsular War.

Here is an extract from his letter, which the reader will note alludes to the title of this book. After first explaining that every army had an officer known as a Provost Marshal, he went on to say:

> I had one with several assistant Provost Marshals. The duty of these officers is to ride about with a detachment of troops (possibly Staff Corps of Cavalry in the later days of the campaign) to prevent marauding and plundering by the soldiers and to inflict punishment on those whom he should find in the act of plundering. In truth, I believe these officers punished but seldom. The plunderers generally ran away as soon as they saw or heard the officer, who was titled the Bloody Provost. As I have stated, it was the duty of the Provost Marshal and his assistants to punish those whom they should find in the act of plundering or marauding; but no officer in the army was permitted to order one of these to punish anybody. Of that I am quite certain, and I do not think I ever ventured myself to order that which I prevented others from ordering. Indeed, I recollect upon one occasion finding fault with one who had ordered a provost to punish a man. I stated that I could not give such an order myself—that the provost could punish no man unless he found him in the act of plundering.
>
> Portugal, in which two or three campaigns were fought, is a country producing everywhere wine. The wine is collected either in jars or in casks, amongst the most opulent of the wine proprietors, in cellars contiguous to the houses in nearly every village. The soldiers were in the habit of breaking into these cellars. They bored holes in the casks and set the wine running; of which each partook and filled his canteen, which every man carried. These were accompanied by their women as usual, with their children in their arms. They were disturbed possibly by a a fresh party and moved off, invariably leaving the cask running, so that at last the cellar itself became full of wine up to their middles, or even to their chests. This went on, party of

plunderers succeeding party of plunderers, till the 'Bloody Provost' hearing of what was going on, in coming there upon his rounds inerrupted their sports. Being there up to the middle in wine, and generally all drunk, they could not get away; and it was probably necessary that the provost should exercise his authority and punish some in order to clear the cellar.

No doubt the point will not have been missed that only a Provost had the right to order a flogging, something that even the commander-in-chief could not do. Even the Provost privilege had little legal basis, a situation remedied by the Army Act of 1879.

It was one hundred years ago, 28 August 1879 to be precise, that the capture of King Cetawayo ended the Zulu War of 1878–79, a struggle that had seen the disaster at Isandhlwana, and victory at Rorke's Drift and Ulundi. We do not know much about Provost presence there other than that the Deputy Provost Marshal of the 2nd Division commanded by Major-General E. Newdigate was Lieutenant R. A. B. French-Brewster, K.D.G., who was present at the capture of Ulundi on 4 July 1879.

However, we have once again gone ahead of our story, so let us go back 25 years to the tragedy mentioned in the title of this chapter.

When, early in 1854 it became apparent that war with Russia was inevitable, a hopelessly inadequate budget was approved for the expected campaign. At this time we had 221 staff officers in the army, and of these only 15 were staff trained, for this comparatively recent innovation was considered completely unnecessary by most senior officers. Our army under Lord Raglan finally landed at Eupatoria on 14 September. The uniforms were splendid, the men valiant, the officers brave, but often incompetent, and support services were almost non-existent. A market was established by the Provost Marshal and, once the inhabitants learned that a fair price was being paid for everything, supplies flowed in. A general advance was ordered, and this led to the battle of the Alma on 20 September which cost the enemy 5,500 casualties, the British 375 dead and many wounded. The French, who had hardly been engaged, sustained very few casualties, but this was because of the circumstances of the battle and was no reflection on our allies.

Our headquarters was eventually established a few miles from the town and port of Balaclava. The Provost Marshal was Captain W. D. MacDonald of the 93rd Highlanders who, when his own regiment took over the church in the village of Kadikoi as a regimental hospital, endeavoured to evict them on the grounds that his permission had not first been obtained. The regimental surgeon appealed to Lord Raglan, who ordered that the hospital was to remain where it was. Doubtless this ruling saved many lives in the bitter winter that followed, throughout which the frustrated Provost Marshal did not miss an opportunity to harass the unfortunate surgeon. This is an early instance of the mentality of many of the Provost Marshals selected for that appointment in this campaign. Possibly this was an accident of circumstances, but whatever the cause the end result was that the men who became victims of the most mismanaged war in our history had the additional burden of overbearing Provost Marshals.

Meanwhile, back in England it had become evident that in this war there was to be very little chance of our forces living off the land. Even had that been possible there was no local transport available for requisitioning. Three new administrative corps were therefore formed. These were the Land Transport Corps, which was to provide transport in the Crimea, but in the event was of little use, until reorganisation locally by a Colonel McMurdo, after which they gave extremely valuable service. The second new unit was the Army Works Corps, similar to the Royal Staff Corps of the Peninsula. These men were Pioneers and were eventually absorbed into the Engineers. The last was the Mounted Staff Corps, formed to assist the Provost Marshal. The majority of recruits came from the Irish constabulary. The uniform devised for them was a fanciful helmet and a red tunic braided with black cord. They were mounted on huge horses, and one contemporary author described them as looking like 'they were the advance troop coming to open a circus in the village'. Their commandant was Major W. C. Grant; other officers were Captain R. S. Baynes and Cornets E. Budgeon and R.W.S.R. Hunton.

The famous Charge of the Light Brigade took place on 25 October, and with the 4th Light Dragoons rode Quartermaster John Hill, whom we last met in these pages as Deputy Provost Marshal of the Bombay column of the army of the Indus. Riding with the 11th Hussars was No. 489 Sergeant Luke Molley, who later in the campaign served as an Assistant Provost, as did No. 1357 Sergeant Gregory Jowett of the same regiment, who survived the Charge and later served as Assistant Provost to the 2nd Division.

On 5 November the bloody battle of Inkerman was fought and nine days later came a hurricane that wrecked many of the store ships waiting to unload in Balaclava. Blankets, clothing, boots, tents, all essential for the oncoming winter, were lost. This would never have happened had there been any sort of organisation in the port, but there was none. Stores were left on board for weeks, and once landed were left exposed to the elements and the rats—both animal and human. The Commissariat had no ideas what supplies they held and would issue nothing without a multiplicity of signatures. Soldiers died through lack of items that were rotting on the quays. Captains would not obey the orders of the harbourmaster; there was no dockyard police; all was chaos and inefficiency, and the lesson was tragically hammered home that gorgeous uniforms do not make an army. Although the weather was bitter in late November and December soldiers were flogged for theft if caught collecting wood from the many hurricane wrecks, and had to watch H.M.S. *Caradoc* being employed in collecting wood for the fires of Lord Raglan and his staff.

After the hurricane the first contingents of the three new corps arrived. The Mounted Staff Corps were sent to assist maintaining order in the port and vicinity. Also arriving shortly afterwards was a party of railway navvies, brought out to construct a line from Balaclava to the front. Their maintenance was the responsibility of the contractor and had been meticulously organised. They flourished while the soldiers died in droves.

The officers of the M.S.C. were unpopular among cavalry officers and when, in December, two were nearly captured by Cossacks, a cavalry officer witness could hardly conceal his delight, and wished they had been caught. Probably it was the young Cornets Budgeon and Hunton whose impetuousness nearly put them in the bag!

Early in January an energetic commandant, Colonel Harding, was appointed for the town and port; the railway was pushed ahead, more navvies arrived, and the hordes of traders were cleared from the ruins of the town and resettled in a controlled area nearby. By 1 March the town was well ordered, with M.S.C. on patrol with drawn sabres. The sutlers were made to charge fair prices and went in terror of the Provost Marshal and his men. The only thing that did not improve much was the postal service, a source of constant complaints by Mr. W. H. Russell, the *Times* correspondent.

At this time murders and robberies of allied servicemen in the Constantinople base had assumed alarming proportions, but a suggestion to send a detachment of M.S.C. there did not find favour.

Off-duty soldiers were employed around Balaclava at extra payment to assist in road-making and rebuilding, and on one occasion considerable amusement was caused to the soldiers by the way in which an Irish railway navvy roared when flogged by the Provost Marshal for a misdemeanour.

The conditions in which the soldiers lived, although much improved by the work of Colonel Harding, caused hundreds of needless deaths. The efforts of Mr. Russell to raise support at home were assisted by the effect of a shipload of casualties arriving at Portsmouth. These men were just dumped ashore and left, and but for the compassion of the townspeople many would have made the journey home to die of neglect in our main naval base.

In February 42 per cent. of soldiers admitted to Balaclava hospitals died, and in March 56 per cent. The ministrations of Miss Florence Nightingale and her ladies, with little official assistance, eventually produced order out of medical chaos. The blame for the terrible medical services lies firmly on the shoulders of the home authorities and on the senior doctor in the Crimea, Dr. John Hall, Inspector-General of Hospitals, who was knighted for his services when it was all over! An example of conditions experienced can be found in the 63rd Regiment, which at one time had only seven men fit for duty.

Colonel Harding was assisted by Major Hall and Captain Powell, and the credit is equally shared by all three for the reconstruction and organisation in Balaclava that was so evident by mid-April. It is a great tribute to the common soldier that a Commission sent by the government to enquire into Crimean mismanagement, specifically reported that although starved, frozen, and half naked, no capital crimes could be laid at their door. The same could not be said, unfortunately, of our French, Turkish and Sardinian allies.

The French could not understand how the navvies, and, in due course, the sutlers, who were the scum of the earth, were generally so well behaved. However, all contemporary writers show the reason for this—the omnipotent Provost Marshal and his staff, with their ready resort to the lash! There was also a very efficient Deputy Judge Advocate General with the army, a Mr. Romaine, a man so meticulous and observant that Lord Raglan considered him the eyes of the army.

When the extent of staff incompetence in the Crimea became known, the Horse Guards kept passing glowing accounts of the progress of the new camp at Aldershot to the Press, in an effort to divert public opinion. The fact that in the new camp temporary tentage accommodation cost £100,000, merely reminded the readers that tentage for the Crimean army lay at the bottom of Balaclava harbour!

During March Mr. Russell was complaining of drunken soldiers hiding from the Provost Marshal behind his hut, where a low wall screened them from view. This sanctuary was soon to be denied them, for by the end of the month the advance of the railway had removed the wall and thus solved his problem. It is said that by this time the policing by M.S.C. patrols in Balaclava would have done credit to any large city at home. A dangerous fire in the port area on 1 April was put out by the men of the 71st Regiment, who five days later had one man killed and several injured in a railway accident. By 28 April the railway was handling 240 tons of stores each day.

As June drew to a close Lord Raglan, worn out by his exertions and illness, died. He was conveyed on board H.M.S. *Caradoc* for the journey home on 29 June. The official order for the funeral cortege from headquarters to the harbour, as published in the *London Gazette* on 18 July, shows that the escort, from all units which had been under his command, included two files of troopers from the Mounted Staff Corps bringing up the rear of the procession.

During August several of our general officers received the K.C.B. for their services, and it is recorded that each was first required to pay £164 13s. 4d. to ensure that their name was put on the list, this being an indication of the corruption then existing and which was particularly apparent in respect of the conditions of supplies. It was in the same month that we put cavalry pickets, each accompanied by an M.S.C. trooper, at the archway on the Woronzoff road. This was in an attempt to apprehend soldiers who rode out into the country to loot unattended houses. Although the French had gendarmes attached to their army they did nothing to discourage looting, and this was a cause of great discontent among our men. We alone of the allies endeavoured to respect private property; but it was often evident that our policy was capable of being thwarted.

Early in September the Redan, the main defensive position before Sebastopol, fell. Killed in the assault was Lieutenant Douglas M'Gregor, 97th Regiment, son of the Inspector of the Irish Constabulary, an official who had done much to secure recruits for the M.S.C. when it was raised. When the enemy evacuated Sebastopol later that month cavalry screens were put out to prevent our soldiers going into the town, but as the French, Turkish and Sardinian authorities did not stop their forces from entering and looting, our troops again felt that they were being discriminated against. Many disregarded the orders and went in, preferring to run the risk of flogging by the Provost Marshal if caught.

The M.S.C. were disbanded within a few days of the fall of the fortress and their spiked brass-bound felt helmets were no longer to be seen in the streets and country around Balaclava. They had gone a good job in the short period of their existence, and soon returned to their beats in Ireland, no doubt regretting the loss of the pay of an Ensign which had been their reward while with M.S.C., and all sporting the Crimea medal in due course.

Coincidentally (for the units were unconnected) the M.S.C. was formed at the same time as history was being made back in England by the raising of a separate Corps of Mounted Police as a distinct arm of the service. M.S.C. appear to have come under the control of the Provost Marshal in Balaclava, but they were not Assistant Provosts, as his military assistants were. It is unlikely that the military opinion of the day was that professional policemen were necessary to protect the few remaining inhabitants of Balaclava for, as we will learn later, one of the reasons for forming a military police unit in Aldershot was 'for the protection of the inhabitants of the neighbourhood'. It is a puzzle, but not without precedent, for the Staff Corps of Cavalry of the Peninsula and Waterloo days co-existed with the established Provost Service.

Many Russian stragglers and deserters came into our lines during October and were placed in the custody of Assistant Provost Gillespie, a sergeant of the 93rd Highlanders. We have met him before during the account of the Indian Mutiny; he was an intelligent and efficient N.C.O. On one occasion he was sent by a Colonel Blane to the Russian stores in Sebastopol to see what he could find for his prisoners of war, and was successful in obtaining a complete new kit for each man, with the exception of boots.

Earlier in 1855 an expedition from the allied army had landed in Kertch, and in October, when fighting had ceased, the Turkish element of the force gave great trouble. The

Provost Marshal of the combined contingents was Captain Guernsay, of the 71st, which regiment represented Britain in the force, and he was greatly troubled at the Turkish practice of digging up long-dead Russians and removing the jewellery customarily buried with them. Despite the publication of orders forbidding this practice, cemeteries were raided almost nightly. One day a party of Turkish soldiers, including an officer, robbed and murdered an old Russian lady and then went to her home, apparently with the intention of dealing similarly with her sister, who also lived there. The Provost Marshal heard of their plans and apprehended them, and as they were being flogged Captain Guernsay and his party were attacked by a large band of Turkish soldiers. A soldier of the 71st was badly injured and the Provost Marshal hurt by stones. He drew his revolver and warned the assailants, but was then attacked by the ringleader, a Turkish officer, wielding a sword. After a struggle the officer and three others were arrested and the remainder fled.

By the end of October excessive consumption of alcohol was posing a problem in Kadikoi. The grant of field allowance of sixpence per day to soldiers, plus the extra money they could earn by working on the railway and roads, was partly responsible. A money order system was started and some took advantage of it to send money home. An order was published that every canteen keeper or store owner on whose premises a drunken soldier was found was to be fined £5 for each soldier. No excuses would be accepted. The money was a perk for the Provost Marshal and there is no reason to doubt that he made a handsome income from this source.

Reports in home newspapers during December of drunkenness in the Crimea so annoyed the commander there, General Codrington, that he wrote a protest to the Horse Guards. He enclosed figures for the months of September, October and November showing that on an average just over one man per hundred had been convicted of drunkenness every two days. However, as these figures were of actual cited cases they covered but a fraction of total drunks. As an excuse he offered the facts that over 10,000 men during the period had received arrears of additional working pay and all men were given more than £2 0s. 0d., as arrears of field allowance. One good result of the shake-up this terribly mismanaged war brought in its train was the separation of the Colonial Department from the War Office, a Secretary of State for War was appointed, and the old Board of Ordinance abolished, becoming a branch of the War Office.

Early in January 1856 the unpopularity of the Provost Marshal in Balaclava soared to great heights, and roused intense hatred among the civilian captains of the transports using the harbour. They were particularly incensed at his brutality and hectoring manner, and the fact that officialdom condoned his conduct. In Balaclava at this time were two Provost Marshals, Captain C. Sherrington of 46th Foot and Captain F. Macbean, 92nd Foot. At army headquarters the military magistrate and principal Provost Marshal was Captain R. S. Baynes, 8th Foot, formerly of the Mounted Staff Corps, and the Provost Marshal was Captain G. L. Carmichael, 95th Foot.

A fire in the lines of the Army Works Corps outside Balaclava on St. Patrick's Day killed 16 men and, as many of our soldiers were from the Emerald Isle, no doubt national celebrations led to the tragedy. The first few days of July saw the departure of the French from the Crimea and the last British embarked on 12 July. The terrible weather there from October 1854 to the end of February 1855 had accounted for thousands of our soldiers, who remained as mute testimony to the inefficiency, incompetence and lack of concern that destroyed half our army of the Crimea.

So much for the Tragedy; let us now turn to the Triumph which was the Abyssinian campain of 1867. Forgotten now by all other than military historians, it stands out from the many small wars of this period as a model of organisation and execution. The war became inevitable when demented King Theodore of Ethiopia arrested our Consul, Captain Cameron, and other Europeans together with their families. Even so force of arms was only resorted to when all other methods of persuasion failed. The expedition was mounted from Bombay, with certain specialists, including a Royal Engineer Signals Company, from the United Kingdom. Staff in Bombay studied the Persian campaign of 1856-57, the post-Mutiny field force organisations and logistics, and the 1860 China expedition. The terrible maladministration and disregard of human life during the Crimea War was not to be repeated. The end result was that the Abyssinian campaign did much to remove the stigma of the Crimea, and there is a great element of truth in the contemporary belief that this was because the home government and Horse Guards had little to do with it!

Planning commenced in July, and the subsequent record of the campaign, published in 1870, summarised the appreciation of the Provost requirement as follows:

> In all operations in a foreign country an efficient Police Force, accompanying the army, has proved to be essential, not only for maintaining discipline when soldiers are out of sight of their Officers, but in order to protect the people.
>
> It had been usual to appoint a Non-Commissioned Officer as Provost Marshal, as these duties were of an unpleasant nature, generally restricted to soldiers; but, as in the present case, the control would be extensive, and looking to the importance of having an experienced Officer at the head of the police, it was considered well to appoint a Superior Officer as Provost Marshal, with efficient N.C.O.s as assistants, and some selected men of other grades.
>
> As regards the power to be exercised by the Provost Marshal's establishment, these had generally been, according to Military Law, defined by the Commander of the Forces in so far as extreme punishment was concerned, but the Provost Marshal had generally been entrusted with considerable discretionary power.

At first sight one wonders why military mounted police were not used. The answer lies in the fact that there were none of the type controlled by Provost Marshals on the Indian establishment, and those at Aldershot were a purely local force.

Lieutenant-General Sir R. Napier was appointed to the command on 17 August, and the plan developed was for a landing at Zula on the Red Sea coast, followed by an advance to Magdala, where the captives were being held, then a return to the base and re-embarkation. Among the specialists brought from England were photographers, a geographer, a zoologist, and an archaeologist. The thorough arrangements included the provision of 300 round shot and a supply of unserviceable hammocks for burials at sea.

Landings at Zula started in the first week of October and gradually built up until the force was 12,000 strong. An Indian army in those days was accompanied by a huge number of followers, and its own bazaar to supply their wants and comforts for the troops. Regulations of bazaars was the duty of the Provost Marshal—indeed, we have already seen how in very early times regulation of prices in camps was one of the Provost Marshal's tasks. The Indian system was a development of this ancient obligation.

Napier's orders for the general control of camps laid down that police must be on duty night and day to keep out natives who were not on official business. Each camp without a bazaar should have a flag denoting the site of the market, and a policeman on duty there to keep order and to forbid access to persons carrying arms. A guard must be conveniently situated to assist the policeman should it be necessary.

The orders specifically stated:

> A Provost Marshal with an efficient establishment will be appointed for every camp. The camp Police will be under his orders. Natives of the country should never be flogged except with the approval of the Chief attached to the station for the settlement of disputes, etc. In the event of a night attack it will be the duty of the Provost Marshal and his assistants to keep order among the camp followers.

Bazaars were established at Zula, Senafe, Antola, and Kumayli. The Provost Marshal received an allowance of 300 rupees monthly, and Major Shepherd, Bombay Staff Corps, was both Principal Superintendent of Bazaars, stationed at the main one in Zula, and Provost Marshal; in addition to this allowance he received staff pay. The station staff officer at Kumayli was appointed to act as Provost Marshal and Superintendent of Bazaars in addition to his normal duties. For this extra commitment he was given an allowance of 50 rupees monthly.

The orders published by the Provost Marshal at Zula for the regulating of bazaars in all camps were as follows:

1. All licensed dealers are permitted to sell by retail (to be drunk on the premises), ale, wine and spirits, to anyone who does not belong to the European Regiments or Batteries, to the Naval Brigade or to the ships in the harbour.
2. All wines, etc., drunk on the premises, should be paid for on the spot, as no complaints for non-payment will be entertained.
3. No wines, spirits or beer can be taken out of the Bazaar, either on board ship or for transport inland, without a pass countersigned by the Superintendent of Bazaars.
4. Officers and others requiring wines, spirits or beer from the Bazaar can obtain stamped passes on application at the Bazaar Office, but it is particularly requested that all passes may be returned to the Bazaar Office or destroyed when no longer required.
5. No ale, wine or spirits, unless drunk on the premises, are to be sold without a stamped pass, signed by the Superintendent of Bazaars.
6. Any man in the Bazaar found with country liquor in his possession will be flogged and turned out of camp, in addition to any other penalty that may be awarded.
7. No shops will be open before six o'clock in the morning or after gunfire in the evening.
8. Dealers and owners of stores will be held responsible for good order on their premises. No excuse whatever will be received, and the Police have orders to enter any house at any hour if they have reason for supposing that the Bazaar Regulations are being infringed.
9. All dealers in wine, beer and spirits are required to keep one sample bottle of every liquor they sell on a table in their stores, where it can be seen by the Police.
10. Anyone giving information to the Police, of the violation of these rules, or any other infringement, will be rewarded.

   The strictest punishments will be enforced after the publication of these rules.

The police were found from members of all units in the force, both European and Indian. Their duties included the enforcement of camp hygiene regulations and patrolling store areas and unit lines. Water point duties were also undertaken, anti-plundering measures enforced, and straggling from the camp areas prevented, but after one muleteer had been murdered by local natives solely for his blanket the troops and followers became less inclined to wander far from camp. By 3 February 1868 the police at the Zula headquarters totalled 77 all ranks, with three horses, for which water was rationed on the scale of 115 gallons a day for all the men and 15 for the horses. Each station, no matter how small, had its complement of policemen, and not the least important of their duties was to ensure the animals in convoys arriving or departing were fed and watered.

The advance commenced and the first camp constructed was at Senafe, the second at Adigral, and the third at Antalo, which became a larger base than the others. The last post was established at Kumayli, where the forces gathered for the final push to Magdala, 400 miles from their starting point at Zula. The long lines of communication had to be constantly patrolled, and on two occasions mail carriers were attacked and the mails stolen. The only recorded case of murder of an European was on 28 May 1868, towards the close of the campaign, when a civilian, Mr. Dufton, employed by 'G' Branch, disobeyed orders and attempted to travel through Kumayli Pass alone, and was robbed and killed by members of the Shobo tribe.

A small post was opened at Dildi for final concentration before the attack on Magdala, and in consequence of a disturbance between troops in March, Lieutenant Warburton, Royal Artillery, was made camp commandant. He appointed a Provost Marshal with a few soldiers as police, and took all necessary precautions for the protection of the camp.

On 10 April 1868 the army of Emperor Theodore met one brigade of the British at Aroge and was decisively beaten, leaving over 2,000 dead and wounded on the field, the British losses being two dead and eight wounded. The comment of the emperor when he saw the ruin of his army has been preserved; he said, 'I have been conquered by the advance guard alone'!

Magdala fell on 13 April for the loss of eight British wounded, and Theodore committed suicide, ironically enough with a revolver presented to him in happier times by his principal captive, Captain Cameron. All the prisoners, a total of 61, were released unharmed. The town was plundered and the loot sold by auction, the proceeds being passed back to the troops in form of prize money. It was decided that the fort at Magdala would be destroyed and this was done as a precise military operation, the orders for which were as follows:

General Orders 1050 of 1868

The following orders for the destruction of the magazine and buildings on Magdala are forwarded to Maj. Gen. Sir Charles Staveley KCB, Commanding 1st Division, for guidance.

1. The Troops, with the exception of the Sappers and Miners, under the direction of Capt. Goodfellow, RE will be entirely withdrawn from Magdala by 4 pm tomorrow, the 7th instant.

2. Capt Goodfellow, RE, will then destroy the Kafirba Gate, and will ascertain by careful observation whether he can explode the powder magazine without injury to the church. He will also consider whether it will be safe to explode the magazine first and then fire the remaining buildings successively, commencing from the Kafirba Gate, or southern part of the fort, and finally, after withdrawing the Sappers, will blow up the northern entrance, under such arrangements as will prevent any injury to his party. Should he be able to blow up the magazine without injury to the church, he will do so, otherwise he will fire the building in such a way as to prevent any injury to his men from the accidental explosion of the magazine.

3. He will then join the withdrawn garrison of Magdala, which will return to the camp occupied by the 23rd Punjab Infantry, where they will rest for the night, and be prepared to march to Talanta under such detailed instructions as they may receive from Major General Sir Charles Staveley on the 18th instant.

4. As the destruction of the buildings of Magdala may be the signal for the Galla's to come forward in considerable numbers, it will be necessary that the garrison should not pass Islamgie until joined by the Sappers.

5. No stragglers however should be permitted to remain behind. A Sergeant of Provost should be in attendance, and inflict summary punishment on any who may attempt to linger behind for the sake of plunder or any other object.

6. Care should be taken that the orders on this point should be made known to the camp followers.

7. No watering parties or picquets should be overlooked, and all baggage should be sent away early enough to be clear of the troops.

Camp before Magdala   By Order,
16th April 1868   T. J. Holland Capt, A.Q.M.G.
                                      in charge of the Quartermaster
                                      General's Office.

Evacuation went according to plan, but the local tribes harassed the rearguard. Several followers who straggled were killed, but frequent raids on the baggage were unsuccessful, many raiders being killed. Dildi was closed on 29 April and the troops slowly withdrew stage by stage to Zula where the last troops arrived in late May. Lieutenant-Colonel Bray of the 4th of Foot was placed in command of the rearguard with authority to execute any marauders attempting to rob the baggage. He was allocated two drummers to carry out any floggings he might order for troops or followers. The commander left on 10 June and the rearguard on the 18th, and so closed the model campaign.

When one considers that complete wooden townships had been imported, a railway constructed, and wells found right up to Dildi, it was a fine piece of organisation. The railway was removed rail by rail and taken back to India or Aden, just a few distorted lines were left behind, and the wells were left to the care of the tribes to utilise or neglect according to their whim.

This campaign was unusual right to the end, for the medal eventually issued bore the recipient's name on the reverse, instead of on the rim, as was customary. The white, red, white ribbon was of a different width to that normally pertaining, and the disc of the medal was suspended from the ribbon by a crown, a complete departure from tradition that has remained unique.

Of interest to those to whom Provost duties and traditions are professionally important is the report of Major R. M. Bonner, of the Bombay Staff Corps, who had relieved Major Shepherd, made after the conclusion of the campaign, the relevant parts of which read:

It now becomes my duty to report to you the working of the Bazaar Establishment in Abyssinia from the arrival of the force in the country.

The largest and most important was the Zula Bazaar, which prior to the termination of the campaign rapidly grew into a town. Almost everything was procurable here, the wants of a large fleet in the bay have been supplied, and the necessaries of life have been obtained at prices generally lower than those prevailing in Bombay, and I hope that it has been of the greatest assistance to the Force, that it has also been a relief to the Commissariat Department.

With the large number of sailors, the Europeans employed on the railway and the very mixed population, a large number of whom were composed of the lowest classes of Egypt and the Mediterranean Seaports, there has been a good deal of Magisterial and Police work, but there were no serious crimes, the principal offences being cases of theft. The Police that have been employed here have been found sufficient to protect the residents and to maintain order.

The other Bazaars have been formed at Kumayli and Senafe. About 70 shops have been opened at Kumayli, which, from being the Headquarters of the Transport Train, has been a place of considerable importance during the last three months.

Owing to the difficulty of procuring carriage there was some delay in getting shops up to Senafe, but about 20 have been established there, which would have proved of immense benefit to the Commissariat had a force been detained there for the rains.

The Kumayli Bazaar was established on 15th of February, after which I proceeded to Senafe and was employed in collecting grass and forage at Guna-Guna, when I was ordered to the front by double marches. On arrival at Ashangi I received an order from His Excellency the C in C to return to Antalo, where I discharged the duties of Provost Marshal and received charge of the Conservancy Establishment there. On Major Shepherd's departure for Bombay I returned here and received charge of the office at Zula.

I am glad to be able to report that the whole of the Bazaars that have been established here have been self supporting, and that the expense of maintaining the Police and establishments have entailed no cost upon the government.

That final sentence of the report must have given the Command Secretary of the day great satisfaction! Sir Robert Napier became Lord Napier of Magdala; and before leaving this episode of British arms it may be of interest to readers to know why Theodore incarcerated the Europeans—apparently he was angry because he had written to Queen Victoria and had not received an answer!

CHAPTER XIV

RAISING OF THE MILITARY POLICE AND THEIR FIRST CAMPAIGN

The Sand of the desert was sodden red,
Red with the wreck of the square that broke,
The Gatlings jammed and the Colonel's dead,
And the Regiment's blind with dust and smoke.

Sir Henry Newbolt

GENERATIONS OF SCHOOLBOYS have thrilled at these lines immortalising the battle of Abu Klea. For The Royal Military Police this battle has a special significance: among the dead was an officer who had commanded military policemen in their first campaign. According to the medal roll there was only one actual military policeman in the battle. However, let us first look in at the birth of the corps, the third birth that is, for the 1813 and 1854 attempts had come to nothing, as we have learned. It is said that the idea for a permanent home for the army in Aldershot was Prince Albert's, and that may well be, for some of his military ideas were very good. However, it was on 13 February 1853 that the first load of materials arrived from the contractors, Heywood and Nixon, and with the subsequent concentration of soldiers in close proximity to the shanty town that sprung up it soon became obvious that regimental pickets were not the answer to the problems arising from garrison life. In due course all home cavalry regiments received a copy of this Horse Guards letter on 13 June 1855:

Sir,

    The General Commanding in Chief, deeming it necessary to form a Corps of Mounted Police for the cantonment of Aldershot, and with a view to the internal organisation *of a permanent Corps,* desires me to call for a return of NC Officers and soldiers, not exceeding five in all, as you may consider fit for this duty. They should be not less than five years service, if of ten the better, of sober habits, intelligent, active and capable of exercising a sound discretion.

They will be organised into one Corps under an Officer, and subject to the immediate orders of the General Officer Commanding the Cantonment.

P. A. Wetherall
Adjutant General

There can be no doubt that this letter is the birth certificate of the Royal Military Police as we now know it. If we disregard Wellington's letter of 24 March 1813 (which I personally consider the birth date) then we must accept Wetherall's letter as one, of which the intent is beyond argument. During July a total of 21 other ranks were selected for service in the new arm, personnel coming from 2nd Dragoons, 3rd Light Dragoons, 16th Lancers, 7th Hussars, and 15th Hussars. Corps pay of 1s. 6d. daily for sergeants and 1s. 0d. for privates was authorised. Junior N.C.O.s appear to have been overlooked. The job specification was defined as:

To be employed as a Corps of Mounted Police for the preservation of Good Order in the camp at Aldershot, and for the protection of the inhabitants of the neighbourhood.

During October No. 541 Troop Sergeant-Major Thomas Trout, 7th Hussars, reported for duty with the new corps. He stayed for 26 years, dying in office as Major T. Trout, Provost Marshal and Commandant of Military Police. By 21 November he had been appointed Acting Provost Marshal at 4s. 6d. daily. An Assistant Provost Marshal was then nominated for each brigade, and regiments in the garrison were authorised to attach men for service with the military police, for which they received an extra 4d. per day. Mr. Trout became an unpaid quartermaster on 13 December 1861, and on 1 April 1869 was commissioned as Provost Marshal at 12s. 6d. per day.

Under an authority of 11 December 1865 the establishment had been increased to 32 all ranks, and in 1872 military police for the first time accompanied troops on exercises. Three years later a set of Orders for the use of military police were published. Control of sutlers and supervision of loose women—ancient responsibilities—still remained, and there was the added task of familiarising themselves with public houses in their area—this possibly a labour of love! An entirely new requirement was the instruction to work in conjunction with the civil police. It is of great interest that these Orders referred only to 'Military Police', the description 'Mounted Police' having fallen into disuse.

A military police corps as a regular component of our army was authorised on 31 July 1877 as the result of a Horse Guards letter, 12709/200 C 10382, dated 12 May 1877. All serving personnel who came up to the standards now set were transferred in on 1 August, those not reaching the standards were returned to their original regiments. There is insufficient space here to note all the founding members, but there is one whose service does deserve commemoration. No. 2 in the new roll was Quartermaster Sergeant George Bell, who was responsible for feeding, clothing, arming and mounting the military police until his retirement on 20 July 1911—34 years of service in one appointment which included two initial raisings of corps and two mobilisations—a remarkable previously unacknowledged achievement! He must have been well loaded with years when he eventually retired.

During 1877 the establishment was again increased to total 75 other ranks, and by then there were military police in Woolwich, Shorncliffe and Portsmouth, in addition to Aldershot. Another quartermaster's commission was granted on 1 April 1878, when No. 1, Sergeant-Major William Silk became the second officer in the corps. He was the son-in-law of Major Trout, whom he succeeded when that worthy died in office on 13 February 1881. Brass tablets commemorating these officers can be seen in the Warriors' chapel of Aldershot garrison church.

As a young soldier, Silk, then in the 9th Lancers, had taken part in the Relief of Lucknow, and later operated in field forces where Bruce's military police were used. He was therefore well aware of the significance of the red turban. Later as a member of the 14th Hussars he had worn a red plume in his helmet. It seems possible that it is to him that we owe the scarlet cap of today's military policemen. There are other theories on its origin, but I favour the Silk connection.

No. 3 on the roll of the corps was Sergeant-Major Charles Broakes. He was commissioned as a quartermaster in the corps on 13 March 1881 to fill the vacancy created by Silk's appointment as Provost Marshal. In due course he became the third Provost Marshal to come from the ranks of the military police.

Following a mutiny in the Egyptian army, and widespread murders of Europeans, the Khedive appealed to England for help. We responded by bombarding Alexandria on 14 July 1882 and landing Marines to protect non-Moslems from slaughter by the rebels, who, under Arabi Pasha, had become a formidable force. Captain Lord Charles Beresford, R.N., was given the task of reforming the Alexandria city police from 300 men who had remained loyal. These he distinguished from their mutinous comrades by tying red ribbons round their arms, thereby continuing the ancient connection of red with law enforcement.

When the advance elements of our army headquarters landed in Alexandria they included Lieutenant-Colonel William Cleland as Provost Marshal. Reinforcements left Aldershot on 2 August, after inspection by the Duke of Connaught, and included military mounted police proceeding on operations for the first time in the history of their corps. Only a few days before this the army reserve had been called out. Many who had been serving with the metropolitan police were ordered to the Military Police Depot at Aldershot, where they formed the nucleus of a new corps, the Military Foot Police.

By 2 August we had installed army headquarters in the Khedives Summer Palace in Ismailia. The capture of Arabi Pasha's second-in-command, Mahmond Fahmi, later that month proved a great asset. He had planned the defences at Tel-El-Kebir and could see no reason why he should not describe them to us, which he did whole-heartedly.

At the end of August M.M.P. and M.F.P. reinforcements arrived, and Lieutenant C. Broakes was appointed Provost Marshal of the Ismailia base, with a Mr. Robert Blattner as his interpreter at one pound a day. Broakes had been summoned from Ireland, where he returned after only six weeks in Egypt. During his short stay he earned a very good reputation, and a written commendation from the Greek Vice Consul. Troops serving in this campaign were awarded the Egyptian General Service medal, with clasps according to engagements in which they were present. They also received a medal awarded by the Khedive, known as the Khedival Star. Broakes received both, but no clasps. His E.G.S.M. is inscribed on the rim 'Lt. C. Broakes Mil. Mtd. Police', and is the first medal to be awarded to a military police officer. This unique award now rests in the R.M.P. museum at Chichester.

A contingent of troops arrived from India with Major H. C. Marsh of the Bengal Staff Corps as their Provost Marshal. Provost Marshal at the battle of Tel-El-Kebir was Lieutenant-Colonel Cleland, with Captain C. E. Becket, 3rd Hussars, commanding military mounted police. There is a reference to his men in *All Sir Garnet*, by J. Lehmann, published by Jonathan Cape in 1967, and to whom I am· indebted for permission to reproduce this extract:

> Looting was proceeding at a furious pace at a large enemy camp a few yards away. By tradition the belongings of the enemy become the property of the victors. Highlanders, Guards and the Royal Irish charged through the many rows of abandoned tents. In comic relief to the serious scenes enacted earlier that day, here a tall Highlander would be garbed in the long flowing robes of a desert Sheik; there a diminutive cockney would be strutting about under an enormous turban, carrying an arsenal of fancy pistols and daggers, in a broad colourful cummerbund. Others rode about on factious horses whose owners, in their haste, had taken off on foot. On returning to their respective units they were forced to surrender what they had taken. An energetic Provost Marshal and his large, stern faced body of Mounted Police, acting under Sir Garnet's strict orders, quickly put an end to the pernicious searching.

A total of 59 military policemen received the medal and
Tel-El-Kebir clasps. Two officers and 15 men received the
medal without clasp.

When Cairo was occupied Lieutenant-Colonel Cleland
became Provost Marshal of Egypt and earned a reputation
for his fondness for hanging. An officer who particularly
distinguished himself with the military foot police was
Lieutenant W. A. Cough, OxLI, who was awarded with a
brevet majority and the Order of Osmanieh 5th Class.

General Wolseley left for home on 21 October and a
period of reorganisation followed. The Egyptian army was
put on sound lines under British officers, but received a
severe setback in October when a body under Hicks Pasha
was annihilated in upper Egypt by the forces of the Mahdi,
whose Moslem revival was sweeping all before it; conquered
people either joined in or were put to death. Shortly after
this a second Egyptian force under General Valentine Baker
was routed, many of his British officers being killed, as were
37 out of 40 seconded British policemen. Demoralised
Egyptian soldiers fled back to the port of Saukim, where
the garrison promptly mutinied and refused to fight.

The British withdrawal from Egypt was halted and Marines
landed at Saukim to assist the remaining loyal members of
the garrison and the civil police to organise defence of the
port and town. A relief force left for Saukim in February
1884 and military police were included. Two N.C.O.s,
No. 1300 Lance-corporal A. Gould and No. 75 Corporal
T. Howse, were present at the second battle of El Teb in
which the latter was wounded. He has the dubious honour of
being the first military police battle casualty. It is recorded
that of General Sir Archibald Graham's four orderlies one
was killed and two wounded. It is possible that Corporal
Howse was one of these, for it was the custom to supply
M.P. N.C.O.s as senior officers' orderlies, a habit started by
Wellington with the Staff Corps of Cavalry.

Meanwhile in England parliament was deciding what to
do about General Charles Gordon, who was besieged in
Khartoum, the Mahdi's base. Our forces withdrew to lower
Egypt, leaving a strong force with naval support to hold

Saukim and patrol the frontier. Fresh troops continued to arrive in Egypt and General Sir Garnet Wolseley returned to assume command again. Lieutenant-Colonel Cleland left to return to his regiment in Ceylon, and Lieutenant-Colonel J. H. Sandwich, Royal Marine's Light Infantry, became Provost Marshal of Egypt. In early summer young Lieutenant C. F. N. Macready, Gordon Highlanders, became Staff Lieutenant Provost in Alexandria, thus commencing a police connection that was to last for many years. The dual appointment of A.P.M. Cairo and officer-in-command military police Cairo was assumed by Captain G. C. P. Freeman Williams, Royal Sussex, with Lieutenant J. Maxwell, Black Watch, becoming Staff Captain Provost, and Lieutenant R. H. Maxwell camp commandant and Provost Marshal at Wolseley's headquarters.

Military police in Cairo were often called on to assist Cairo city police during riots, which have always been a popular pastime in that city. The A.P.M. there was given the added task of superintendent of a military prison we had established in the citadel. Alexandria also came in for its share of civil disorder; one common cause being our refusal to pay compensation for our bombardment. Crowds there had a great respect for the huge horses of our mounted military police, who on one occasion saved the chief of police, a Swiss officer named Major Marks. His men had abandoned him in the midst of a hostile mob. Our M.M.P. arrived just in time to prevent him being lynched. Alexandria with its constant turnover of foreign seamen, simmering local population, and popularity with the dregs of the Levant, was an ideal training area for crowd control and internal security duties.

Troops continued to arrive from the United Kingdom, India, Malta and Gibraltar, and on 7 October Canadian voyageurs disembarked. These men, many of whom were full-blooded Red Indians, had come to man boats on the Nile. Lieutenant Macready was obliged to augment his military police with a company of Guards Camel Corps with fixed bayonets to keep the new arrivals away from native liquor sellers crowding the dockyard perimeter fence.

During October the expeditionary force started moving up country, the mounted military police detachment being led by No. 113 Sergeant-Major J. L. Burke, soon to be commissioned. On arrival at Saukim Lieutenant-Colonel R. W. F. Gordon, Argyll and Sutherland Highlanders, became Provost Marshal. Captain R. H. Maxwell established a military police post at Dongola, where Wolseley set up his headquarters. Maxwell also followed the Provost Marshal's traditional role when he organised a camp market.

The historic battle of Abu Klea was fought on 17 October 1885. Near disaster occurred when the enemy broke into our square and the Gatling gun jammed. A gentleman volunteer, Colonel Fred Burnaby, died a hero's death, under circumstances recorded for all time in a poem by Sir Henry Newbolt, part of which heads this chapter. The only military policeman present at the battle was No. 23 Corporal W. Harris, M.F.P. His medal with the unique Abu Klea clasp is among the collection in the R.M.P. museum.

With the news of the murder of General Gordon plans to advance to Khartoum were shelved. A Saukim field force was formed to hold that port and watch the frontier. Captain Freeman Williams joined the force in a non-Provost capacity, and Lieutenant Macready took over his appointment in Cairo. The S.S. *Persian Monarch* arrived in Saukim on 13 March with a draft of 13 M.M.P. and their horses.

In Cairo Macready was ordered to arrest Zubir Pasha, a slave trader turned diplomat who, it was feared, might embrace Mahdism and incite the country against us. At 5.10 p.m. on 14 March, accompanied by 16 M.F.P. and 12 M.M.P., Macready arrested all the suspect's sons. One dived out of the opposite door of the carriage into which he had been put, straight into the arms of a huge military policeman, waiting there for just such an eventuality. At the same time the father was arrested in Alexandria and the following day the family left in H.M.S. *Iris* for exile in Gibraltar.

In Saukim the Hadendowa tribe, the main local adherents to the Mahdi's cause, started creeping into our lines at night, naked and greased all over. During one such raid they stole the Provost Marshal's horse and murdered his native servant. Osman Digma, the Mahdi's local commander, was well beaten near Nasheen on 22 March, and on 2 April, after a body of 591 volunteers from New South Wales joined, his home town of Tamai was captured and razed. The campaign then ended as there was no reason, politically or otherwise, to proceed into the Sudanese hinterland. Wolseley again returned home, and local tribes were levied to guard Saukim and the frontier. Appropriate clasps were issued for the various desert actions, and one for Saukim.

Any danger remaining of a resurgence of Mahdism vanished on 29 June when that worthy died of smallpox, thus removing the threat to Egypt. On return to Cairo Captain Freeman Williams resumed his old appointment and Macready, now a Captain, became Staff Captain Provost at Alexandria, where he organised a very efficient anti-vice squad. Two military police N.C.O.s were employed in plain clothes, this being possibly the first occasion that N.C.O.s in civilian clothing were used on duty. A register was maintained of all local prostitutes and each woman was issued with a card. Volunteer medical officers periodically examined them and gave treatment when necessary, making an appropriate entry on the card. One such volunteer was Captain Mungo Park, later to lose his life in Central Africa when on an expedition with Stanley. In a very short time V.D. casualties were reduced to two per cent. of the normal sickness rate. Unfortunately, the arrival of a less enlightened district commander caused disbandment of the vice squad, and in no time the infection rate was back to the original eight per cent. History repeated itself during the Second World War, when a similarly bigotted commander closed licensed brothels in Egypt. Casualties inflicted by the whores of the country soon rivalled those sustained in the Western Desert.

In both Cairo and Alexandria barracks were built for our forces; those allocated to the military police in Cairo, Bab-el-Habid, became the home of the corps until evacuation of Cario in 1947. They then became a school for illiterate Egyptian soldiers until they were eventually demolished.

Under Horse Guards letter 407/1885, dated 2 July 1885, M.F.P. became a permanent corps of our regular army, at which time there were nine United Kingdom detachments.

Three days later Provost Marshal William Silk died and was succeeded by Captain Charles Broakes who came over from Ireland where he had been A.P.M. In December the following year the commander-in-chief wrote to express his satisfaction with the work of M.F.P. As a measure of protection it was decided in March 1887 that all M.P. privates should be appointed acting-lance-corporals. Only a percentage received the pay of appointment until February 1953, when all lance-corporals became paid. The mid-1880s saw an upsurge of violence in Ireland and an increase in subversion among Irish regiments. M.P. establishments were therefore increased to 75 M.M.P. and 197 M.F.P., a total of 272 for both corps. A section of 15 N.C.O.s were permanently stationed in Egypt, and large detachments were maintained in Dublin, The Curragh, Cork and Belfast.

After the commissioning of Sergeant-Major John L. Emerson as a quartermaster and honorary lieutenant in 1889, he fought a long paper battle with the Horse Guards before he won his point, and became a Q.M. of M.P. instead of being a General List appointment. By then M.P.s were familiar figures on State occasions and at the annual Royal Tournament at the Royal Horticultural Hall in London. Whenever the army put on a big parade M.P.s were to be seen. Most civilian police forces with whom they came into contact recognised their professionalism and dedication. In 1892 the pernicious practice of bringing men in from other corps to fill senior N.C.O. vacancies ceased; henceforth promotions were to come from within. Unfortunately, soon the corps were to start looking outside for its officers. This state of affairs continued until 1953 when an R.M.P. Corps of Officers was formed.

In Africa a para-military police force, the Mashonaland Military Police, was raised during 1893 in Fort Salisbury—now Salisbury, capital of Zimbabwe-Rhodesia. Later the name was changed to British South Africa Police, and they suffered heavy casualties during the Mashonaland Rebellion of 1896 and the Matabelle Rising the following year. In these operations the force won a V.C., a D.S.O. and a C.M.G.

The *Graphic* newspaper published an illustration of Major Broakes and some of his men on duty in Aldershot on 25 August 1894. On his retirement not long afterwards he was personally thanked by H.R.H. the Duke of Connaught for his devoted service. Major J. L. Emerson then became Provost Marshal, the last to do so from the ranks of the military police.

One of the more humorous military police commitments in Aldershot was that of running a garrison pound for stray animals. Before an impounded animal was released there was a fee of 2s. 6d., payable to the Provost Marshal. As the area was and still is favoured by gipsies, there were many amusing, and occasionally ugly, scenes as gipsy owners tried to repossess their stock without paying.

October 1896 saw the departure of the first military police for service on Malta, and by March the following year the detachment comprised a sergeant, three corporals, and 16 lance-corporals. Military police remained on the island for over eighty years.

The Diamond Jubilee of Queen Victoria in 1897 saw a very large military police presence, and by then military police were permanently stationed in 17 locations:

Aldershot	Chatham	Dover	Portsmouth
Alexandria	Colchester	Dublin	Shorncliffe
Belfast	Cork	Edinburgh	The Currah
Cairo	Devonport	Gosport	Valetta
			Woolwich

Corps Order No. 7 on 10 October 1899 was no doubt received with satisfaction by all ranks, for it permitted retention of corps pay for up to 61 days while in hospital because of injuries received on duty, provided that a court of enquiry confirmed that such was the case. Previously corps pay ceased on admission to hospital no matter what the reason for the indisposition.

CHAPTER XV

THE BOER WAR AND BEYOND

THE CAUSES of the South African War of 1899–1902 (better known as the Boer War) were many. Some regarded it as phase two of the Boer War of 1880, a campaign in which we received some severe jolts. Possibly that received psychologically by Captain Campbell, 94th Regiment, Provost Marshal of Pretoria, stayed with him for some time. With the peace his Boer prisoners changed overnight from being rebellious subjects to members of a foreign nation. The Provost Marshal, together with the British garrison, had to quit the city, now the capital of the Transvaal Republic, in a hurry, no doubt to the accompaniment of suitable comments from the erstwhile prisoners!

Be that as it may, when we did not reply by 1700 hours on 11 October 1899 to an ultimatum from President Kruger, war was on. Only two days later Captain (Quartermaster) J. W. M. Wood was transferred from 1st Dragoons to the military police and appointed Provost Marshal to succeed Major Emerson, who had retired. He came to a Corps in the throes of mobilisation. Most mainland United Kingdom detachments returned to Aldershot, leaving only the sick behind, and about half the strength of the Irish establishment headed for home. The first draft of a sergeant-major and 10 N.C.O.s of M.F.P. sailed on the S.S. *Trojan* on 18 October with the headquarters staff of the commander-designate, General Redvers Bullers, V.C. Three days later a sergeant-major and 14 N.C.O.s of M.M.P. followed on the S.S. *Moor*. Also on board was Major Hon. J. H. G. Byng, 10th Hussars, going out as the army Provost Marshal.

By 22 November the total strength of military police in or en route for South Africa was 150 all ranks, disposed as follows:

	W.O.s	S./Sgt.	Sgt.	Cpl.	L/cpl.	Corps
Army H.Q.						
Staff	1	1	—	1	8	M.F.P.
Staff	1	—	1	2	11	M.M.P.
P.M.s Orderly	—	—	—	—	1	M.M.P.
A.A.Q.M.G.s Orderly	—	—	—	—	1	M.M.P.
L. of C.	—	—	1	1	8	M.F.P.
H.Q. 1st Division	1	—	1	2	7	M.M.P.
H.Q. 2nd Division	—	—	1	1	8	M.M.P.
H.Q. 3rd Division	—	—	1	2	7	M.M.P.
H.Q. 1st Cavalry Division	—	—	—	1	3	M.M.P.
H.Q. 1st Brigade	—	1	—	2	7	M.F.P.
H.Q. 2nd Brigade	—	—	1	1	8	M.F.P.
H.Q. 3rd Brigade	—	—	1	1	8	M.F.P.
H.Q. 5th Brigade	—	—	1	1	6	M.F.P.
H.Q, 6th Brigade	—	—	1	—	8	M.F.P.
H.Q. 10th Brigade	—	—	1	—	9	M.F.P.
H.Q. 1st Cavalry Brigade	—	—	1	1	3	M.M.P.
HQ. 2nd Cavalry Brigade	—	—	1	1	3	M.M.P.
Totals	3	2	13	19	113	= 150

These figures included a few reservists and nine N.C.O.s due for discharge who re-engaged voluntarily in order to proceed on active service. Medically unfit men were sent to keep a small presence in the United Kingdom detachments, and 25 cavalry men, together with 20 from infantry regiments, were posted to Aldershot to assist the remnants of the military police. These soldiers were called 'Lent Men' and wore their original uniforms with the addition of an M.P. armband worn above the left elbow when on duty. All were made lance-corporals, and the order implementing this is quite unique in that it records the absence of the corps from England. The preamble read:

Corps Orders by Major J. W. M. Wood, Commanding Military
Police Corps, Aldershot.

18th November 1899

The Commanding Officer is pleased to make the following
appointments during the absence of the Military Police Corps
in South Africa. The appointments carry with them the pay
of the rank and the Extra Duty Pay provided for their temporary
ranks in Article 863 of the Pay Warrant etc., etc.

In South Africa the onrush of the enemy had been
dramatic and unexpected; nothing of this mode of warfare
appeared in the text books and he soon overran vast areas of
our territory. Several important towns were besieged and
British morale was reduced to a low ebb. The only good thing
was that at home the war produced a flood of patriotic songs,
many of which are still with us today.

Our troops bottled up in Ladysmith, where Lieutenant-
General Sir George White commanded, were formed into the
4th Infantry Division, the Provost Marshal of which was
Captain H. N. Robinson, King's Liverpool Regiment. He
continued in this appointment in a mobile column after the
division, in common with the others, was broken up into
these handy-sized hard-hitting little formations. Captain
Robinson was present at the battle of Laings Nek and
throughout the operations in Natal.

Military police serving in Malta and Egypt were moved to
South Africa, but had not arrived by the time our 1st, 2nd
and 3rd Infantry Divisions moved off. General Buller's plan
was to pacify Natal with the 3rd Division under Lieutenant-
General W. Gatacre, and for the 1st and 2nd Divisions, under
Lieutenant-Generals Lord Methuen and Sir C. F. Clery respectively, to march to relieve the diamond town of Kimberley.
We suffered a defeat on the Modder River and again at
Rosmead on 28 November. It was during the former action
that Major H. F. Coleridge, Loyal North Lancs., serving as an
A.P.M., won the D.S.O., as far as is known this being the first
to be won by a Provost officer. It was in the reforming period
after these actions that the mobile columns were instituted.
Major Coleridge joined one as its A.P.M. and served throughout the war in that capacity.

With the arrival of military police reinforcements, the dispositions of the N.C.O.s were changed and they were posted nominally to the headquarters of divisions for re-deployment as the requirements dictated—general headquarters had 12 M.F.P. and 12 M.M.P.; each division had 20 M.F.P.; and 12 M.M.P. went to the cavalry division. In certain locations on the lines of communication M.F.P. to a total of 16 overall were posted. As there were eight divisional headquarters this gives a total of 212 appointments. In addition there was a large detachment of M.M.P. and M.F.P. in Cape Town, with smaller detachments in other parts. Many N.C.O.s were used as orderlies; indeed, General Buller's own orderly was a military policeman.

These figures include, as they arrived, the N.C.O.s detailed for service with the 5th Division; Lieutenant-General Sir C. Warren (6th Division); Lieutenant-General T. Kelley-Kenny, and the 7th Division; Lieutenant-General C. Tucker; and the 9th Division (Lieutenant-General H. Colville), which was created from troops already in South Africa. The 8th Division never went out, but some of its militia battalions arrived to man the lines of communication. It appears that the maximum strength of the military police in South Africa rose to well over three hundred at the height of the campaign, and there is no doubt that but for the arrival of the A.P.M. Egypt and his men in the early days the military police strength would have been unequal to the tasks the corps was called upon to undertake.

When Major Byng went off as A.P.M. and column commander, the office of A.P.M. at G.H.Q. was assumed by Major A. G. Chichester, Royal Irish Rifles. At that time a junior intelligence officer at G.H.Q. was Captain J. F. C. Fuller, who as a major-general later became a well-known military writer. He is recorded as having received a pass from the A.P.M. authorising him to 'go anywhere, at any time, by any means'. Add 'in any dress' and we have the endorsement found in the Special Investigation Branch warrant cards issued in Egypt during the Second World War!

On 10 January 1900 Field-Marshal Lord Roberts, V.C. became commander-in-chief and, realising that mobility was the answer to the Boers' unconventional methods of warfare, he ordered that one company from every infantry battalion be converted to mounted infantry. These were then formed into a mounted infantry division, but operated in columns.

Holders of Provost appointments in divisions in January 1900 were:

APM	1st Division	Captain R. J. Ross	Middlesex Regt.
APM	2nd Division	Major G. F. Ellison	Royal Warwicks
APM	3rd Division	Captain J. R. F. Sladen	East Yorks
APM	4th Division	Major E. C. J. Williamson	East Kents
APM	5th Division	Major M. G. Williamson	King's Own Scottish Borderers
APM	6th Division	Major F. Wintour	Royal West Kents
APM	7th Division	Lt.-Col. R. H. Morrison	
APM	Cavalry Division	Captain P. A. Kenna, V.C.	21 Lancers

General Buller, who was in the field when Roberts arrived, assumed command of what became the Natal Field Force. The majority of his troops came from the commands of Lieutenant-Generals Clery and Warren. Force headquarters was established at Springfield on 11 January. Provost Marshal at headquarters was Major B. Williams, R.E., and he was present at both unsuccessful battles of the River Tugela and Spion Kop, the latter being an absolute disaster for British arms, which, instead of opening the way to the relief of Ladysmith as planned, halted Buller in his tracks. Mounted military police were utilised, as were other mounted troops, to patrol water-holes, as it was discovered that Boers were poisoning them whenever an opportunity arose. By 28 January the main force had moved off to the base that Field Marshal Roberts had decided to establish between the Modder and Orange rivers. After maintenance and adjustments he advanced into the Orange Free State on 12 February. The majority of troops on this occasion came from the 6th and 7th Divisions, freshly arrived from England. The A.P.M. at Force headquarters was Major R. M. Poore, 7th Hussars, who was graded as an A.A.G. on the staff.

Kimberley was relieved on 17th February, and 10 days later the entire Boer army operating in that area, together with its commander, General P. A. Cronje, was encircled and forced to surrender. Success breeds success, and on 1 March the town of Ladysmith was relieved. The force paused a while to reorganise before pushing on for Bloemfontein, the State capital. Orders for the advance were issued on 11 March. Paragraph 5 reads:

> The baggage of the units in Para 3 will march at 6.30 a.m., in the same order as the Corps, Headquarters baggage leading, under Major R. M. Poore, Provost Marshal, with an escort of four Companies, Col. Martyr's Mounted Infantry, and one battalion Guards Brigade.
> By Order
> J. M. Grierson, Lt. Col.
> A.A.G. for C of S.

A spirited little action had occurred on 8 March when a large commando unit under Commandant J. Theron attacked the lines of communication town of Piquetberg. The defenders, commanded by Major A. F. Pilson, numbered only 86, many of whom were convalescents. Others were N.C.O.s of M.M.P. based on the town. At 1620 hours the attackers withdrew having failed to gain access to the town. Field Marshal Roberts continued to advance and took the surrender of Bloemfontein on 13 March, appointing Major-General G. Prettyman as military governor. Personnel of the Cape police, who had remained loyal throughout the siege of Kimberley, were brought in to organise a police force. It was here that the proposal was made to organise a military police force for service in the Orange Free State. No doubt the Field Marshal bore in mind the success of military police raised by Major Herbert Bruce in Bengal after the Mutiny. Apart from ascertaining that there were 30,284 military police available currently in India, nothing further seems to have been done.

In England there had been a public outcry at what appeared to be inadequate medical facilities for the troops. *The Times* newspaper therefore commissioned Mr. W. Burdett-Coutt, M.P., to go to the front and report on the situation as he found it. His reports caused an uproar, for it was very obvious that some lessons of the Crimea War had been forgotten. He showed that the medical arrangements after the battle of Bloemfontein were sketchy in the extreme. The War Office acted energetically and medical services were completely overhauled, soon becoming the best available under the circumstances. We must not forget that the man on the spot can only do his best with the facilities provided. Those at home, responsible for providing resources and out of touch with reality, act within predetermined limits that they are not willing or able to widen, and must bear the blame. Later on in this chapter figures will be given that illustrate the inadequacy of our financial and manpower estimates for the war.

Once the base in Bloemfontein was established and his army rested, Field Marshal Roberts again advanced, moving towards Kroonstad on 3 May, his ultimate target being Pretoria, capital of Transvaal, some three hundred miles away. Johannesburg fell on 31 May, and army headquarters were established in the district called Orange Grove. A military governor was appointed, and steps taken to re-establish the police force, always a priority task when urban areas are occupied.

Pretoria capitulated on 5 June, and Brigadier-General J. Maxwell became military governor. His work as staff captain military police in Cairo years before no doubt stood him in good stead when he reorganised the city's police. Smart deduction by his staff officer, Captain Ivor Maxse, broke up a conspiracy to kidnap Lord Roberts. The leader of the miscreants, a German national, was a former Boer policeman who had been granted his freedom on his promise to take no further part in the war. He was brought before a military court and eventually shot, his custody and execution arrangements being the responsibility of the Provost Marshal.

Lieutenant-General Sir Charles Warren was appointed military governor of Griqualand, a part of Cape Colony. His available forces included 30 M.M.P., whom he used mainly as cavalry during his pacification of the area. At the town of Konig on 20 June a 200-strong commando unit under Commandant De Villiers surrendered. The cleared area was governed under martial law from Griquatown, but once the reformed civil police were functioning efficiently control was returned to the civil authorities, under the watchful eye of the local lines of communication area commander. The governor and the majority of his troops then returned to Cape Town.

At one time, when G.H.Q. was stationed in the Lydenburg area, occasional visits were made by officers of the opposing sides on humane or other grounds. When such contact was sponsored by the British it was usual for the envoy to be accompanied by a mounted policeman carrying a white flag. On one occasion when an officer went to see the Boer General Schoemann, commander of an enemy force in the Steenkampburg mountains, they were obliged to wait for a day until the general arrived, and while waiting they were well looked after. When they eventually met General Schoemann he said that one of his party was seriously ill. The M.M.P. N.C.O. was sent back to the British lines for transport and on return escorted the sick man to a British hospital, where, despite an immediate operation, he died. The fact that he was then given a military funeral greatly impressed the Boers.

Following a successful action at Hartebeestefontein by troops under Lord Methuen, Klerksdorp, a Transvaal town, was occupied on 19 February 1901, and a vast quantity of stores and many Boer families fell into our hands. The occupying force was only 750 strong, mainly soldiers of the 1st Battalion Loyal North Lancashire Regiment, one of whose officers was the Column A.P.M., Major H. E. Coleridge, D.S.O., who now became A.P.M. of the town and surrounding area, a position he held until after the end of the war. We are fortunate that records remain giving full details of Major Coleridge's service as a Provost officer, which covered almost the entire war, and were as follows:

> As APM and I.O. of a Column he was on operations in Cape Colony, north and south of the Orange River, from late 1899 until the spring of 1900. This period covered the advance on Kimberley, including actions at Belmont, Enslin, Modder River and Magersfontein. Operations in the Orange Free State followed during April and May, and in Orange River Colony from then

until July, embracing actions at Lindley on 1 June and the Rhenoster River later. From July until November he was in action west of Pretoria in the Transvaal, where he remained until the end of hostilities, being based on Klerksdorp once it was occupied. In addition to receiving the DSO, he was mentioned in Despatches on 10th September 1901 and was awarded the Queen's South African Medal with four Clasps, and the King's with two.

Few Provost officers in those days experienced such a sustained period of service. Both his parent regiment, and Provost, should be proud of the contribution made to their respective history and tradition by this Victorian gentleman. During March No. 191 Sergeant W. Tyrer, M.F.P., was transferred to the Imperial Military Railway Police, which appears to have been a locally-raised Empire force, about which nothing is known.

Lord Kitchener became commander-in-chief and set about denying supplies and reinforcements to the enemy. Strings of blockhouses and wire fences were erected across the country, and Boer families were detained in camps which were the original concentration camps. Cattle were impounded. All these measures reduced the enemy's mobility and denied him facilities for rest and recuperation, there being literally nowhere he could go to be dry in the rainy season. Desertion became rife, for it had been customary for the burghers to return home now and then for a break before returning to the war. Thousands of homesteads across the veldt were reduced by this policy to abandoned, weed-covered, piles of rubble.

Major C. F. N. Macready, whom we last encountered in this story as a military police officer at Alexandria, was serving on the staff at the Cape. On 6 June 1901 he was appointed to head a Commission to Zululand to investigate a dispute between the Acting High Commissioner there and the Natal government. A member of his Commission was Major Amber, L.F., an A.P.M. from Natal. The Commission duly returned and reported to the government.

As part of his plan to cut off Boer supplies Lord Kitchener decided to put the ports of Cape Town, Port Elizabeth and Port London under martial law. It was proved that supplies of all kinds, volunteers and information were coming through these three ports. The application of martial law would also be of assistance in controlling behaviour in the base area, for a recent scandal involving certain service wives in the *Mount Nelson* hotel had caused a stir both at home and locally. It was therefore proposed that there be a Base Provost Marshal in Cape Town, and an A.P.M. in each of the ports, all of whom would operate under a central regulatory system.

Major Macready was offered the position of Base Provost Marshal on 13 October 1901, but as a result of representations by Sir Gordon Sprigg, Prime Minister of Cape Colony, the plan was modified inasmuch as each port A.P.M. operated independently and martial law was not proclaimed. Macready has left his opinion of the modification in his memoirs, *Annals of an Active Life*, published by Hutchinson in 1926, to whom I am very grateful for permission to reproduce the following passage:

> It is a great pity that the change was made. After the First World War there were many serving Officers highly trained in Provost duties and their value was recognised by the Staff, but in Boer War days ideas on Provost work were extremely vague, going little beyond the custody of prisoners and the arrest of soldiers for disciplinary offences. Had there been a strong Provost Marshal in Cape Town at this time the scandals at the Mount Nelson Hotel, which anti-British elements used to vilify British Officers, would never have occurred.

Under the revised scheme Major Macready became A.P.M. Port Elizabeth, and by close liaison with his counterparts appointed to the other ports their operations were conducted almost as originally planned. It was proved that Americans were going to South Africa as members of ships' crews, deserting, and joining the Boers, or deserting to join British auxiliary forces and when fully armed and equipped, again deserting to join the enemy. By close collaboration with the port authorities in each area this source of enemy reinforcement was cut off. Another scheme was that of detailing military police patrols to confiscate items of service clothing found in the possession of natives. This closed another avenue of enemy recruitment, for in the past Boer sympathisers had found no difficulty in equipping themselves with clothing obtained from natives and, by passing themselves off as members of our Colonial forces, used British movements facilities to get them to the front, where they made their way across to their friends—our enemies. We must never forget that the Empire rallied round the Mother Country, and military contingents came from far and wide, and without their assistance it is possible that the war may not have been won. The Australians in particular were most valuable; good horsemen, excellent shots, and unfettered by the discipline of tradition that often brought the British their finest, but most disastrous, hours.

As a further remedial measure Macready turned attention to the brothels—his military police service in Alexandria in the 1880s had taught him no doubt that these can become centres of intrigue—and so it was in this case. British soldiers seldom obtained leave in South Africa, and when they did their low rate of pay normally confined them to the locality of their station. It was not so, however, with the Colonials, who were exceedingly well paid. Once on furlough they made a bee-line for the coast and the brothels, where they regularly left their arms for no other reason than that they were fed up with carrying them. The Boers had an organised collection system, and thus a constant trickle of small arms went from the ports to the hinterland. The institution of regular military police searches and patrols soon eliminated this source of supply to the enemy. The final regulatory improvement was the introduction of control of Boer prisoners at large in coastal towns on parole. These were made to report daily to military police headquarters to sign in, thus curtailing their freedom of movement and ability to act against us. Communications were such that it now became impossible for them to travel between towns on subversive business, and be back to report at the stipulated time.

Major Quentin Agnew, R.S.F., took over as A.P.M. Port Elizabeth on 14 December 1901, and Macready went to another staff appointment and subsequent promotion. Captain W. Childs became officer-in-charge of military police in Cape Town, an appointment that lasted for a long time after the war, as deserters kept coming to light requiring repatriation.

In January 1902 a camp was opened for Boer dependants in Klerksdorp, where Major Coleridge was still A.P.M., though as often as not he was away on operations with a column. As the last stages of the war were being fought within some miles of Klerksdorp its importance gradually increased. The concentration camp population was in the region of 3,000 people, and the A.P.M. arranged that milk from captured cattle should be made available regularly for the inmates' children, and for their hospital.

Late in January a large British convoy of empty wagons, proceeding to Klerksdorp to draw supplies, was attacked and destroyed when only a day's march away. Of an escort numbering 338 all ranks, one wounded officer and 108 men were all that eventually reached our lines. The attackers had been a 2,000-strong commando unit led by General H. J. de la Rey, a famous Boer leader. The garrison commander, Brigadier-General J. C. Barker, organised a force, in which M.M.P. were included, to scour the countryside for survivors, but although there were encounters with small bodies of the enemy, nothing was found. de la Rey struck again at 5 a.m. on 7 March when he completely destroyed a column commanded by Lord Methuen, who was wounded and captured. He was treated correctly and sent into Klerksdorp under a flag of truce.

This incident is typical of our failure to learn from experience. Dawn was a favourite Boer time for attack, yet troops commanded by an officer who had served throughout the entire campaign were surprised and defeated. A story is told about this period in the war when a M.M.P. N.C.O., acting as courier, had his horse shot dead by a Boer patrol. Before the enemy came up to him he pushed his despatches under his dead horse. The Boers stripped the N.C.O. naked and left him. Once they had gone he retrieved his documents and set off on foot, reaching his destination four days later and handed over the despatches—still stark naked.

Lord Kitchener sent a Highland brigade to reinforce Klerksdorp, and on 19 March marched in and set up his headquarters. Large numbers of troops now concentrated in the area and in consequence the supply depot was moved in from Bloemfontein. Obviously these were hectic days for the A.P.M.—they certainly were for his poor horse, for a veterinary certificate exists showing that on 27 March 1902 an animal was destroyed because of fever and exhaustion. The area now swarmed with punitive columns and the remaining enemy bands were slowly eliminated. Early in April, Louis Botha, de la Rey, and members of the Transvaal government went to Klerksdorp for peace negotiations. These proved long and tiresome, but finally at 1555 hours on 31 May 1902 peace was signed in Pretoria, on very generous terms for the Boers.

We had lost 21,579 men, of whom only one-third were battle casualties, the remainder dying of disease. A total of 24,000 Boers died, and of these 20,000 were dependants incarcerated in our camps, where epidemics had been commonplace. At the commencement of the war it was estimated that £10,000,000 would cover the cost, but final expenditure was in excess of £200,000,000. Our military planners had thought that 75,000 men would suffice; actually it required 450,000 to bring the war to a conclusion.

Looting had been rife, the Boers doing so on every occasion, often relying on it for re-provision. Lord Roberts was against it, but Lord Kitchener had said, 'Loot like mad', and his advice was followed whenever possible.

There were seven military police fatal casualties, and a stained glass window in the Garrison church of St. George, Aldershot, commemorates them. A memorial tablet was erected in the new Corps chapel in the R.M.P. depot, Chichester, during 1965, in order that the men would not be forgotten as the home of the Corps had left the Aldershot area.

Distinguished Conduct Medals were awarded to:

No. 338	Cpl. F. Jones	M.F.P.
No. 421	Cpl. A. H. Northeast	M.M.P.
No. 140	C/Sgt. A Gale	M.F.P.

Mentions were made in Despatches to the following:

No. 421   Cpl. A. H. Northeast   M.M.P (twice)
No. 338   Cpl. F. Jones   M.F.P. (twice)
No. 366   L/Cpl. G. Ashley   M.M.P. (twice)
           Q.M. (Hon. Lieut.) C. Burroughs   M.M.P.
No. 352   Cpl. R. Rowbottom   M.M.P.
No. 140   C/Sgt. A Gale   M.F.P.
           Sgt. W. Howard   18 H., attached to M.M.P.
                                             (for his work as a
                                             Provost Sergeant)

(In addition Q.M. and Hon. Lieut. C. Burroughs was promoted to
Hon. Captain.)

Let us leave the final word on the Provost Service in this
war to about 130 inhabitants of Klerksdorp, all of whom
were former enemies or foreign members of this Transvaal
community. When Major Coleridge eventually left the town
he was presented with an Illuminated Address. We have
already seen that this officer was unique, but for an officer
of an occupation force to be awarded a testimonial by those
over whom for so long he held the power of life or death must
be quite exceptional, and a true measure of his humanity.

Both mounted and foot military police made good names
for themselves during this war, although four members did
fall from grace and were court martialled. The senior, an
S.S.M., who had come from Egypt was reduced and given
84 days' hard labour in Cape Town early in 1900.

By the end of the war Provost officers were beginning to
be considered as military police officers, but a great opportunity had been lost to speed the process, as the reader will
no doubt have appreciated on reading the complaint of
Major Macready on page 217. However, it was not until
1953 that R.M.P. officers first appeared in the army; until
then only quartermasters had worn the badges of the Corps.

Let us leave this story in Aldershot, where in the closing
days of the 19th century public houses stayed open until
midnight, with only men on pass or absentees encountered
on the streets after 2100 hours. Each evening every regiment
of the garrison provided a picket of 10 men to control
members of their units who were in town, or to assist the
military police if requested. On pay night double pickets
were ordered, for on those nights feuds were pursued or new

ones hatched. Overall responsibility in our largest garrison town lay with the military police, and local newspaper archives will prove how well they discharged their duties. The days of 'Bloody Provost' were long gone, but who was to know that within 45 years the military police were to suffer immense casualties in two World Wars, that Provost Marshal and military police officers were to become synonymous, that M.M.P. and M.F.P. were to become one—the Corps of Military Police, and later the Corps of Royal Military Police?

Shortly before the Second World War the Corps of Military Police's claim to be considered combatant was contemptuously dismissed with a fatuous comment about them 'claiming to be combatant merely because they are armed with revolvers with which to protect themselves'. Today the combatant Corps of Royal Military Police has Her Majesty the Queen as its colonel-in-chief. But all this is the saga of 'Bloodied Provost', and that is another story!

SELECT BIBLIOGRAPHY

Archer, T., *The War in Egypt and the Sudan,* Blackie, 1886.

Atkyns and Young, *The Civil War,* Longmans, 1967.

Aydelotte, F., *Elizabethan Rogues and Vagabonds,* London, 1913.

Bagwell, H., *Ireland under the Tudors,* Holland, 1885.

Bagwell, H., *Ireland under the Stuarts,* Holland, 1909.

Baines, H., *Manuel of Monumental Brasses,* Adams and Dart, 1861.

Barnett, C., *Britain and Her Army,* Allen Lane, 1970.

Beatty, W., *With Shame Remembered,* Cassell, 1962.

Beer, G. L., *The Old Colonial System,* New York, 1912.

Bell, G., *Rough Notes of an Old Soldier,* Bell, 1867.

Bell, G., *Soldier's Glory,* Bell, 1956.

Bennett, G., *Nelson—the Commander,* Batsford, 1972.

Bentley, N. (ed.), *Russell's Despatches from the Crimea,* Deutsch.

Berner, Lord (trans. and ed.), *Chronicles—J. Froissart,* London, 1812.

Bingham, R., *James V—King of the Scots,* Collins, 1971.

Black, C., *The Story of Jamaica,* Collins, 1965.

Bowling, A. H., *Indian Cavalry Regiments,* Almark, 1971.

Brett-James, A., *Wellington at War,* Macmillan, 1961.

Brett-James, A., *Military Memoirs of Edward Costello,* Longmans, 1967.

Bryant, A., *The Great Duke,* Collins, 1971.

Bryant, A., *Jackets of Green,* Collins, 1972.

Burne, A. H., *The Agincourt War,* Eyre and Spottiswoode, 1956.

Carswell, J., *The Descent on England,* Barrie and Ratcliffe, 1964.

Carte, —, *The Life of James, Duke of Ormonde,* O.U.P. 1851.

Childs, W., *Episodes and Recollections,* Cassell, 1930.

Chillende, E., *The Inhumanity of the King's Prison Keeper at Oxford,* London, 1643.

Clarendon, —, *History of the Rebellion,* O.U.P.

Clarke, A., *The Old English in Ireland,* McGibbon and Kee, 1966.

Cleig, C. R., *The Life of Arthur, Duke of Wellington,* Methuen, 1862.

Coate, M., *Cromwell in the Great War and Inter Regnum,* B. Bradford Barton, 1963.

Cole, H. N., *History of Aldershot,* Gale and Polden, 1951.

Coleman, T., *The Railway Navvies,* Hutchinson, 1965.

Coley, J., *The Journal of the Sutlej Campaign, 1845-6,* Smith Elder, 1856.

Collier, R., *The Sound of Fury,* Collins, 1963.

Colville, H. E., *History of the Sudan Campaign,* H.M.S.O., 1889.

Creighton, L., *Life of the Black Prince,* London, 1874.

Cruickshank, C. G., *Elizabeth's Army,* Clarendon, 1966.

Cundall, F. (ed.), *Lady Nugent's Journal,* London, 1906.

Curran, W. H., *The Life of the Rt. Hon. J. P. Curran,* Constable, 1819.

Curtis, E., *History of Ireland,* Methuen, 1936.

Davies, C., *Wellington and his Army,* Blackwell, 1952.

De Wattville, H., *The British Soldier,* Dent.

Edwardes, M., *A Season in Hell,* Hamilton, 1973.

Edwardes, M., *Red Year,* Hamilton, 1973.

Featherstone, D., *MacDonald of the 42nd,* Seeley, 1971.

Firth, C., *Regimental History of Cromwell's Army,* Clarendon, 1940.

Fitzherbert, C., *Clifford, V.C.,* Joseph, 1956.

Fuller, J., *Memoirs of an Unconventional Soldier,* Nicholson, 1936.

Gardner, W. J., *History of Jamaica,* London, 1909.

Gilbert, J. T., *A History of the City of Dublin,* McGlashen, 1854.

Gillingham, J., *The Life and Times of Richard I,* Weidenfeld, 1973.

Godley, A., *Life of an Irish Soldier,* Murray, 1939.

Gordon Alexander, W., *Recollections of a Highland Subaltern,* Arnold, 1898.

Grant, M. H., *History of the War in South Africa, 1899–1902,* Hurst and Blackett, 1910.

Griffiths, C. J., *Narrative of the Siege of Delhi, with an account of the Mutiny at Ferozepore in 1857,* Murray, 1910.

Griffiths, P., *To Guard my People,* Benn, 1971.

Grose, H., *Military Antiquities of the English Army,* London, 1786.

Gurwood, J. (ed.), *The Despatches of the Duke of Wellington,* Murray, 1936.

Hamley, E., *The War in the Crimea,* Seeley, 1907.

Harrison, H., *Recollections of Life in the British Army during the latter part of the 19th century,* Murray, 1908.

Hart, L. (ed.), *Letters of Pte. Wheeler, 1809–26,* Joseph, 1951.

Haswell, J., *The First Respectable Spy,* Hamilton, 1969.

Helm, P. J., *England under the Yorkists and Tudors, 1471–1603,* Bell, 1968.

Hewitt, H. J., *The Organisation of War under Edward III,* M.U.P., 1966.

Hibbert, C., *Corunna,* Batsford, 1961.

Hibbert, C., *The Whatley Diary,* Longmans, 1974.

Hickson, M., *Ireland in the XVIIIth Century, or the Irish Massacres,* Longmans, 1884.

Holland and Hozier, *Records of the Expedition to Abbyssinia,* H.M.S.O., 1870.

Huxford, H., *History of the 8th Gurkha Rifles,* Gale and Polden, 1952.

Jackson, B., *Notes and Reminiscences of a Staff Officer,* Dutton (New York), 1903.

Jackson, T., *Ireland Her Own,* Lawrence and Wishart, 1971.

Jenkins, E., *Elizabeth and Essex,* Gollancz, 1961.

Jenkins, E., *Elizabeth and Leicester,* Gollancz, 1961.

Jones, J., *Journal of the Sieges carried out by the Army under the Duke of Wellington,* Wheale, 1816.

Kaye, J., *A History of the Sepoy War in India,* Allen, 1880.

Kaye and Malleson, *History of the Indian Mutiny,* Longmans, 1906.

Kendall, P., *Richard the Third,* Allen and Unwin, 1955.

Kingslake, A., *The Invasion of the Crimea,* Tauchnitz, 1863.

Lawrence Archer, J., *Commentaries on the Punjab Campaign, 1848-49,* Allen, 1878.

Leeper, A., *Historical Handbook of Monuments Inscriptions, etc., of the Cathedral Church of St. Patrick, Dublin,* Dublin, 1890.

Lehmann, H., *All Sir Garnet,* Cape, 1967.

Lindsay, J., *1764,* Muller, 1959.

Lodge, E., *Gascony under English Rule,* Methuen, 1926.

Longman, W., *The History and Times of Edward III,* Longmans, 1869.

Love, H., *Vestiges of Old Madras,* Murray, 1913.

Ludlow, E., *Memoirs of Edward Ludlow,* Oxford.

Lummis and Wynn, *Honour the Light Brigade,* Hayward, 1973.

Lunt, J., *The Scarlet Lancer,* Hart Davies, 1964.

Mackinnon, J., *History of Edward the Third,* London, 1900.

Mackinnon and Shadbolt, *The South African Campaign of 1879,* Eyre and Spottiswoode, 1882.

Macready, N., *Annals of an Active Life*, Hutchinson, 1926.

MacWilliam, H., *The Records of the Black Watch Mutiny,* Forster Groom, 1910.

Maitland, W., *History of London,* Vol. I, London, 1756.

Markham, F., *Five Decades of Epistles of War,* London, 1622.

Mattingly, G., *The Defeat of the Spanish Armada,* Cape, 1959.

Maurice, J., *History of the Campaign of 1882 in Egypt,* H.M.S.O., 1889.

Maxwell, C., *Dublin under the Georges,* Faber, 1936.

McCall, T., *The Rising in the North,* York Archaeological Journal, 1905.

McGuffie, T., *Peninsula Cavalry General,* Harrup, 1951.

McGuffie, T., *The Siege of Gibraltar,* Batsford, 1965.

Mercer, C., *Journal of the Waterloo Campaign,* Dautes, 1929.

Milton, R., *The English Ceremonial Book,* David and Charles, 1972.

Mitchell, J., *The Court of the Connetabilie,* 1947.

Money Barnes, R., *The Soldiers of London*, Seeley, 1963.

Montgomery, J., *Toll for the Brave*, Parrish, 1963.

Moore Smith, G. (ed.), *The Autobiography of Lieutenant-General Sir Harry Smith*, Murray, 1903.

Munro, W., *Records of Service in many Lands*, Hurst and Blackett, 1881.

Naipal, V., *The Loss of El Dorado*, Deutsch, 1969.

Napier, W., *The Life and Opinions of Sir Charles J. Napier*, Murray, 1857.

Neilson, G., *Trial by Combat*, Hodge, 1890.

Newhall, R., *The English Conquest of Normandy, 1416–24*, Yale, 1924.

Newhall, R., *Muster and Review*, Harvard.

Noble, T., *Huntingdonshire and the Spanish Armada*, London.

Nolan, E., *The Illustrated History of the War against Russia*, James and Virtue, 1857.

Official, *Ancient Criminal Trials in Scotland*, Vol. I, 1524–84, Edinburgh, 1833.

Oliver, S., *Jamaica—Blessed Isle*, London, 1937.

Oman, C., *Sir John Moore*, Hodder, 1953.

Oman, C., *History of the Art of War in the 16th Century*, Methuen.

O'Sullivan, M., *Barnebe Googe—Provost Marshal of Connaught, 1582–85*, Vol. 18, Galway Historical Society Journal, 1938.

Parry and Sherlock, *A Short History of the West Indies*, MacMillan, 1956.

Pakenham, T., *The Year of Liberty*, Hodder, 1969.

Peacock, H., *The Army Lists of the Roundheads and Cavaliers*, Camden Hotten, 1864.

Pennybacker, M., *The Two Spies*, New York, 1932.

Phillips, I., *The Journal of Sir Samuel Luke*, Oxford Record Society, 1947.

Phillips, W., *Papers Relating to the Trained Soldiers of Shropshire in the Reign of Queen Elizabeth*, Shropshire Archaeological and Natural History Society, 1891.

Pitman, F., *The Development of the British West Indies*, New Haven, 1917.

Pollock, J., *Way to Glory—The Life of Havelock of Lucknow*, Murray, 1957.

Porter, M., *Overture to Victoria*, Redman, 1961.

Powick, H., *Military Obligations in Medieval England*, O.U.P., 1962.

Ribton Turner, C., *A History of Vagrants*, London, 1887.

Round, J., *King's Sergeants and Officers of State*, Nisbet, 1911.

Rouse, A., *The Elizabethan Renaissance*, Macmillan, 1971.

Russell, W., *My Indian Mutiny Diary*, Cassell, 1858.

Russell, W., *The British Expeditionary Force to the Crimea*, Routledge, 1857.

Savoury, R., *His Britannic Majesty's Army in Germany during the Seven Year's War*, O.U.P., 1967.

Selby, J. (ed.), *The Napoleonic Wars of Thomas Morris*, Longmans, 1967.

Shadbolt, S., *The Afghan Campaign of 1878-80*, Eyre and Spottiswoode, 1882.

Sharpe, C., *Memorials of the Rebellion of 1569*, London, 1840.

Sherer, J., *Daily Life in the Indian Mutiny*, Swan, 1898.

Scott Thompson, G., *Lord Lieutenants in the 17th Century*, London, 1923.

Simon, E., *Henry VII*, Muller, 1968.

Stewart Brown, R., *Sergeants of the Peace in Medieval England and Wales*, M.U.P., 1936.

Smith, J., *The Parish, its Obligations and Powers at Law*, Sweet, 1857.

Smith Dorrien, H., *Memories of Forty Eight Years' Service*, Murray, 1925.

Squibb, G., *The High Court of Chivalry*, London, 1959.

Stocquellor, J., *A Personal History of the Horse Guards*, Hurst and Blackett, 1873.

Stow, J., *The Annals of England*, London, 1601.

Stubbs, —, *Bishop Select Charters*, London, 1890.

Strickland, A., *Lives of the Queens of England*, London, 1843.

Sylvester, J., *Recollections of the Campaigns of Malwa and Central India*, Bombay, 1860.

Thompson, G., *The Crime of Mary Stuart,* Hutchinson, 1967.

Tisdale, E., *Mrs. Duberley's Campaign,* Jarrolds.

Touch, D., *Last Years of a Frontier,* Clarendon, 1928.

Tugwell, M., *The Unquiet Peace,* Wingate, 1957.

Turner, A., *Sixty Years of a Soldier's Life,* Methuen, 1912.

Turner and Power, *Tudor Economic Documents,* London, 1924.

Turner, E., *Gallant Gentlemen,* Joseph, 1956.

Underwood, D., *Somerset in the Civil War and Inter Regnum,* David and Charles, 1973.

Wake, J., *Montague Musters Book,* Northants. Record Society, 1931.

Wake, J., *Muster, Beacons and Subsidies,* Northants. Record Society, 1926.

Warner, P. (ed.), *The Fields of War,* New York, 1932.

Ward, S., *Wellington's Headquarters,* O.U.P., 1957.

Wedgwood, C., *The King's War, 1641-47,* Collins, 1958.

Williams, N., *Sir Walter Raleigh,* Butler and Tanner, 1962.

Wrong, H., *Government in the West Indies,* O.U.P., 1925.

Wylie, J., *History of England under Henry IV* (Vols. I and III), Longmans, 1884.

Wylie, J., *The Reign of Henry V* (Vol. I), C.U.P., 1914.

INDEX

Where a person held a Provost appointment this is indicated after the name with a known date of incumbency, and the initials of the post held.

Initials used for this purpose are:

PMG	Provost Marshal General
PM	Provost Marshal
VPM	Vice Provost Marshal
DPM	Deputy Provost Marshal
APM	Assistant Provost Marshal
RPM	Regimental Provost Marshal

LIST OF SUBSCRIBERS

W.O.2 John Abbott
Lt. Col. N. C. Allen, R.M.P.—former student of Major Tyler
W.O.2 S. Armstrong, S.I.B., R.M.P.
Capt. J. Clifford Atkinson, A.R.I.B.A.
P. R. Attridge
Maj. J. E. Ayres, R.M.P.
The Badge Club, Maendy Junior School, Cowbridge
Lt. Cdr. (X) (Reg.) P. B. Bayliss, R.N.
Maj. J. K. Bonell, R.M.P.
W.O.1 (R.S.M.) D. C. Boyd, S.I.B.
Brig. J. W. Bridge
Horace E. Bromwich
Rosemary and Tweedie Brown
4607338 Cpl. E. (Buck) Buckley, ex 204 Provost Coy. 1940
C/Sgt. J. Buckley, R.R.F.
Maj. H. Burden, M.B.E., M.S.M.
Col. A. V. Burge, M.B.E., B.E.M., F.I.I.M., F.A.A.I., M.B.I.M., A.I.T.D.
John Byrne, Esq.
Carol Campbell-Smith
Mrs. R. K. Cooley
Lt. M. Cuthbert-Brown, R.M.P.
W.O.2 B. Davies, R.M.P., S.I.B.
E. E. Davis, 103 Provost Coy. C.M.P.
Norman Dawson, ex S/Sgt. S.I.B., R.M.P.
Ronald Day
Lt. Col. J. C. DeVine (retd.)
Col. P. A. W. G. Durrant
Lt. Col. S. G. Edwards, R.M.P., Commandant R.M.P. Training Centre
Mrs. A. Elvidge (nee Whale)
P. J. Emms, Esq.
Capt. S. G. Evans
Graham P. Fletcher
Cpl. G. W. Flint, R.M.P.
Maj. Charles Garraway, Army Legal Corps.
E. J. Geary, W.O.1
Lt. Col. W. S. Godden, R.M.P.
Maj. J. Graham
P. Hargreaves—remembering those who stayed (Cyprus 1957-60)
J. D. Harmon, D.C.M.
B. J. Harries—to comrades and friendship in Provost
W.O.2 S. M. Haskins, S.I.B.
Col. P. W. le S. Herring, O.B.E., R.M.P.
Jim and Glynis Hill
Cpl. Hopper, J., 174 P.R.O. Coy., R.M.P.
Maj. R. Jackson, R.E.
W.O.2 K. W. Jobson, S.I.B., R.M.P.
A. G. K. Johnson
S/Sgt. Johnson, B. J., S.I.B., R.M.P.
Sgt. J. T. Keen, R.M.P.
Maj. J. B. Keenan, R.A.
Cpl. King, S.A.R.
Sgt. L. Kynaston, R.M.P.
Mr. Walter E. Lee, St. Albans
Col. D. J. London, '1882 and all that'
David Lovell, Colchester R.M.P.A.
Miss E. McHale
Capt. A. C. McIntosh, R.M.P.
Peter McKenna, Ex 247 Provost Coy. 1951-53
George L. McKie, R.M.P., 1957-69
A. McD. McKinnon
Lt. Col. Leslie W. Mason (retd.), R.M.P.

Brig. M. Matthews, M.B.E., R.M.P., Provost Marshal 1977-80
Robert R. Millar, Edinburgh
David Morgan
P. Murphy
Lt. Col. M. L. Nicholls, R.M.P. (retd.)
J. O'Donnell
Pat O'Reilly
Capt. D. E. Page, R.M.P.
W.O.1 (R.S.M.) N. C. Pamplin
Maj. J. E. D. Parminter, R.M.P., 21C S.I.B., R.M.P., B.A.O.R.
J. R. Pavitt
Col. G. E. Pillitz, Provost Marshal B.A.O.R. 1961-64
Mr. W. Pitfield, M.M.
D. Poulton (S/Sgt.), R.M.P.
Mrs. Mary Powell
Brig. D. B. Rendell, C.B.E., M.C., Provost Marshal 1974-77
Brig. L. F. Richards, C.B.E., Provost Marshal 1968-71
Michael G. Riley
Mark Roberts
Maj. A. S. Robertson, R.M.P. (retd.) M.A., M.I.L.
Maj. E. G. Rolt, A.P.M. 1942-46
H. Romeijn, B.A., F.I.L., F.R.S.A.
Royal Military Academy Central Library
W.O.1 B. F. Samways, R.M.P., S.I.B.
Wg. Cdr. J. L. Schooling (retd.), late R.A.F. Provost branch
Lt. Col. W. J. Scoging, M.B.E., R.A.O.C., M.O.D.
W.O.1 (R.S.M.) M. Seabourne, R.M.P.
Sgt. B. Shaw, R.M.P.
W.O.2 P. G. Smith, R.M.P., S.I.B.
Standing of Schneverdingen
S/Sgt. H. J. Storer, 3/778136 Royal Australian Army Provost Corps.
Peter J. Stubbs
Terence N. Suckling
Cpl. J. H. Summers
Maj. J. H. Taylor, late 5th Royal Gurkha Rifles (F.F.) & A.P.M. H.Q. Burma Command
L. C. Taylor
Col. B. Thomas, O.B.E., R.M.P.
Sgt. D. L. Thomas, R.M.P. 1960-83
Col. J. F. Thomas, O.B.E., R.M.P.
James E. Thornton, B.E.M.
S/Sgt. R. Tickner, R.M.P.
W.O.1 (R.S.M.) A. I. Truckle, R.M.P.
S/Sgt. B. M. C. Tyler, S.I.B., R.M.P.
Clive Wainwright (ex W.O.1, R.M.P., S.I.B.)
Maj. A. E. F. Waldron, M.B.E.
Bernie Wallis (ex W.O.1)
W.O.1 D. A. Ward
S/Sgt. J. Weir, R.M.P.
Cpl. S. M. Wells, 2nd Reg. & 110 P.R.O. Coy., R.M.P.
Capt. C. G. Whatman, R.M.P.
Sgt. G. C. Wilkins, R.M.P., S.I.B.
Wilkinson Sword, Ltd.
Dennis A. Williams
J. Wood, M.B.E.
John Wright, G.C.H.Q., Cheltenham
Maj. R. J. Wyatt, T.D.
Capt. D. S. Young, LLB, R.M.P.